DEEP LEARNING NEURAL NETWORKS

Design and Case Studies

DEEP LEARNING NEURAL NETWORKS

Design and Case Studies

Daniel Graupe
University of Illinois, Chicago, USA

NEW JERSEY • LONDON • SINGAPORE • BEIJING • SHANGHAI • HONG KONG • TAIPEI • CHENNAI • TOKYO

Published by

World Scientific Publishing Co. Pte. Ltd.
5 Toh Tuck Link, Singapore 596224
USA office: 27 Warren Street, Suite 401-402, Hackensack, NJ 07601
UK office: 57 Shelton Street, Covent Garden, London WC2H 9HE

British Library Cataloguing-in-Publication Data
A catalogue record for this book is available from the British Library.

DEEP LEARNING NEURAL NETWORKS
Design and Case Studies

ISBN 978-981-3146-44-0
ISBN 978-981-3146-45-7 (pbk)

Printed in Singapore

To Dalia,
To Menachem-Henny, Pelleg, Oren, Laura, Betsy and Rachel
and to my Grandchildren

Acknowledgements

It is a pleasure to acknowledge the assistance in my deep learning neural network and related work to Dr. Hubert Kordylewski, a friend and past assistant, who was instrumental in making the LAMSTAR a reality.

I am greatly indebted to many colleagues at different Universities who collaborated with me in work related to this book and enriched my knowledge and understanding related to this work. Especially to my teacher, colleague, and friend, Dr. John (Jack) Lynn (Liverpool), and to Dr. Kate Kohn, MD, an inspiration and a tower of strength with whom I worked for 24 great years at Michael Reese Hospital, Chicago, Dr. Boris Vern MD, a colleague and an inspiration to my work (Univ. of Illinois, Chicago — UIC), Dr. George Moschytz (ETH, Zurich and Tel Aviv), Dr. Ruey Wen (Notre Dame Univ.), Dr. Yi Fang Huang (Notre Dame), Dr. Kosnstntin Slavin MD (UIC), Dr. Daniela Tuninetti (UIC) and Dr. Qiu Huang (Notre Dame).

I learnt a lot from all my assistants over the years and cannot forget their dedication and help. I must mention those directly associated with this work: Dr. Yunde Zhong, Dr. Aaron Field MD, Dr. Jonathan Waxman MD, Dr. Ishita Basu, Jonthan Abon, Mary Smollack and Nevidita Khobragade.

Not least am I indebted to the students in my Neural Networks a Classes at UIC who agreed that I use programs and results from their Final Projects in these classes in the Appendix to this book: Arindam Bose, Jeffrey Tran, Debasish Bose, John Caleb Somasundaram, Nidamulo Kudinya, Anusha Daggubati,

Aparna Pongoru, Saraswathi Gangineni, Veera Sunitha Kadi, Prithvi Bondili, Dhivya Somasundaram, Eric Wolfson, Abhinav Kumar, Mounika Racha, Yudongsheng Fan, Chimnayi Deshpande, Fangjiao Wang, Syed Ameenuddin Hussain, Sri Ram Kumar Muralidharan, Xiaouxiao Shi and Miao He.

Preface

This text is based on my lectures in classes ECE/CS-559 in the departments of Electrical and of Computer Engineering and Computer Science at the University of Illinois at Chicago over the last several years.

The book is directed to graduate students and researchers in the fields of Computer Science and Electrical and Computer Engineering.

Deep learning neural networks were created for its potential in solving problems in many fields where current methods, theoretical or algorithmic where insufficient. It was felt that an approach that can deal with problems that simultaneously involve nonlinearity, chaos, non-stationarity and even totally non-analytical elements is called for. It was also noted that the human brain can deal with such problems via its own neural networks. Such situations abound in problems in medicine, finance, image understanding, nonlinear control, speech recognition and beyond.

The teaching of the field of Deep Learning neural networks (DLNN) does not and cannot end with learning its theory and design principles. It only starts there. The teaching of DLNN must provide insight into what DLNN can do. This text attempts to give a bit of this insight because this is what it is all about.

In my graduate classes above, I heavily rely on mini-research projects, as in the case studies of this book, where students write their own programs and apply them to problems that are far from their field of study or of knowledge – from medicine, finance, even astronomy.

Therefore, and within the space of a one-semester text, 20 such case studies are included herewith. These were all carried out within 2–3 weeks as class-projects by the author's students in a graduate-level class.

It is hoped that these Case studies will demonstrate to the reader that the field of Deep Learning Neural Networks can be conveniently and successfully applied, with the knowledge provided in this book, to a wide range of concrete problems.

The unique architecture of DLNN is demonstrated by the case studies or by literature quoted in the book, to be a powerful and easily-applicable tool in problems-solving and in academic research. The case studies cover areas as far apart as financial engineering or medical diagnosis and prediction. The case studies and the literature quoted show the effectiveness of DLNN in 2D and 3D vision (still and video), in speech recognition and filtering, in games, in security (including computer security), in industrial fault detection and well beyond. Indeed, it has been widely applied as such at the authors research in several medical problems, as quoted in the text.

It should be noted that the DLNN architecture, especially when implemented with parallel computing, is sufficiently fast in its computing time for real time decisions and can be realized in devices and sensors in medicine and which may be patient-borne or even implanted.

I believe that appending program codes used in the case studies (even if not the full programs, which would have turned this book into a 1000-page volume), is essential for making the teaching of the material complete. The discussions of the case studies in the main text, and the sources given in these discussions, together with the codes or code-sections given in the appendices, will hopefully allow interested readers to reconstruct these case studies.

Every case study that is given in the book, compares several deep-learning neural network methods, concerning their computational speed and success rate (using same data, computation language and PC per study). In some cases, non-neural-network architectures are also compared.

With more and increasingly complex further applications, the field of DLNN will surely expand and develop beyond its present status in the coming years. It is only at its early stages, though it has already done a lot. It already is an, if not *the* established leader in machine intelligence.

Contents

CHAPTER 1

Deep Learning Neural Networks: Methodology and Scope

1.1. Definition

Deep Learning neural networks (DLNNs) may be defined as neural networks architectures that can facilitate deep learning, retrieval and analysis of data that is deeply buried in input information and not otherwise easily retrievable. Their ability to dig deeply in the input data is often superior and/or faster to other (non-neural-network) computational methods due to their efficient integration of several and often many mathematical, logical and computational methods, linear, nonlinear, analytic or heuristic, deterministic or stochastic, for a given task.

Another definition of deep learning neural networks is that, [Dong and Yu, 2014] "DLNNs are a class of machine learning techniques that exploit *many layers* of nonlinear information processing for supervised and unsupervised feature extraction and transformation and for pattern analysis and classification". Also, DLNN networks are usually feedforward networks in their design.

By its name, Deep Learning is needed when simple methods are insufficient, where one must dig deep. This usually requires a "heavy arsenal" of knowledge. This "heavy" arsenal must be of varied, though strong tools. These tools must, however, be intelligently integrated. Integration must not be biased, but depend on unbiased learning by results.

Artificial neural networks can learn. Deep learning neural networks must learn and adaptively rank a whole arsenal by learning. This is their purpose, and this is what the present text is about.

Like other neural network architectures, DLNN architectures generally attempt to imitate the architecture of the biological brain to a certain degree, sometimes more and sometimes less. Their integration of algorithms that certainly do not reside in the biological brain is not too dis-similar from the way that the brain itself receives inputs from pre-processors from outside pre-processors. Light inputs are pre-processed in the retina and sound inputs are pre-processed in the cochlea (for color discrimination or sound frequency discrimination, respectively). Similarly, chemical pre-processing of odors or taste is performed in the nose or in the tongue, before being sent to the central nervous system (CNS). In some way, one may even consider literature that one reads, scientific or otherwise, as a pre-processor of knowledge.

1.2. Brief History of DNN and of its Applications

Deep Learning was one of the main goals of machine intelligence from its very beginning. It was therefore also one of the main purposes of artificial neural networks. The hope was that artificial neural networks can utilize the speed electronic computers and their related programming power to dig deeper into information than man can and that it can integrate various mathematical methods and directly apply them to data. Unveiling of the non-obvious which may however, be important to a specific application was always the expectation of scientific advancement and electronic computers were considered to be a tool for achieving it. Furthermore, it was hoped that the basis for fulfilling this purpose might be sought in a machine based on imitating the general architecture of the human brain, namely, in an artificial neural network architecture.

The first artificial neural network that was designed to be general enough for deep learning was the Back-Propagation (BP) Neural Network, proposed in 1986 by David Rumelhart *et al*. [Rumelhart, 1986]. (A similar design was already proposed by Paul Werbos in his 1974 Ph.D. thesis in [Werbos P J, 1974] and then by D B Parker in 1982 [Parker D B, 1982]). Back Propagation (BP) is based on Richard Bellman's Dynamic Programming theory [Bellman, 1961], and is still employed in several major Deep Learning neural network architectures. However, despite its generality, in itself it is too slow and cannot efficiently integrate many pre-filtering or pre-processing mathematical algorithms as may be needed for deep learning.

In 1975, Kunihiko Fukushima [Fukushima K, 1975] proposed the Cognitron Neural Network to imitate the functioning of the retina for machine visual pattern recognition. He extended Cognitron in 1980, proposing the Neocognitron [Fukushima K, 1980], which was still very cumbersome and rather slow, and which, like its predecessor Cognitron, was still limited to visual pattern recognition. It was not a deep-learning network, and although it was also not a convolutional network, it later served as a basis for the most important convolutional neural networks to be discussed in Chapter 5.

The convolutional neural networks (CNN) became the most recognized and most popular deep learning neural networks. Historically, the CNN network was inspired by modelling of the visual cortex [Fukushima *et al.*, 1980]. It originated with the work by Yann LeCun and his associates, which was concerned with image (zip-code) recognition [LeCun *et al.*, 1989]. Therefore, it is hardly surprising that till today CNN was mainly applied to **image-related problems**.

In this 1989 work, the LeCun *et al.* incorporated convolution in their 5-layer BP-based design, thus achieving deeper and faster learning than afforded by BP alone. Though the training time for this early design was approximately 3 days, today's CNN designs based on LeCun's Le-Net 5 [LeCun *et al.*, 1998] take only minutes to train (depending on the complexity of the problem involved), especially if parallel processing is employed.

Hinton and his co-workers extended the range of applications of the CNN-based architecture to **speech recognition** and **natural language processing** problems [Hinton *et al.*, 2012]. Thus, CNN soon became the leading approach for use in (still and video) image processing and in speech processing, overshadowing other architectures, such as those based on Support Vector Machine (SVM) or on other algorithms in most such problems. Presently, the range of CNN applications spreads to many other applications, as long as these can be represented or reformulated into a 2D or higher-dimensional spatial form, namely, into matrix or tensor notation or any other suitable feature-map. Therefore, CNN became the most widely used neural network for solving complex deep learning problems.

Among the many applications of CNN that appear in the literature, we mention just a few, as follows (in addition to those mentioned earlier):

Still images and Video applications: LeCun's application that launched CNN [LeCun *et al.*, 1089], Ciresan's record breaking application to handwritten text [Ciresan, 2012], the **3D application** by Ji *et al.* [Ji, 2012] and Simonyan and Zisserman's application to video [Simonyan, Zisserman, 2014]. Of the applications to speech we mention [Abdel Hamid *et al.*, 2013].

Of the other fields of applications are applications to **fault detection** [Calderon-Martinez *et al.*, 2006]; **finance** [Dixon *et al.*, 2015]; **search engines** [Rios and Kavuluru, 2015], **Medicine** [Wallach *et al.*, 2015] and many others in many more areas. Also see Chapter 5 and the Case Studies in Chapter 8.

In 1996 Graupe and H Kordylewski proposed a design for the Large Memory Storage and Retrieval Neural Network (LAMSTAR, or LNN) deep-learning network of unrestricted number of layers [Graupe and Kordylewski, 1996]. This neural network (NN) was developed to serve as generalized NN-based learning machine for computing prediction, detection and operational decisions from varied data sources. Data can be deterministic, stochastic, spatial, temporal, logic, time-varying, non-analytic, or a combination of the above. The LAMSTAR is a Hebbian [Hebb, 1949] NN. It follows a 1969 machine intelligence model [Graupe and Lynn, 1969] which was inspired by Emanuel Kant's concept of "Verbindungen" ("interconnections") in Understanding [Kant E, 1781] and by the neuronal interconnections between different cortexes and layers of the brain. Its computational power is due to its ability to integrate and rank parameters from carious co-processors, stochastic, analytic or non-analytic, including entropy, wavelets and beyond. Its speed is derived from employing the Hebbian-Pavlovian principle, Kohonen's winner-takes-all principle [Kohonen, 1984] and from the ease that it lends itself to parallel computing.

The LAMSTAR neural network was successfully applied to problems ranging from **medical prediction and diagnosis** [Nigam, 2004], [Waxman *et al.*, 2010], **financial computing** [Dong F, *et al.*, 2012] to **video processing** [Girado *et al.*, 2004], **computer intrusion** [Venkatachalam V, 2007] and to **speech** [Graupe and Abon, 2003]. Also see Chapter 6 and the Case Studies in Chapter 8.

The basic LAMSTAR structure (LAMSTAR 1, or LNN-1) was normalized in 2008 by Schneider and Graupe [Schneider N, Graupe D, 2008] to yield a modified LAMSTAR version (LAMSTAR-2, or LNN-2). This resulted in considerably improved performance with no effect on computational speed.

1.3. The Scope of the Present Text

Despite the short history of Deep Learning Neural Networks (DLNN), several different architectures have been proposed for it. Even within the different methodologies used in these architectures, programming an algorithm for a given problem is often a very major task. Furthermore, whereas Neural Networks are supposed to follow or to approximate a general architecture based on the organization of the biological Central Nervous System (CNS), many if not most DLNN architectures have little in common with any CNS architecture. Also, our knowledge of the CNN itself is still too weak to allow modeling of its deep learning. Many DLNN designs borrow from the broad range of mathematical techniques and fit these into a network-like algorithm. Rigid limits on architecture are therefore often too restrictive for such integration in any but simple cases, deep learning, by its definition, requires "all the tools possible". Hence, there is no other way but to borrow from any advances in mathematics that we can. After all, mathematical knowledge, as we know it, is available to us through someone's human brain. The price lies in the degree of convenience in integrating it all.

This leads us to divide deep leaning neural networks into three classes:

(a) DLNNs where integration is smooth and intelligent, and where the network is computationally fasts and of a wide range of applicability;
(b) DLNNs whose design incorporates or is based on only specific tools, to allow deep learning for only specific classes of problems, even if, in some cases, in a speedy manner;
(c) DLNNs where integration is complex and the networks is slow and therefore of limited appeal.

Deep learning can also be achieved with non-NN (non-neural-network) architectures, such as SVM (Support Vector Machines) which are general in range of applications, but usually slow (see Case Studies in Chapter 8), especially in very complex problems, or as ad-hoc algorithms for very specific problems.

This book focuses mainly on DLNNs of class (a) above. Indeed, we intend to show that these DLNN's are capable to deliver excellent performance in reasonable speed to a wide range of problems that require deep learning, which is their goal. Not only is their design very fast due to their NN (neural network) architecture, even allowing for integrating external mathematical and algorithmic tools, but their performance and speed is competitive with ad-hoc algorithms whose design is obviously very time consuming. Deep learning techniques that do not follow this design framework, specifically, generative unsupervised techniques are not considered as DL neural networks (Dong and Yu, 2014] and are beyond the scope of this text.

The DLNN designs on which this text focuses should be satisfactory in performance and speed to serve as a product within many industrial and medical tools and devices, such as airplanes, automobiles, nonlinear controllers, robots, medical implants, medical prediction and diagnosis tools, trading and financial analysis tools, etc. In most of these, ad hoc designs are too slow, too dependent on exactly same input data, or too in efficient in adaptation to real-world and on-line situations. And all this is achievable via DLNN without compromise of their performance and of their deepness.

In this text we therefore discuss in depth the following DLNN networks:

(1) The **Back-Propagation Neural Network** (BP)
(2) The **Convolutional Neural Network** (CNN)
(3) The **LAMSTAR** (Large Memory Storage and Retrieval)
Neural Network (LNN)

We comment that Back-Propagation has a very broad range of applications. Also, it is potentially a deep learning neural network, but it is too slow to serve for deep learning it itself. However, it serves as a learning unit in CNN, which is the most popular DLNN, and it also plays an important role other deep learning networks, especially in deep recurrent neural networks and in deconvolution/wavelet neural network. Its understanding is therefore most important for the understanding of later networks.

We also present three other neural networks, namely,

(5) **Deep Boltzman Machine** (DBM)
(6) **Deep Recurrent Neural Network** (DRNN)
(7) **Deconvolution/Wavelet Neural Network** (DCNN or WNN)

However, of the last three networks, DBM and the Deconvolution/Wavelet Neural Network are limited in the fields of application to which they can be applied. DBM, while DRNN networks are very slow in applications to complex problems. DBM and deconvolution networks also cannot integrate a multitude of tools.

Historically, the **Back Propagation Neural Networks (BP)** is the first neural network to demonstrate generality.

1.4. Brief Outline

This text is organized as follows:

In **Chapter 2** we shall present and briefly explain some **basic concepts** in **neural networks** and which are used in deep learning neural networks.

In **Chapter 3** we introduce Fukushima's **Cognitron** and its extension neural network, the **Neocognitron**. These two neural networks were the first attempt to dig deep into a very complex system, namely the biological retina, by using a neural network architecture. It was not intended to serve as a generalized learning machine and its computation was extremely time-consuming. However, the Cognitron and the Neocognitron inspired the development of the most recognized DLNN, namely, the Convolutional Neural Network (CNN).

Chapter 4 is a detailed exposition of the **Backpropagation (BP)**, whose theory follows Richard Bellman's Dynamic Programming Theory and made BP the first truly generalized neural network. The BP Dynamic-Programming-based learning algorithm is later shown to provide the learning engine for CNN and to other deep learning networks.

The **Convolutional Neural Network (CNN)** is described in **Chapter 5**. CNN neural networks were first developed for the purpose of image recognition. Still, they became during their short history almost synonymous with Deep Learning machines, having been applied over a wide field of areas and of topics. Backpropagation is employed as the learning engine in the convolutional neural network.

Chapter 6 describes the **LAMSTAR** (Large Memory Storage and Retrieval) Neural network **(LNN)**. The LAMSTAR differs from the other neural networks of this text by its employment of Hebbian-trained link-weights that serve to integrate Back and to rank inputs from an unrestricted number of pre-processing filters. The chapter presents two versions of the LAMSTAR network, namely, **LAMSTAR-1 (LNN-1)** and its normalized version, **LAMSTAR-2 (LNN-2)**.

Chapter 7 presents the principles of three deep learning neural networks, the Deep Boltzmann Machine (DBM), the Deep Recurrent Neural Network (DRNN) and the Deconvolution Neural Network (DCNN), which is also known as the wavelet Neural Network (WNN) in certain applications. The generality of these networks, in terms of range of applications, is more limited than that of the earlier deep learning covered in this text due to structure or computational speed. These networks are deep learning in the sense that they can dig deep, but they cannot integrate tools beyond their direct scope. Therefore, they are given shorter coverage than the networks of the last three chapters and no Case Studies if these are given for these three networks.

Chapter 8 serves to describe 20 **case studies** on a wide range of applications of the DLNN networks discussed in this text. All these case studies involve two or more different neural networks. Each case study compares the resultant performance (accuracy, success-rate) and the computational times for the networks involved in that case study, for exactly the same data, same PC/laptop and same programming language (per a given case study). The case Studies that are discussed do not cover the deep learning networks whose range of applications is limited, such as the Deconvolution Neural Network, the Deep Boltzmann or the Deep Recurrent Neural Network.

Twenty **program codes** for the **case studies** are presented in the **APPENDIX** to this chapter. These programs are not the complete programs for their respective studies since complete programs of 20 case studies may in themselves need several book volumes. Still, together with the additional referenced codes and related URLs provided in each study's discussion in Chapter 8, they should allow full understanding of the programming of any given case study that is being discussed.

The case studies are based on individual final reports by graduate students in the author's one-semester classes CS-559 and ECE-559 at the University of Illinois, Chicago, over the last 2–3 weeks of these courses. The codes were written by these students on their own PCs or laptops, as was mentioned earlier. The case studies cover a broad field of applications and, as such, they serve to illustrate the generality of DLNN and also the generality of the major deep learning networks above. This is also why no case studies for the networks of Chapter 7 are included.

The comparisons below are in terms of performance and of computational speed relative to the same input data. It must be emphasized that the cases considered are of low-complexity. They do not reflect necessary hold for more complex cases. Also, in all cases, an expert in the field may do better as would a highly skilled programmer. The case studies use mostly straightforward and standard programs, as presented in this text (with pre/co-processing that is explained per given case, rather than specialized, designs. However, the idea of a neural networks is that they are a tool of fixed architecture that can be used without special expertise and which can be applied easily to most problems even on a PC, but which will yield "good" results. Still, a network that gives 100% success rate for a given problem (which is achieved in a few of these case studies) and that is faster than another, is as "good" as one may looks for in the given application.

A summarizing discussion with concluding observations and comments are given in **Chapter 9**.

References

Abdel-Hamid O, Deng L, Yu D, "Convolutional neural network structures and optimization techniques for speech recognition", *Interspeech Conf.* (2013), pp. 3366–3370.

Bellman R, *Dynamic Programming* (Princeton University Press, 1961).

Calderon-Martinez J A, Campoy-Cervera P, "An application of convolutional neural networks for automatic inspection", *IEEE Conf. on Cybernetics and Intelligent Systems* (2006), pp. 1–6.

Dixon M, Klabian D , Bang J H, "Implementing deep neural networks for financial market prediction on the Intel Xeon Phi", *Proc. 8th Workshop on High Performance Computational Finance*, Paper No. 6 (2015).

Dong L, Yu D, "Deep learning methods and applications", *Foundations and Trends in Signal Processing* 7(3–4):197–387 (2014).

Dong F, Shatz S M, Xu H, Majumdar D, "Price comparison: A reliable approach to identifying shill bidding in online auction", *Electronic Commerce Research and Applications* **11**(2):171–179 (2012).

Fukushima K, "Cognitron: A self-organizing multi-layered neural network", *Biological Cybernetics* **20**:121–175 (1975).

Fukushima, K, "Neocognitron: A self-organizing neural network model for a mechanism of pattern recognition unaffected by shift in position", *Biological Cybernetics* **36**(4):193–202 (1980).

Girado J I, Sandin D J , DeFanti T A, Wolf L K, "Real-time camera-based face detection using modified LAMSTAR neural network system", *Proc. IS&T/SPIE 15th Annual Symp. on Electronic Imaging* (2003).

Graupe D, Abon J, "Neural network for blind adaptive *filtering* of unknown noise from speech", *Proc. ANNIE Conf.*, Paper WP2.1A (2002).

Graupe D, Kordylewski H, "A large memory storage and retrieval neural network for browsing and medical diagnosis applications", *Intelligent Engineering Systems through Artificial Neural Networks,* eds. Dagli C H *et al.*, Vol. 6 (ASME Press, 1996), pp. 711–716.

Graupe D, Lynn J W, "Some aspects regarding mechanistic modelling of recognition and memory", *Cybernetica* **3**:119 (1969).

Hebb D, *The Organization of Behavior* (John Wiley, 1949).

Hinton G E, Deng L, Yu D, Dahl G *et al.*, "Deep neural networks for acoustic modeling in speech recognition", *IEEE Signal Processing Magazine* **9**(6):82–97 (2013).

Kant E, *Critique of Pure Reason* (Koenigsbarg, Germany, 1781).

Kohonen T, *Self-Optimizing and Associative Memory* (Springer Verlag, 1984).

LeCun Y, Boser B, Denker J S, Henderson D, Howard R E, Hubbard W, Jackel L D, "Backpropagation applied to handwritten zip code recognition". *Neural Computation* **1**(4):541–551 (1989).

LeCun Y, Bottou L, Bengio Y, Haffner P, "Gradient-based learning applied to document recognition", *Proceedings of the IEEE*, Vol. 86, Issue 11 (1998), pp. 2278–2324. doi:10.1109/5.726791.

Nigam P V, Graupe D, "A neural-network-based detection of epilepsy", *Neurological Research* **26**(1):55–60 (2004).

Parker D B, "Learning Logic", *Invention Report 5-81-64*, File 1, Office of Technology Licensing, Stanford University, 1982.

Rios A, Kavuluru, R, "Convolutional neural networks for biomedical text classification: application in indexing biomedical article", *Proc. 6th ACM Conf. on Bioinformatics, Computational Biology and Health Informatics* (2015), pp. 258–267.

Rumelhart D E, Hinton G E, Williams R J, "Learning internal representations by error propagation", in *Parallel Distributed Processing: Explorations in Microstructures of Cognitron*, eds. Rumelhart D E and McClelland J L (MIT Press, 1986), pp. 318–362.

Schneider N A, Graupe D, "A modified LAMSTAR neural network and its applications", *International Jour. Neural Systems* **18**(4):331–337 (2008).

Simonyan, K, Zisserman, A, "Two-stream convolutional networks for action recognition in videos", *arXiv:1406.2199* [cs.CV], 2014.

Venkatachalam V and Selvan S, "Intrusion detection using an improved competitive learning Lamstar neural network", *IJCSNS, International Journal of Computer Science and Network Security* 7(2):255–263 (2007).

Waxman J A, Graupe D, Carley D W, "Prediction of Apnea and Hypopnea using LAMSTAR artificial neural network", *Amer. Jour. Respiratory and Critical Care Medicine* **181**(7):727–733 (2010).

Wallach I, Dzamba M, Heifets A, "AtomNet: A deep convolutional neural network for bioactivity prediction in structure-based drug discovery", *arXiv:1510.02855* [cs.LG], 2015.

Werbos P J, Beyond Recognition: New Tools for Prediction and Analysis in the Behavioral Sciences, PhD Thesis, Harvard University, (1974).

CHAPTER 2

Basic Concepts in Neural Networks

Before we proceed to discuss specific deep-learning neural networks, we introduce certain concepts used in the coming chapters.

2.1. The Hebbian Principle

First among these is the Hebbian Learning principle [Hebb, 1949] that used implicitly in most neural networks and is explicitly, fundamental to the weight setting in the LMSTAR 1 and LAMSTAR 2 deep learning neural networks.

Hebb's learning principle states that "when an axon of a neuronal cell ***A*** is near-enough to excite some neuronal cell ***B***, and when cell ***A*** repeatedly and consistently takes part in the firing of that cell B, then some growth process or metabolic change takes place in one or both of these two cells such that the efficiency of cell ***A*** with respect to cell ***B*** is increased".

This Hebbian principle can be understood by means of Pavlov's (1901) dog observation [Pavlov, 1927], where "cell ***B*** causes ***salivation*** of the dog and is excited by cell ***F*** which, in turn, is excited by the ***sight of food***. Furthermore, cell ***A***, which is excited by the ***sound of a bell***, is connected to cell ***B***. However, cell ***A*** cannot cause cell ***B*** to fire. Eventually, after repeated firing of cell ***B*** by cell ***F*** while cell ***A*** also happens to be firing, being excited, as always, by the sound of the bell). Subsequently, cell ***A*** which fires, as always, due to the sound of the bell, will be able to cause cell ***B*** to fire — without the firing of cell ***F***, namely, without sight of food ".

Hence, the Hebbian learning principle assumes that a connection between neuronal cells is a weighted connection, the value of the weight being a function of the number of times that neuronal firing passes through connection between these cells (say, from cell A to cell B). The existence of such learnt connections between biological cells in the CNS was physiologically and even biochemically established over the years [Stock, Zhang, 2013].

2.2. The Perceptron

The Perceptron model of a neuron [Rosenblatt, 1958] serves directly or indirectly, as the neuronal model in practically every artificial neural network, as described in Fig. 2.1.

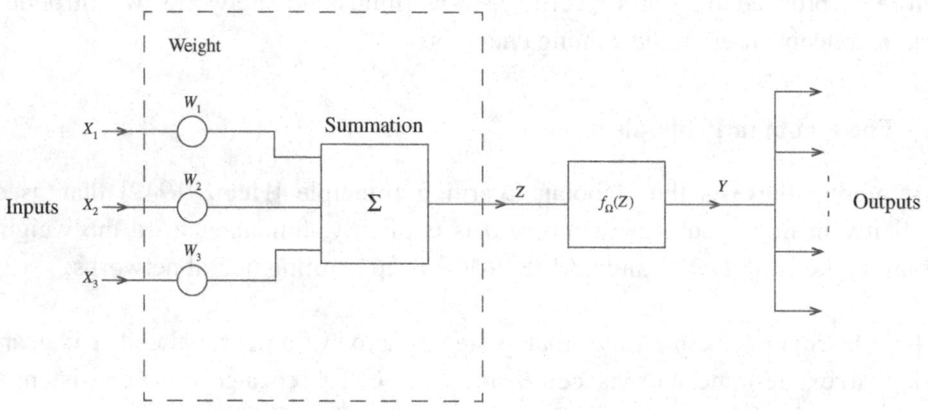

Fig. 2.1. Model of the perceptron.

As shown in Fig. 2.1, the neuronal model of the perceptron has n inputs (3 inputs in Fig. 2.1) denoted as x_i, $i = 1, 2, 3, \ldots, n$, and n weights w_i, where

$$i = 1, 2, 3, \ldots, n \tag{2.1}$$

The weighted inputs $w_i\, x_i$ undergo summation, such that

$$z = \sum_i (w_i\, x_i) \tag{2.2}$$

And the subsequent z is operated upon by a nonlinear operator $F(z)$ to yield the neuron's output y:

$$y = F(z) \tag{2.3}$$

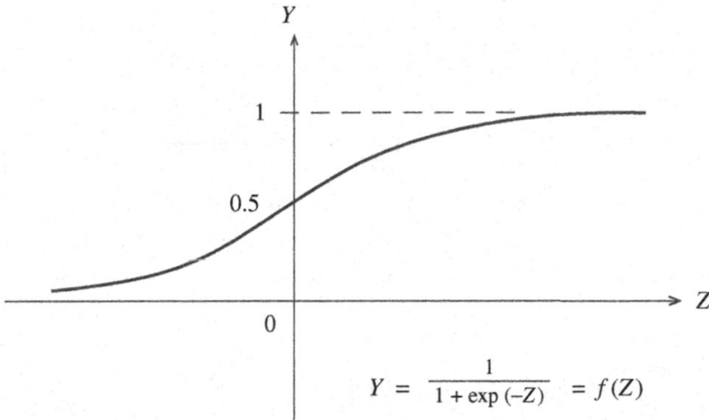

Fig. 2.2. Activation function 1 (soft switch from 0 to 1).

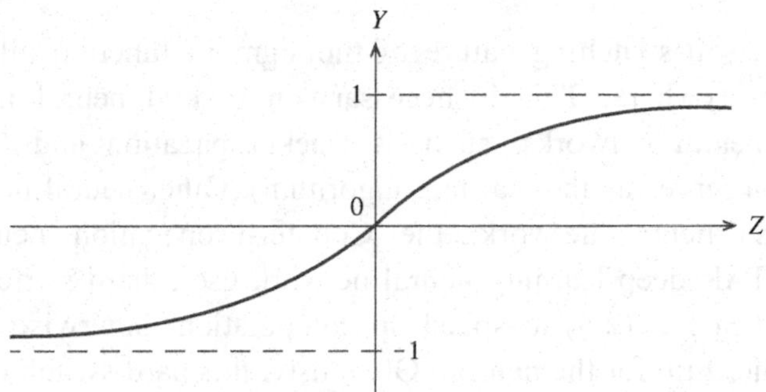

Fig. 2.3. Activation function 2 (soft switch from −1 to +1).

The Perceptron is based on the McCulloch-Pitts principles on the binary (0, 1) nature of the neural output [McCulloch and Pitts, 1943], which conforms with the binary firing/no-firing nature of the biological neuron. Also, it incorporates weights to be learnt regardless of the learning algorithm. For this purpose, it employs a continuous sigmoid activation function $F(z)$, as in Figs. 2.2, 2.3; Eqs. (2.4a) and (2.4b), respectively, which serves as a soft switch, z denoting the input to a sigmoid switch, while y is the neuron's output. This activation function converges to binary limits, say, (0, 1) or (−1, +1).

$$F(z) = 1/\,[1 + \exp(-z)\,] \tag{2.4a}$$

for soft switching between 0 and +1, and

$$F(z) = 2/[1 + \exp(-z)] - 1 \tag{2.4b}$$

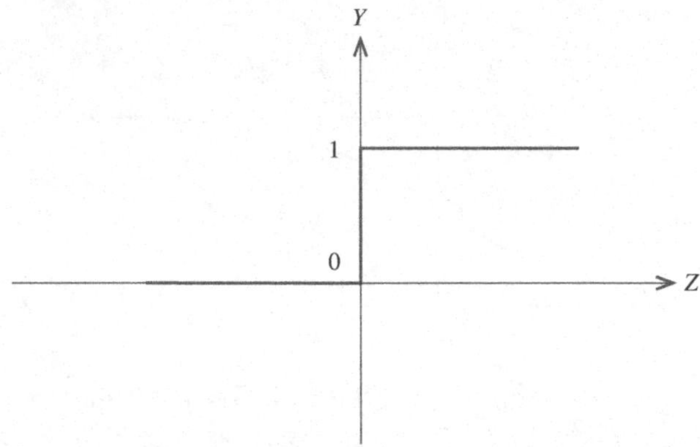

Fig. 2.4. Hard switch activation function.

The continuous, soft-switching nature of the sigmoid function allows it to be differentiable everywhere. This is necessary in several neural networks and deep learning neural networks, such as Backpropagation and CNN (where Backpropagation serves as the learning algorithm). Other neural networks, such as the Hopfield neural network, the Counter-Propagation neural network and the LAMSTAR deep learning neural network use a hard switch instead, as in Fig. 2.4, and in Eq. (2.5) to speed up computation, otherwise adopting the Perceptron architecture for the neuron. Obviously, this hard-switch design is also fully in line with the McCulloch-Pitts principles.

$$F(z) = \text{sign}(z) \tag{2.5}$$

Both the soft switch of the Perceptron and its hard switch equivalent satisfy the Perceptron's model of the artificial neuron as in Eqs. (2.2)–(2.5), and Fig. 2.1 above.

2.3. Associative Memory

The concept of Associative Memory (AM) is again taken from the anatomy of the central nervous system (CNS). Input information (memory) entering the CNS, say, a certain color of light hitting a photo-cell in the retina, is being stored in specific neurons or in a limited group of neurons of the visual cortex, that appear to fit the given input information (color) like a key fitting a lock. Other colors will then be stored elsewhere. The same holds for other types of information, say in the auditory cortex and elsewhere in the brain, as can be observed by functional MRI. Obviously, this feature contributes significantly to the efficiency of the CNS. This concept was first proposed to be used in artificial neural networks by Longuett-Higgins [Longuett-Higgins, 1968] and extended by Kohonen [Kohonen, 1977], still well before the advent of functional MRI, for improving efficiency of storing and of retrieving information in artificial neural networks. This method of storage is known Associative Memory (AM) or as Bidirectional Associative Memory (BAM) and is employed on the Hopfield neural network, in Counter-Propagation neural networks and in the LAMSTAR deep-learning neural network [Graupe, 2013]. AM can be derived via the equations below:

$$\boldsymbol{W} = \textstyle\sum_i \boldsymbol{y}(i)\, \boldsymbol{x}^T(i) \tag{2.6}$$

where $\boldsymbol{W}$ is a weights matrix of the form

$$\boldsymbol{W} = [w(i, j)] \tag{2.7}$$

$w(i, j)$ being the (i, j) element of the matrix, and $\boldsymbol{y}(i)$ and $\boldsymbol{x}(i)$ are input and output vectors of dimensions M and N respectively.

Furthermore, if

$$\boldsymbol{y}(i) = \boldsymbol{x}(i) \tag{2.8}$$

as is the case in the feedback configuration of the Hopfield neural network [Hopfield] and as in the Counter-Propagation neural networks [Kohonen, 1984] and in the LAMSTAR deep learning network of the present Chapter 6 [Graupe, 1997], then:

$$\boldsymbol{W} = \textstyle\sum_i \boldsymbol{x}(i)\, \boldsymbol{x}^T(i) \tag{2.9}$$

where superscript T denotes transposition.

Consequently, assuming that the input vectors $\boldsymbol{x(i)}$ are orthonormal (say, after normalization), then:

$$\boldsymbol{x}^T(\boldsymbol{i})\, \boldsymbol{x}(\boldsymbol{i}) = \delta(i, j) \tag{2.10}$$

$\delta(i, j)$ being the Kronecker delta function, and

$$\boldsymbol{W}\boldsymbol{x}(\boldsymbol{j}) = [\, \textstyle\sum_i \boldsymbol{x}(i)\, \boldsymbol{x}^T(i)]\, \boldsymbol{x}(\boldsymbol{j}) = \boldsymbol{x}(\boldsymbol{j}) \tag{2.11}$$

to simplify storage and retrieval of a particular information vector (namely, attribute, set).

This will be further explained via the concept of Winner-Takes-All, as discussed in the next sub-section.

2.4. Winner-Takes-All Principle

Another popular design concept in neural networks and subsequently, in deep learning neural networks is the concept of Winner-Takes-All (WTA) introduced by Kohonen in his SOM (Self-Organizing-Map) design [Kohonen, 1984]. By this concept, input information sent to a given WTA layer of neurons will be stored only in that neuron whose (trained or pre-assigned) input weights yield the maximal output to that input information. Hence, all other neurons in that layer will output 0 when faced with that input information.

Noting the concept of Associative memory of the previous sub-section, the WTA setting can be implemented, as follows:

Let all input vectors $\boldsymbol{x}$ are normalized to length 1 in the vector space, say via Eq. (2.12), to yield normalized vectors $\boldsymbol{x}'$, such that the elements $x(i)$ of a vector $\boldsymbol{x}$ become:

$$\boldsymbol{x}'(i) = \boldsymbol{x}(\boldsymbol{i})/sqrt\ \textstyle\sum_j [x^2(j)]\} \tag{2.12}$$

Hence, assuming normalized vectors $\boldsymbol{x}'$, we have that

$$(\boldsymbol{x}')^T \boldsymbol{x}' = 1 \tag{2.13}$$

This implies that any vector other than the one whose input weights conform with the incoming vector will yield an output smaller than 1, which will be rejected (by some fast algorithm — see p. 187 in [Graupe, 2013]), while keeping (storing) only the one that fits the weights of the given neuron. The result is a great reduction in computation in both biological neural networks and in artificial ones. The concept of Winner-Takes-All is used Counter-Propagation and Adaptive-Resonance-Theory (ART) neural networks [Graupe, 2013] and in the LAMSTAR 1 and LAMSTAR-2 deep learning networks of Chapter 6.

2.5. The Convolution Integral

The convolution integral is a folding function that serves to compute the output the operation of a filter function over a dynamic signal.

Consider a filter given in Laplace transform form as $G(s)$, s being a Laplace operator — see Section 7.2 in [Graupe, 1979] on Laplace transform form, whereas $U(s)$ denotes a signal operated upon by that filtering function.

The passing of the signal $U(s)$ through the filter $G(s)$ yields the output $X(s)$, where:

$$X(s) = G(s)\, U(s) \tag{2.14}$$

In discrete time, when using the z-transform operator (z), Eq. (2.14) becomes

$$X(z) = G(z)\, U(z) \tag{2.15}$$

The mathematical operations of Eq. (2.14) and ((2.15) are mathematically known as convolution operations or as transfer functions.

Applying the inverse Laplace transform to Eq. (2.14) yields the continuous time-domain output:

$$x(t) = \int_0^t g(\tau)u(t-\tau)d\tau \tag{2.16}$$

Similarly, applying the inverse z-transform to Eq. (2.15), yields the discrete time domain output x_j where:

$$x_j = \sum_{i=1}^{N} g_i u_{j-i} \tag{2.17}$$

It should be noted that u and g are fully interchangeable in Eqs. (2.16) and (2.17), without affecting the output.

Equation (2.16) is known as the convolution integral and Eq. (2.17) is its discrete time equivalent, known as the convolution sum. Both are used in the convolutional neural network (Chapter 5), and the deconvolution neural network (Chapter 7), where g_j and i of Eq. (2.17) are derived with the deconvolution network.

The above convolution integral/sum implies that the most recent sample of the input u is operated upon for least time by the filter g (namely, u just arrived at the filter and only starts to be affected by it or be "indoctrinated" by it), while the earliest arriving sample of the input u has been operated upon (affected) by that filter for the longest duration.

The convolution equations above are for the scalar (signal) case. They can be extended into vector/matrix form. Furthermore, Eqs. (2.16) and (2.17) may include a nonlinear operation $g(u)$ rather than a multiplication inside the integral/sum of these equations.

It is important to observe that the convolution Eqs. (2.16) and (2.17) are of the same form and meaning when g and *u are both signals or images*. In that case they become **cross-correlation** (even auto-correlation) equations (integrals/sums).

Furthermore, if g is a wavelet or has properties of a wavelet, then Eqs. (2.16) and (2.17) become continuous or discrete **wavelet transform** equations, respectively.

References

Graupe D, *Identification of Systems* (Krieger Publishing Co., 1979).

Graupe D, *Principles of Artificial Neural Networks* (World Scientific Publishing, 1997, 2013).

Hebb D, *The Organization of Behavior* (John Wiley, 1949).

Hopfield J J, "Neural computation of decisions in optimization problems", *Biol. Cybernetics* **52**:141–152 (1982).

Kohonen T, *Associated Memory: A System Theoretical Approach* (Springer Verlag, 1977).

Kohonen T, *Self-Organization and Associative Memory* (Springer Verlag, 1984).

Longuett-Higgins H C, "Holographic model of temporal recall", *Nature* **217**:104 (1968).

McCulloch W S, Pitts W, "A logical calculus of the ideas imminent in nervous activity", *Bull. Math. Biophysics* **5**:115–133 (1943).

Pavlov I P, *Conditional Reflexes* (1927), in Russian. English translation (Oxford University Press, 1927, Dover Press, 1962).

Rosenblatt F, "The perceptron, a probabilistic model for information storage and organization in the brain", *Psychol. Rev.* **65**:386–408 (1958).

Stock J B, Zhang S, "The biochemistry of memory", *Current Biology* **23**(17):R741–R745 (2013).

CHAPTER 3

Back-Propagation

3.1. The Back Propagation Architecture

The back propagation (BP) algorithm was proposed in 1986 by Rumelhart, Hinton. and Williams for setting weights and hence for the training of multi-layer perceptrons. This opened the way for using multi-layer ANNs, nothing that the hidden layers have no desired (hidden) outputs accessible. The BP algorithm of Rumelhart [Rumelhart *et al.*, 1986] is based on a gradient form of Richard Bellman's Dynamic Programming [Bellman, 1961] and is very close to algorithms proposed earlier by Werbos [Werbos, 1974] in his Ph.D. dissertation in Harvard in 1974 and then in a report by D B Parker [Parker, 1982] at Stanford in 1982, both unpublished at the time. It goes without saying that the availability of a rigorous method to set intermediate weights, namely to train hidden layers of ANNs gave a major boost to the further development of ANN, opening the way to overcome the single-layer shortcomings that had been pointed out by Minsky and Papert [Minsky and Papet, 1969] and which nearly dealt a death blow to ANNs. BP was the first neural network that could be applied to a broad range of problems from different areas. It was therefore, with adequate preprocessing the first neural network with a claim to be regarded as a deep learning network. However, as is the case with many dynamic programming-based algorithms, and especially since BP is based on gradient dynamic programming, it was too slow to satisfy the machine learning needs. Still, it was rehabilitated later on [LeCun, 1989], when it became the learning engine of the far faster Convolutional deep learning neural network (CNN) that is the subject of Chapter 5 below, which became the most popular deep learning neural network. Indeed, one of the creators of BP, Geoffrey Hinton is also one of the leading creators of CNN.

3.2. Derivation of the BP Algorithm

The BP algorithm starts, of necessity with computing the *output layer*, which is the only one where desired outputs *are* available, but the outputs of the intermediate layers are unavailable (see Fig. 3.1), as follows:

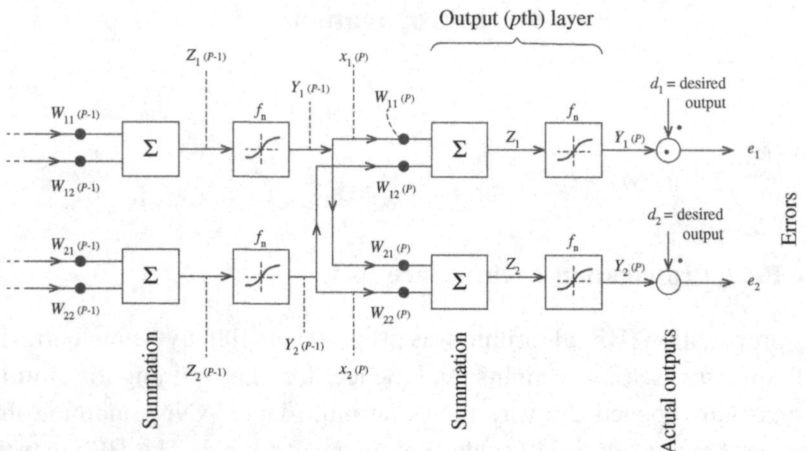

Fig. 3.1. Two hidden layers of a BP neural networks.

Let ε denote the error-energy at the output layer, where:

$$\varepsilon \triangleq \frac{1}{2}\sum_k (d_k - y_k)^2 = \frac{1}{2}\sum_k e_k^2 \tag{3.1}$$

$k = 1 \ldots N$; N the number of neurons in the output layer. Consequently, a gradient of ε is considered, where:

$$\nabla \varepsilon_k = \frac{\partial \varepsilon}{\partial w_{kj}} \tag{3.2}$$

Now, using the steepest descent, we have that

$$w_{kj}(m+1) = w_{kj}(m) + \Delta w_{kj}(m) \tag{3.3}$$

j denoting the jth input to the kth neuron of the output layer, where, by the steepest descent procedure:

$$\Delta w_{kj} = -\eta \frac{\partial \varepsilon}{\partial w_{kj}} \tag{3.4}$$

The minus (–) sign in Eq. (3.4) indicates a down-hill direction towards a minimum. We note from the perceptron's definition that the k's perceptron's node-output z_k is given by

$$z_k = \sum_j w_{kj} x_j \tag{3.5}$$

x_j being the jth input to that neuron, and noting that the perceptron's output y_k is:

$$y_k = F_N(z_k) \tag{3.6}$$

F being a nonlinear activation function as discussed in Chapter 2 and must be continuous to allow its differentiation. We now substitute

$$\frac{\partial \varepsilon}{\partial w_{kj}} = \frac{\partial \varepsilon}{\partial z_k} \frac{\partial z_k}{\partial w_{kj}} \tag{3.7}$$

and, by Eq. (3.5):

$$\frac{\partial z_k}{\partial w_{kj}} = x_j(p) = y_j(p-1) \tag{3.8}$$

p denoting the output layer, such that Eq. (3.7) becomes:

$$\frac{\partial \varepsilon}{\partial w_{kj}} = \frac{\partial \varepsilon}{\partial z_k} x_j(p) = \frac{\partial \varepsilon}{\partial z_r} y_j(p-1) \tag{3.9}$$

Defining:

$$\Phi_k(p) = -\frac{\partial \varepsilon}{\partial z_k(p)} \tag{3.10}$$

then Eq. (3.9) yields:

$$\frac{\partial \varepsilon}{\partial w_{kj}} = -\Phi_k(p) x_j(p) = -\Phi_k y_j(p-1) \tag{3.11}$$

and, by Eqs. (3.4) and (3.11):

$$\Delta w_{kj} = \eta \phi_k(p) x_j(p) = \eta \Phi_k(p) y_j(p-1) \tag{3.12}$$

j denoting the jth input to neuron k of the output (p) layer. Furthermore, by Eq. (3.10):

$$\Phi_k = -\frac{\partial \varepsilon}{\partial z_k} = -\frac{\partial \varepsilon}{\partial y_k}\frac{\partial y_k}{\partial z_k} \tag{3.13}$$

But, by Eq. (3.1):

$$\frac{\partial \varepsilon}{\partial y_k} = -(d_k - y_k) = y_k - d_k \tag{3.14}$$

whereas, for a sigmoid nonlinearity:

$$y_k = F_N(z_k) = \frac{1}{1+\exp(-z_k)} \tag{3.15}$$

we have that:

$$\frac{\partial y_k}{\partial z_k} = y_k(1 - y_k) \tag{3.16}$$

Consequently; by Eqs. (3.13), (3.14) and (3.16):

$$\Phi_k = y_k(1 - y_k)(d_k - y_k) \tag{3.17}$$

such that, at the output layer, by Eqs. (3.4), (3.7):

$$\Delta w_{kj} = -\eta \frac{\partial \varepsilon}{\partial w_{kj}} = -\eta \frac{\partial \varepsilon}{\partial z_k}\frac{\partial z_k}{\partial w_{kj}} \tag{3.18}$$

where, by Eqs. (3.8) and (3.13):

$$\Delta w_{kj}(p) = \eta \Phi_k(p) y_j(p-1) \tag{3.19}$$

Φ_k being as in Eq. (3.17), to complete the derivation of the setting of output layer weights.

Back-propagating to the rth hidden layer, we still have, as before

$$\Delta w_{ji} = -\eta \frac{\partial \varepsilon}{\partial w_{ji}} \tag{3.20}$$

for the ith branch into the jth neuron of the rth hidden layer. Consequently, in parallelism to Eq. (3.7):

$$\Delta w_{ji} = -\eta \frac{\partial \varepsilon}{\partial z_j} \frac{\partial z_j}{\partial w_{ji}} \tag{3.21}$$

and noting Eq. (3.8) and the definition of Φ in Eq. (3.13):

$$\Delta w_{ji} = -\eta \frac{\partial \varepsilon}{\partial z_j} y_i(r-1) = \eta \Phi_j(r) y_i(r-1) \tag{3.22}$$

such that, by the right hand-side relation of Eq. (3.13)

$$\Delta w_{ji} = -\eta \left[\frac{\partial \varepsilon}{\partial y_j(r)} \frac{\partial y_j}{\partial z_j} \right] y_i(r-1) \tag{3.23}$$

where $\frac{\partial \varepsilon}{\partial y_j}$ is inaccessible (as is, therefore, also $\Phi_j(r)$ above).

However, ε can only be affected by upstream neurons when one propagates *backwards* from the output. No other information is available at that stage. Therefore:

$$\begin{aligned} \frac{\partial \varepsilon}{\partial y_j(r)} &= \sum_k \frac{\partial \varepsilon}{\partial z_k(r+1)} \left[\frac{\partial z_k(r+1)}{\partial y_j(r)} \right] \\ &= \sum_k \frac{\partial \varepsilon}{\partial z_k} \left[\frac{\partial}{\partial y_j(r)} \sum_m w_{km}(r+1) y_m(r) \right] \end{aligned} \tag{3.24}$$

where the summation over k is performed over the neurons of the next (the $r + 1$) layer that connect to $y_j(r)$, whereas summation over m is over all inputs to each k'th neuron of the $(r + 1)$ layer.

Hence, and noting the definition of Φ, Eq. (3.24) yields:

$$\frac{\partial \varepsilon}{\partial y_j(r)} = \sum_k \frac{\partial \varepsilon}{\partial z_k(r+1)} w_{kj} = -\sum_k \Phi_k(r+1) w_{kj}(r+1) \tag{3.25}$$

since only $w_{kj}(r + 1)$ is connected to $y_j(r)$. Hence, ϕ becomes

$$\Phi_j(r) = \frac{\partial y_j}{\partial z_j} \sum_k \Phi_k(r+1) w_{kj}(r+1)$$

$$= y_j(r)[1 - y_j(r)] \sum_k \Phi_k(r+1) w_{kj}(r+1) \tag{3.26}$$

and, via Eq. (3.19):

$$\Delta w_{ji}(r) = \eta \Phi_j(r) y_i(r-1) \tag{3.27}$$

to obtain $\Delta w_{ji}(r)$ as a function of ϕ and the weights of the $(r + 1)$ layer, noting Eq. (3.26).

Note that we cannot take partial derivatives of ε with respect to the hidden layer considered. We thus must take the partial derivatives of ε with respect to the variables upstream in the direction of the output, which are the only ones that affect ε. This observation is the basis for the Back-Propagation procedure, to facilitate overcoming the lack of accessible error data in the hidden layers.

The BP algorithm thus propagates backwards all the way to $r = 1$ (the first layer), to complete its derivation. Its computation can thus be summarized as follows (see Fig. 3.2).

Apply the first training vector. Subsequently, compute $\Delta w_{kj}(p)$ from Eqs. (3.17) and (3.19) for the output (the p) layer and then proceed through computing $\Phi_j(r)$ and $\Delta w_{ji}(r)$ from Eqs. (3.26) and (3.27) for $r = p - 1, p - 2, \ldots, 2, 1$.

Using Eq. (3.26) to update $\Phi_j(r)$ on the basis of $\Phi_j(r + 1)$ upstream (namely back-propagating from layer $r + 1$ to layer r), etc. Next, update $w(m + 1)$ from $w(m)$ and $\Delta w(m)$ for the $m + 1$ iteration via Eq. (3.3) for the latter training set. Repeat the whole process when applying the next training vector until you go through all L training vectors. Then repeat the whole process for $(m + 2)$, $(m + 3)$, … until adequate convergence is reached.

The ***learning rate*** η should be adjusted stepwise, considering stability requirements resulting from the Dvoretsky Stochastic Approximation Theorem

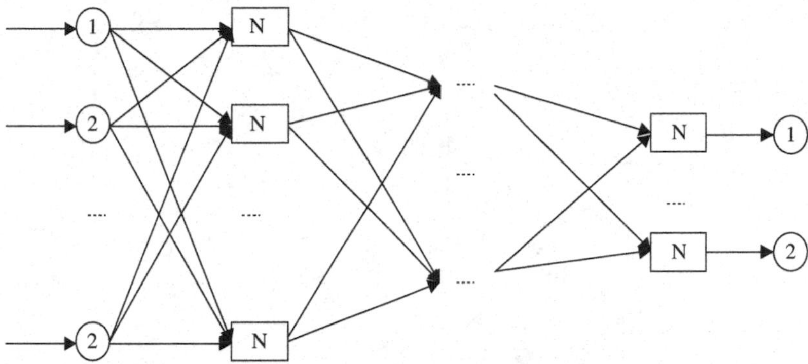

Fig. 3.2. Schematic BP neural network.

[Dvoretsky, 1956], [Graupe, 1989]. However, since convergence is usually rather fast when the error becomes very small, it is advisable to reinstate η to its initial value before proceeding.

Initialization of $w_{ji}(o)$ is accomplished by setting each weight to a low-valued random value selected from a pool of random numbers, say in the range from −5 to +5.

The number of hidden layer neurons should be higher rather than lower. However, for simple problems, one or two hidden layers may suffice.

3.3. Modified BP Algorithms

3.3.1. Introduction of bias into NN

It is often advantageous to apply some bias to the neurons of a neural network (see Fig. 3.3). The bias can be trainable when associated with a trainable weight to be modified as is any other weight. Hence the bias is realized in terms of an input with some constant (say +1 or B) value, and the exact bias b_i (at the ith neuron) is then given

$$b_i = w_{oi}B \tag{3.28}$$

w_{oi} being the weight of the bias term at the input to neuron i. Note that the bias may be positive or negative, depending on its weight.

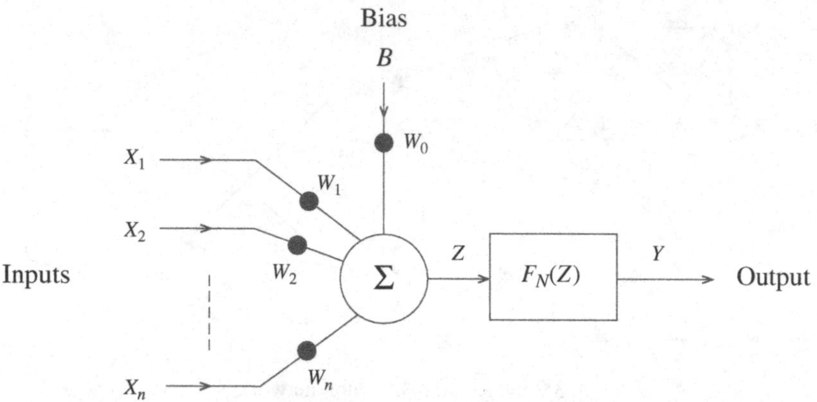

Fig. 3.3. A biased neuron.

3.3.2. Incorporating momentum or smoothing to weight adjustment

The backpropagation (BP) algorithm to compute weights of neurons may tend to instability under certain operation conditions. To reduce the tendency to instability Rumelhart [Rumelhart *et al.*, 1986] suggested to add a momentum term to Eq. (3.1). Hence, Eq. (3.12) is modified to:

$$\Delta w_{ij}^{(m)} = \eta \Phi_i(r) y_j(r-1) + \alpha \Delta w_{ij}^{(m-1)} \tag{3.29}$$

$$w_{ij}^{(m+1)} = w_{ij}^{(m)} + \Delta w_{ij}^{(m)} \tag{3.30}$$

for the $m + 1$ iteration, with $0 < \alpha < 1$; α being the momentum coefficient (usually around 0.9). The employment of α will tend to avoid fast fluctuations, but it may not always work, or could even harm convergence.

Another smoothing method, for the same purpose and also not always advisable, is that of employing a smoothing term as proposed by Sejnowski and Rosenberg [Sejnowski *et al.*, 1987], is given as follows:

$$\Delta w_{ij}^{(m)} = \alpha \Delta w_{ij}^{(m-1)} + (1-\alpha) \Phi_i(r) y_j(r-1) \tag{3.31}$$

$$w_{ij}^{(m+1)} = w_{ij}^{(m)} + \eta \Delta w_{ij}^{(m)} \tag{3.32}$$

with $0 < \alpha < 1$. Note that for $\alpha = 0$ no smoothing takes place whereas causes the algorithm to get stuck. η of Eq. (3.32) is again between 0 and 1.

3.3.3. Other modification concerning convergence

Improved convergence of the BP algorithm can often be achieved by: *modifying the range of the sigmoid* function from the range of zero to one, to a range from –0.5 to +0.5.

1. ***Feedback*** may sometimes be used, via a recurrent architecture such as in [Graupe, 2013]. (See Section 7.2) may sometimes be used.
2. Modifying step size can be employed to avoid the BP algorithm from *getting stuck* (learning paralysis) at a local minimum, or from oscillating. This is often achieved by reducing step size, at least when the algorithm approached paralysis or when it starts oscillating.
3. Convergence to ***local minima*** can best be avoided by statistical methods where there always exists a finite probability of moving the network away from an apparent or a real minimum by a large step.
4. Use of ***Resilient-BP*** algorithms, such as RPROP [Riedmiller and Braun, 1993] may greatly speed up convergence and reduce sensitivity to initialization. RPROP considers signs of partial derivatives (see Section 3.2 above) to compute weights by BP, rather than their actual values.

References

Bellman R, *Dynamic Programming* (Princeton University Press, 1961).

Dworetzky A, "On stochastic approximation", *Proc. 3rd Berkeley Symposium on Mathematical Statistics and Probability,* University of California Press, 1956.

Graupe D, *Time Series Analysis, Identification and Adaptive Filtering* (Krieger Publishing Co., 1989).

Graupe D, *Principles of Artificial Neural Networks* (3rd edition), (World Scientific Publishing Co., 2013).

LeCun, Y, Boser B, Denker J S, Henderson D, Howard R E, Hubbard W, Jackel L D, "Backpropagation applied to handwritten zip code recognition". *Neural Computation* **1**(4):541–551 (1989).

Minsky M, Papert S, *Perceptrons* (MIT Press, 1969).

Parker D B, "Learning Logic", *Invention Report 5-81-64*, File 1, Office of Technology Licensing, Stanford University, 1982.

Riedmiller M, Braun H, "A direct adaptive method for faster backpropagation learning: The PROP algorithm", *Proc. IEEE Conference on Neural Networks* (1993), pp. 586–591.

Rumelhart D E, Hinton G E, Williams R J, "Learning internal representations by error propagation", in *Parallel Distributed Processing: Explorations in Microstructures of Cognitron*, eds. Rumelhart D E and McClelland J L (MIT Press, 1986), pp. 318–362.

Senjowski T J, Rosenberg C R, "Parallel networks that learn to pronounce English text", *Computer Systems* **1**:145–168 (1987).

Werbos P J, Beyond recognition: New tools for prediction and analysis in the behavioral sciences, PhD Thesis, Harvard University, (1974).

CHAPTER 4

The Cognitron and Neocognitron

4.1. Introduction

The cognitron, as its name implies, is a network designed mainly with recognition of patterns in mind. To do this, the cognitron network employs both inhibitory and excitory neurons in its various layers. It was first devised by Kunhiko Fukushima [Fukushima, 1975], and is an unsupervised network such that it imitates the biological retina to perform what may be considered as deep learning for the purpose of recognizing images.

The Neocognitron was also developed by Fukushima [Fukushima, 1980, 1983] to revise and to extend the capabilities of the Cognitron. It was inspiration for the later development of the Convolutional deep learning neural network in 1989 [LeCun, 1989], which became the leading deep learning neural network.

4.2. Principles of the Cognitron

The cognitron basically consists of layers of inhibitory and excitory neurons. Interconnection of a neuron in a given layer is only to neurons of the previous layer that are in the vicinity of that neuron. This vicinity is termed as the connection competition region of the given neuron. For training efficiency, not all neurons are being trained. Training is thus limited to only an elite group of the most relevant neurons, namely to neurons already previously trained for a related task.

Whereas connection regions lead to overlaps of neurons, where a given neuron may belong to the connection region of more than one upstream neuron, competition (for "elite" selection) is introduced to overcome the effect of the overlaps.

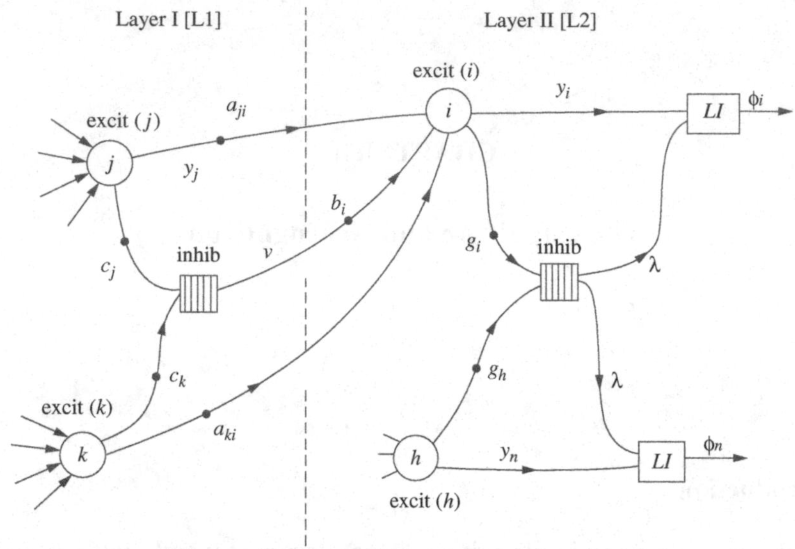

Fig. 4.1. Schematic description of a cognitron network.
(a competition region with two excitory neurons in each layer).

Competition will disconnect the neurons whose responses are weaker. The above feature provides the network with considerable redundancy, to enable it to function well in the face of "lost" neurons.

The cognitron's structure is based on a multi-layer architecture with a progressive reduction in number of competition regions. Alternatively, groups of two layers, L-I and L-II may be repeated n times to result in $2n$ layers in total (L-I1, L-II1, L-I2, L-II2, etc.). See Fig. 4.1 for a schematic diagram of the network, having a competition region LI with 2 excitory neurons.

4.3. Network Operation

(a) Excitory neurons

The output of an excitory neuron is computed as follows:

Let $y(k)$ be the output from an excitory neuron at the previous layer and let $v(j)$ be the output from an inhibitory neuron at its previous layer. Define the output components of the excitory i'th neuron as:

$$x(i) = \sum_k [a(i, k)\, y(k)] \qquad \text{due to excitation inputs} \qquad (4.1)$$

$$z(i) = \sum_k [b(i, k)\, v(k)] \qquad \text{due to inhibition inputs} \tag{4.2}$$

$a(i, k)$ and $b(i, k)$ being relevant weights, that are adjusted when the neuron concerned is more active than its neighbors, as discussed in Section 4.4 below. The total output of above neuron is given as:

$$y(i) - f[N(i)] \tag{4.3}$$

where:

$$N(i) = [1 + x(i)]/[1 + z(i)] - 1 = [x(i) - z(i)]/[1 + z(i)] \tag{4.4}$$

while

$$F[N(i)] = \begin{cases} N(i) & \text{for } N(i) \geq 0 \\ 0 & \text{for } N(i) < 0 \end{cases} \tag{4.5}$$

Hence, for small $z(i)$

$$N(i) \sim x(i) - z(i) \tag{4.6}$$

while, for v very large x, z

$$N(i) \sim [x(i)/z(i)] - 1 \tag{4.7}$$

Furthermore, if both x and z increase linearly with some γ, namely:

$$x = p\,\gamma \tag{4.8}$$

$$z = q\,\gamma \tag{4.9}$$

p and q being constants, then

$$y = [(p - q)/2q]\{1 + \tanh[\log(pq/2)]\} \tag{4.10}$$

which is of the form of the Webber-Fechner Law that approximates responses of biological sensory neurons — see Guyton, 1971, pp. 562–563.

(b) Inhibitory neurons

The output v of an inhibitory neuron is given by

$$v(i) = \sum_i [c(i)\, y(i)] \tag{4.11}$$

where

$$\sum_i [c(i)] = 1 \tag{4.12}$$

$y(i)$ being an output of an excitory neuron. The weights $c(i)$ are *pre-selected* and do not undergo modification during the network's training.

4.4. Cognitron Training

The $a(j, i)$ weights of the excitory neuron in a 2-layer cognitron structure are iterated by δa as in Eq. (4.13), but *only* if that neuron is a winning neuron in a region where $a(i, j)$, $y(i)$ and $c(j)$ are as in Eqs. (4.1), (4.3) and (4.11), respectively:

$$\delta a(j, i) = qc^*(j)\, y^*(i) \tag{4.13}$$

the parameter q being pre-set, asterisks denoting previous layer.

One should note that there are several excitory neurons in each competition layer L1 while there is only one inhibitory layer.

The inhibitory weights $b(j)$ going to excitory neurons are iterated according to Eq. (4.14):

$$\delta b(i) = q \sum_j [a(ij)\, y^2(j)]/2v^* \tag{4.14}$$

where $b(i)$ are the weights on the connection between the inhibitory neuron of layer L1 and the i'th excitory neuron in L2, $\sum_j$ denoting the summation on the weights from all excitory neurons of L1 to the same i'th neurons of L2. Also, v denotes the value of the inhibitory input as in Eq. (4.11), q being a rate coefficient.

If no neuron is active in a given competition region, then Eqs. (4.13) and (4.14) are replaced with Eqs. (4.15) and (4.16), respectively:

$$\delta a(j, i) = q'c(j)\, y(i) \tag{4.15}$$

$$\delta b(i) = q'v(i) \tag{4.16}$$

where

$$q' > q \tag{4.17}$$

such that now the higher the inhibition output, the higher is its weight, in sharp contrast to the situation according to Eq. (4.13).

Initialization

Initially all weights are set at zero and no neuron is active (none is providing an output). Hence, the first output goes through, since at the first layer of excitory neurons, network's input vector serves as the *y* vector of inputs to L1, to start the process via Eq. (4.15) above.

Lateral Inhibition

An inhibitory neuron is also located in each competition region as in layer L2 of Fig. 4.1, to provide lateral inhibition whose purpose (similar to the use of lateral inhibition in Adaptive Resonance (ART) neural networks — see Chapter 10 in [Graupe, 2013]. This inhibitory neuron receives inputs from the excitory neurons of its layer via weights $g(i)$ to yield an output λ as in Eq. (4.18) below:

$$\lambda = \sum_j [g(i)\, y(i)] \tag{4.18}$$

$y(i)$ denoting the output of the excitory neuron of the previous (say, L1) layer, and:

$$\sum_j [g(i)] = 1 \tag{4.19}$$

Subsequently, the output λ of the L2 inhibitory neuron above, modifies the actual output of the i'th L2 excitory neuron from $y(i)$ to $\phi(i)$ where

$$\phi(i) = f\{[y(i) - \lambda]/[1+\lambda]\} \tag{4.20}$$

where $y(i)$ is as in Eq. (4.3) above, $f\{\ldots\}$ being as in Eq. (4.5), to result in a feed-forward form of lateral inhibition and which is applicable to all layers.

4.5. The Neocognitron

A more advanced version of the cognitron also developed by Fukushima *et al.* [Fukushima, 1983], is the neocognitron. It is hierarchical in nature and is geared toward simulating human vision.

Recognition is arranged in a hierarchical structure of groups of 2 layers, as in the case of the cognitron. The two layers now are a simple-cells-layer (S-layer) and a concentrating layer (C-layer), starting with an S-layer denoted as S1 and ending with a C layer (say, C4). Each neuron of the S-layer responds to a given feature of its input layers (including the overall network's input). Each of the arrays of the C layer processes in depth inputs from usually one S layer array.

The number of neurons and arrays generally goes down from layer to layer. This structure enables the neocognitron to overcome recognition problems where the original cognitron failed, such as images under position or angular distortions (say somewhat rotated characters or digits in handwriting recognition problems). See Fig. 4.2.

Few applications of the Cognitron or of the Neocogntrom are available in the literature and these appear to be all in the field of image recognition. Long computing time and progress in other neural networks and especially the advent of CNN (Chapter 5 below) may be the reasons for this. Therefore, none of the case studies in this text is using either the Cognitron or the Neocognitron. However, its pioneering ideas inspired the whole field of deep learning neural and specifically, the development of the CNN deep learning neural network [LeCun *et al.*, 1989].

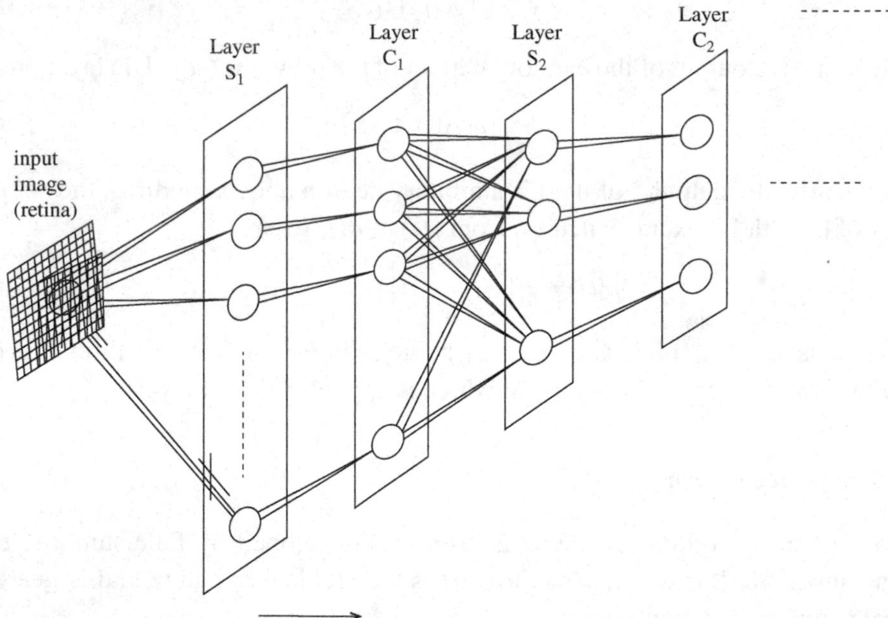

Fig. 4.2. Schematic of a neocognitron.

References

Graupe D, *Principles of Artificial Neural Networks* (3rd edition), (World Scientific Publishing Co., 2013).

Guyton A C, *Textbook of Medical Physiology* (14th edition), (W B Saunders Publishing Co., 1971).

Fukushima K, "Cognitron: A self-organizing multi-layered neural network", *Biological Cybernetics* **20**:121–175 (1975).

Fukushima K, "Neocognitron: A self-organizing neural network model for a mechanism of pattern recognition unaffected by shift in position", *Biological Cybernetics* **36**(4):93–202 (1980).

Fukushima K, Miyake S, Ito T, "Neocognitron: A neural network model for a mechanism of visual pattern recognition", *IEEE Transactions on Systems, Man, and Cybernetics* **13**(3):826–834 (1983).

LeCun, Y. Boser B, Denker J S, Henderson D, Howard R E, Hubbard W, Jackel L D, "Backpropagation applied to handwritten zip code recognition", *Neural Computation* **1**(4):541–551 (1989).

Minsky M, Papert S, *Perceptrons* (MIT Press, 1969).

CHAPTER 5

Deep Learning Convolutional Neural Network

5.1. Introduction

The convolutional deep-learning neural network (ConvNet, CNN) is the most widely used and most popular deep learning neural network. It is a true deep learning network, in contrast to the convolutional NN for decomposition (Chapter 4), which is discussed in this text mainly for introducing convolution itself and the power of convolution in learning. The term "convolutional neural network" is often considered as synonymous with the term "deep learning neural network". It applies to the class of neural networks based on and derived from the work of Yann LeCun and his associates in 1989 [LeCun *et al.*, 1989] and with the La-Net algorithms [LeCun, 1998]. As was mentioned in Chapter 1, CNN was inspired by the models of the biological retina [Hubel and Wiesel, 1959] and by Fukushima's Cognitron and Neocognitron [Fukushima, 1975], [Fukushima, 1980], which are discussed in Chapter 4 of this text and its computation uses the Back-Propagation algorithms, as discussed in Chapter 3 above. It employs the convolution integral in its discrete-time form — see Section 2.5 above, where the convolution function (filter) is the algorithmic form of certain (3D) volumes of numbers (parameters), as suggested by LeCun *et al.*

The Hubel/Fukushima origin and the geometric convolution function used all indicate that the CNN (ConvNet) was developed with vision/imaging (2D/3D) applications in mind, where indeed it is still most powerful and most used. Hinton *et al.* showed that it can be equally effective in speech and natural language processing. This obviously opened the field to other applications, many of which are illustrated in the Appendices of Case Studies at the end of this text. Whereas there are many variants on the ConvNet, considering the specific application in mind (and even for a given application), we shall present it in a form that follows, more-or-less, the widely used LeNet 5, with some variations. The CNN design of Krizhevsky, Sutskever and Hinton [Krizhevsky *et al.*, 2012], which is based on the LeNet architecture but with several convolutional layers stacked together, (rather than being immediately followed by a pooling layer — see below) won the ImageNet Challenge in 2012.

In some of the Case Studies below some other variations do appear, but they still follow the basic structure discussed below.

5.2. CNN Structure

5.2.1. Basic architecture

The CNN structure is based on the CNN design as related image recognition, as in Fig. 5.1. Other applications require a process to reformulate the input such that an input-feature map is constructed (Fig. 5.2).

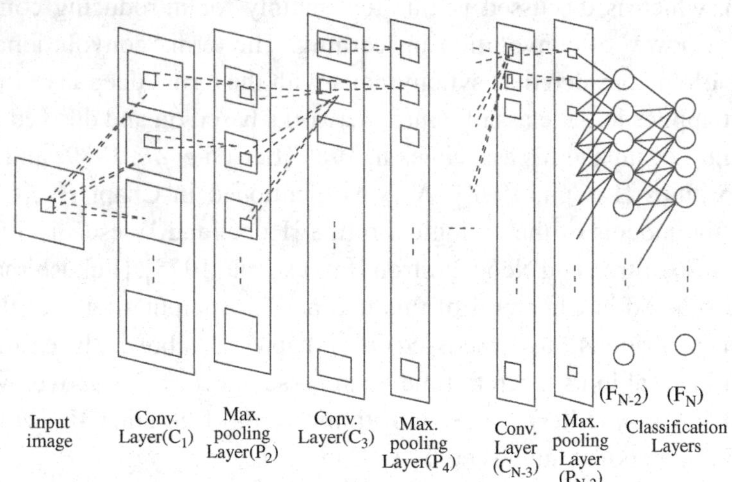

Fig. 5.1. Basic structure of CNN.
(ReLu layer follows each Convolution layer — not shown separately in Figure)

The main elements in the CNN design can be summarized as:

Convolution Layers — of which there are usually many, depending on the problem's dimensions and complexity.

ReLU (Rectified Linear Unit) Layers — usually follow each convolution layer and are repeated with them.
Pooling Layers — of which are also many repeated layers, and which follow the pair convolution and ReLu layers.
Fully Connected (FC) Layer — is a single, fully-connected output layer for classification and decision, which follows at the end.
Back Propagation (BP — see Chapter 3 above) is used to the learning by its repeated computing of the weight between the various neurons in the Convolution Layers. It is not a layer per-se, but an algorithm for weight setting of a given layer. The BP algorithm itself is not affected by ReLu.

Another important aspect of CNN is **Parameter Sharing**, which has an important role in speeding-up this neural network whenever its use can be justified. CNN is not necessarily restricted to visual inputs. As long as the input can be converted into a feature map even if not necessarily a 2D feature map, the Input-Image of Fig. 5.1 above can be replaced by that feature map. It thus becomes an "equivalent input image" and processed by any CNN network.

The layers of a ConvNet consider neurons arranged in volumes of 3 dimensions: **width, height, depth**.

The most popular CNN architecture (Fig. 5.1) is in terms of a repeated arrangement of the following three distinct types groups of layers:

CONVOLUTIONAL-LAYER/RELU-LAYER/POOLING-LAYER

The number of repetitions depends on the problem to be solved and its complexity. In all cases the arrangement of layers starts with an INPUT FEATURE MAP (say, image) and is terminated by a Fully-Connected output (decision) layer. The improved ImageNet design [Krizhevsky *et al.*, 2012]. Which won the ImageNet 2012 yielded improved performance through modifying the grouping of three layers above such that the pairs {Convolutional-Layer/RELU-Layer} are repeated twice (or more) before being followed by the Pooling Layer above. A consequent arrangements of repetitions of the modified group of

{[(CONV/RELU)/(CONV/RELU)]-[Pooling]}

is described in [Karpathy *et al.*, 2016], which was mentioned in Section 5.1 above. Each of the individual layers receives an input that is a 3D volume and after processing it (as described below) transfers it as a 3D volume at its output to the next layer.

The Convolution-Layer and the Fully-Connected (FC) output layer at the end of the CNN network have weight (parameters) that are being learnt (trained), while the RELU and the Pooling layers have none, although the Pooling-Layer has hyper-parameters.

In this way, CNN networks transform the original image layer by layer from the original pixel values to the final scores. The Convolution-Layers and the FC Output-Layer perform transformations that are a function of the activations in the input volume and of the parameters that are learned via Backpropagation. In contrast, the RELU-Layer and the Pooling Layers implement fixed functions.

All layers mentioned above are discussed in the later sections of this chapter as are features, such as Backpropagation and Parameter Sharing, that are incorporated in these layers.

5.2.2. Further design details

5.2.2.1. *Depth dimension in the CNN architecture*

Depth of volume in any layer is given by the number of parallel Feature Maps at that layer. In ***color*** Image recognition applications this may be in terms of the RGB (Red-Green-Blue) intensities. In ***Grey-Scale*** images it can be based on grey-level ranges of intensity between 0 and 1. In ***3D applications***, depth will be based on slices of the images in a 3D space.

Also, when employing preprocessing filters at the CNN input, the number of such preprocessors will be counted in the depth dimension. Furthermore, in applications where input feature maps (FMs) at certain points of time or space must be jointly entered to solve a given problem (say, a financial prediction problem requiring input of financial parameters distributed over a time period), these can serve as layers in the feature map entered into the first (and therefore, of subsequent) convolution layer FMs, as is also common practice in applications of the LAMSTAR neural network (see Chapter 8).

5.2.2.2. *Design extension to allow generality of applications — Input preprocessing array*

Initially, CNN was based on models of biological retina for image recognition [LeCun, *et al.*, 1989]. However, as we show later in this chapter, by now CNN has already been successfully applied to almost any field if knowledge.

In certain applications, especially those relating to speech and to signal processing, CNN may employ pre-filters (say, spectrograms) that transform the input (say, speech) into a frequency or wavelet domain, to produce a feature map in a different domain than the data itself. In this case, the multiple filters should be operating in series, each on the output of the earlier one, which is not always feasible.

Furthermore, in certain applications CNN can employ an approach similar to that used in the LAMSTAR design of Chapter 6 below [Graupe and Kordylewski, 1996], [Graupe, 1997], where any kind of input data is pre-processed with an array of different filters, mathematical, logical or of other algorithmic form — see Chapter 6 below. The output parameters of these filters will then become additional dimensions of the CNN's input tensor, which may have nothing to do with images. They will thus form an array of Feature Maps (FM's) at the input of the ***first Convolution Layer*** of the CNN network, as in Fig. 5.2 and not unlike the input tensor to a 3D CNN. Obviously the number of preprocessors employed will increase the ***depth dimension*** in the first Convolution Layer and in all subsequent layers.

Alternatively, in some applications, one may use the matrix entry of winning neurons in the various SOM layers of LAMSTAR as its input "image" (map), thus integrating outputs of different pre- or co-processors.

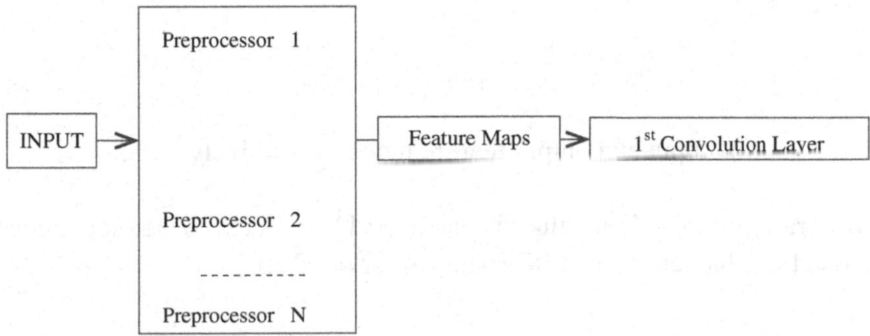

Fig. 5.2. Integration of preprocessors as *n*-dimensional CNN input.

The above extensions can easily employ parallel computing for their co/pre-processing, as is the case in the LAMSTAR design. Parameter sharing (as discussed later in the next subsection and in subsection 5.8 of the present Chapter) may not be valid in most applications beyond Image Processing.

5.3. The Convolutional Layers

5.3.1. Filter design for convolution

By its definition, Convolution requires a **filter** (function) to convolve the layer's input with, as discussed in Section 4.1 above. In the deep-learning CNN network, the functions considered as volumes.

The input at each convolution layer (CL) is convolved using a filter (see Section 2.5 above). In image processing problems, the filter is a kernel (matrix or tensor) comprising of learned (trained) weights. It convolves (folds) the input image by applying the matrix discrete convolution operation (see Section 4.1) as in Eq. (5.1) element-wise on input feature-maps of the CL to yield the outputs of this layer, as follows (see Sections 5.3.2 and 5.3.3 for further details).

$$\omega_{rq} * x_q = z \tag{5.1}$$

$\omega(rq)$ and $X(q)$ denoting the convolution (matrix) function and input, respectively

$$z(m,n) = \sum_{k=0}^{K-1}\sum_{l=0}^{L-1} \omega_{rq}(k,l)x_q(m+k,n+l) \tag{5.2}$$

with

$$q = 1, 2, \ldots, Q \tag{5.3a}$$

and

$$r = 1, 2, \ldots, R \tag{5.3b}$$

where Q, R are the input and output feature maps, respectively.

Learning (training) of weight values is performed by a Backpropagation algorithm as discussed in Chapter 2 above [Karpathy A, *et al.*, 2016].

Another important component of CNN is that of full or partial **Parameter Sharing**, which contributes to the speeding-up of CNN, noting the "curse of dimensionality" that is a major reason for the slowness of the Backpropagation neural networks of Chapter 2 and its consequent limited use as a stand-alone **deep learning** neural network, despite its obvious generality. However, as stated above in the present Section, **Backpropagation (BP)** is still an essential tool in CNN since it provides its learning feature. BP is used for forward or backward propagation in CNN, depending on where the input to the BP section of the algorithm appears in the computation.

Parameter Sharing and Backpropagation, as used in CNN, are further discussed in Sections 5.4 and 5.9 below, respectively.

5.3.2. Output of convolutional layers

Consider an image recognition problem, where the input feature map at the first convolution layer is of dimension $N \times N \times D$, D being the depth of the input Image, and a set of weights (kernels) of dimension $K \times K \times D$ at the same layer. The number of neurons (V) along each row of the output is given by [Karpathy *et al.*, 2016]:

$$V = (N - K + 2P)/S + 1 \tag{5.4}$$

P being the number of empty neurons (pixels) at the edges of the row (**zero-padding**, when employed) and S denoting the **stride** used in that row, namely the distance between neighboring kernels (number of pixels between the beginning of one kernel and the next). The stride (S) employed in the horizontal row of an image need not be the same as employed between columns.

5.3.3. Role of kernels of weights in convolution layers

The outputs of a convolutional layer (CL) are computed from the input of the region (receptive field) of their corresponding feature map via the (trained/learnt) weights. These sets of weights serve as the convolution filters (convolution function in the sense of Section 4.1 above) of the CNN network and are known as the **kernels** of the convolutional layers in CNN terminology (see Fig. 5.3).

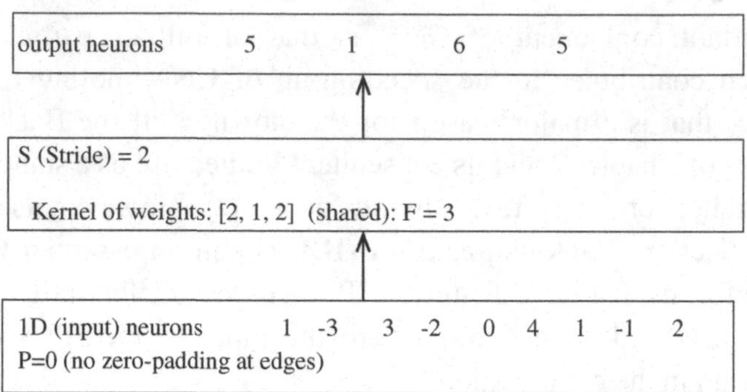

Fig. 5.3. Input and output of the convolution layer.
(case of 1-dimensional feature map)

5.4. Back Propagation

All weight training (updating) in CNN is done by Backpropagation (BP). The error is propagated from the output layer through all layers of the CNN network. Weight training takes place only in the Convolutional Layers and in the Fully-Connected output layer. The details of the Backpropagation procedure are given in Chapter 3 and are therefore not be repeated here.

We note that BP is used both for forward and for backward propagation, depending on the side where inputs are located. During the forward pass of a pooling layer it is advisable to keep track of the index of the max activation to allow efficient operation during the backward operation.

5.5. ReLu Layers

RELU (Rectified Linear Unit) is a function $f(x)$ satisfying:

$$F(x) = \max(0, x) \tag{5.5}$$

The ReLu layer that applies the non-saturating activation function as in Eq. (5.5) to its input received from the Convolution Layer. No learning is performed in the RELU layer, nor are any other functions or hyper-functions being applied.

The RELU function is a hard Max function that serves to enhance the nonlinear properties of the decision function and of the overall CNN network without affecting the receptive fields of the convolution layer. The incorporation of repeated RELU Layers in the CNN structure (see Section 5.2) is reported to increase the network speed with no affecting convolution or training [Krizhevsky, 2012].

5.6. Pooling Layers

In order to speed-up computation in CNN for complex deep-learning problems, especially for many-pixel image, pooling layers are integrated in the CNN architecture, as explained in Section 5.2. Pooling serves progressively reduce the size and the resolution of the representation and the computational effort in the convolutional layers thus speeding-up computation and controlling overfitting. It operates independently on each input slice. No learning is performed in the pooling layers, whose task is limited to subsampling only.

The Pooling Layer is repeatedly set within the CNN network as discussed in Section 5.2 above.

5.6.1. Max pooling

The usually preferred pooling method in CNN is Max-Pooling [Scherer, 2010]. It allows considering the most responsive node of a given region of interest. There is biological and psychological evidence to indicate that such focusing is also employed in human vision.

The principle of Max Pooling is that of reducing a set (see Fig. 5.4)

5	2	9	4
7	1	0	3
4	2	7	4
3	5	8	6

Fig. 5.4. 4 × 4 region of pixels.

into a lower-dimension set (see Fig. 5.5):

7	9
5	8

Fig. 5.5. 2 × 2 region of pixels.

where each maximal value (say image strength) within of a region (square) section is replaced by its maximal pixel-value (element-value, namely, image strength). Consequently, the larger (square) region is replaced by a smaller one which then consists of the maxima (strength-wise) of the smaller regions (squares) within that larger region. This can be mathematically expressed as [Scherer *et al.*, 2010]:

$$a_j = \max_{N\times N}\{a_j^{n\times n}u(n,n)\} \tag{5.6}$$

where $u(n, n)$ denoted the window function concerned.

In **max pooling layers**, the error is only at $\arg\max_{N\times N}\{a_j^{n\times n}u(n,n)\}$. Therefore, error maps in max pooling layers are sparse. If overlapping pooling windows are used, it is advisable to accumulate several error signals in one unit. [Scherer *et al.*, 2010].

5.6.2. Average pooling

One of the alternatives to Max Pooling in CNN is the Average Pooling method. It differs from Max Pooling by replacing the term "Maximal" by "average" throughout the discussion given in Section 5.4.1 above, or, in general:

$$a_j = \text{ave}_{N\times N}\{a_j^{n\times n}u(n,n)\} \tag{5.7}$$

5.6.3. Other pooling methods

Other pooling methods also exist, where the pooling function is given by [Scherer *et al.*, 2020]:

$$a_j \tanh\left(\beta\sum_{N\times N} a_i^{n\times n} + b\right) \tag{5.8}$$

However, Max Pooling is the most common and its performance is superior to other pooling methods [Scherer *et al.*, 2010] in most situations.

5.7. Dropout

Dropout was introduced by Hinton *et al.* to reduce overfitting in deep learning neural networks serves to reduce overfitting of the *NN*.

When employing dropout, the feed-forward operation is gated by a vector of independent Bernoulli random variables at probability p, namely, any neuron in the network will be disconnected at that probability. Hence, the gating vector is sampled and the randomly selected probability multiplies element-wise with the outputs of a given layer, to create a reduced (thinned) number of operational neurons and hence, a reduced number of outputs. The thinned outputs serve as inputs to the next layer. This process is applied at each layer, to yield a sub-network from a larger network and therefore to considerably reduce the computational effort in setting parameters and speed up computation, if properly executed. Dropout neural networks can be trained using stochastic gradient descent by BP in a manner similar to standard neural nets to set (learn) the rate of dropout [Srivastava, 2014].

5.8. Output FC Layer

The Output (Decision Layer of CNN is a Fully Connected (FC) layer. It serves for decision and classification purposes. The weights of the Output Layer undergo training (using Backpropagation, as in the Convolution Layers). Its output volume is of size $(1 \times 1 \times n)$, n being the number of classes to be output (classified).

5.9. Parameter (Weight) Sharing

In many image recognition problems using CNN, each filter h_i is replicated across the entire visual field. The replicated filters share the same parameterization (weight vector and bias) and form a *feature map*. Weight sharing affects the convolution and the subsampling (pooling) layers.

The basic assumption: of parameter sharing is that parameter (weight) set that is useful with respect to some spatial position of an input feature map is also useful at a different position.

This assumption is not reasonable if the task is to differentiate between rare aspects in detail or if there is one central characteristic net likely to relate to what is around it. Hence it is not relevant in many cases. On the other hand, it may be relevant also beyond image processing, depending on the details of the task [Karpathy A, *et al.*, 2016].

If the above holds only for a particular (sufficiently large) region of an image, then we may still employ **Partial Parameter Sharing** (also called **Limited Parameter Sharing**) over that region.

Parameter sharing yields considerable speeding-up of computation in CNN, when applicable [Abdel-Hamid O, *et al.*, 2013].

5.10. Applications

Whereas most applications of CNN are in the field of vision, which inspired the development of this architecture in 1989, numerous applications were in the field of speech recognition. Still applications now cover many other fields. Below we list some of these applications below:

Image Recognition (2D and 3D)
First and foremost, CNN was developed with image recognition in mind [LeCun *et al.*, 1989] and from there it spread to numerous areas. A 2003 application of CNN to image recognition Matusugu *et al.*, 2003] reported a 2.4% error rate on recognizing 5600 still facial images of 10 subjects [Matusugu M, 2013]. In 2012 a 0.23% error rate for a CNN application by Ciresan *et al.* to the handwritten text MNIST (Mixed National Institute of Standards and Technology) database [Ciresan, 2012]. The list of applications of CNN to image recognition in 2D and 3D is never ending. We just mention the 3D application by Shuiwang Ji *et al.* [S. Ji *et al.*, 2012] to Human Action Recognition [S. Ji, 2012].

Video Processing
Among the applications of CNN to video, we mention the 2014 papers by Karpathy *et al.* [Karpathy, 2014] and by Simonyan and Zisserman [Simonyan K; Zisserman A, 2014].

Speech Recognition
One of the papers in this field is the study by Abdel-Hamid *et al.* in the 2013 Interspeech Conference [Abdel-Hamid *et al.*, 2013].

Games: A recent paper [Clark and Storkey, 2014] reported that CNN, when trained with database of human professional database was far faster and outperforms some **GO games** against Monte-Carlo-based Fuego 1.1.

Other fields of application include:
Natural language processing [Collobert *et al.*, 2006], **Finance** [Dixon *et al.*, 2013], [Siripurapu, web] **Fault Detection** [Calderon-Martinez *et al.*, 2006], **Search Engines** [Rios and Kavuluru, 2015], **Drug Discovery** using 3D representation of chemical connections [Wallach *et al.*, 2015], **Human Action Recognition** [S. Ji, 2013], and beyond.

5.11. Case Studies (with program codes)

In the Appendices at the end of this text we present 14 case studies covering a broad range of applications of CNN. Many of which compare CNN with other architectures for the same case and using the same data.

The topics of the case studies in the appendices covering face recognition, fingerprint recognition, cancer detection, and protein (DNA) classification, human activity recognition, scene classification, 3D depth retrieval from 2D images, butterfly species and leaf classification, financial prediction, epilepsy seizure detection, speech recognition and music genre classification.

References

Abdel-Hamid O, Deng L, Yu D, "Convolutional neural network structures and optimization techniques for speech recognition", *Interspeech Conf.* (2013), pp. 3366–3370.

Calderon-Martinez J A, Campoy-Cervera P, "An application of convolutional neural networks for automatic inspection". *IEEE Conf. on Cybernetics and Intelligent Systems* (2006), pp. 1–6.

Ciresan D, Meier U, Schmidhuber J, "Multi-column deep neural networks for image classification", *EEE Conference on Computer Vision and Pattern Recognition* (2012).

Clark C, Storkey A, "Teaching deep convolutional neural networks to play go", *arXiv preprint arXiv:1412.3409* (2014).

Collobert R, Weston J, "A unified architecture for natural language processing: Deep neural networks with multitask learning", *Proceedings of 25th ACM International Conference on Machine Learning* (2008).

Dixon M, Klabian D, Bang J H, "Implementing deep neural networks for financial market prediction on the Intel Xeon Phi", *Proc. 8th Workshop on High Performance Computational Finance*, Paper No. 6 (2015).

Dong L, Yu D, "Deep learning methods and applications", *Foundations and Trends in Signal Processing* 7(3-4):197–387 (2014).

Fukushima K, "Cognitron: A self-organizing multi-layered neural network", *Biological Cybernetics* **20**:121–175 (1975).

Fukushima K, "Neocognitron: A Self-organizing neural network model for a mechanism of pattern recognition unaffected by shift in position", *Biological Cybernetics* **36**(4):193–202 (1980).

Graupe D, *Principles of Artificial Neural Networks* (World Scientific Publishers, 1997).

Graupe D, Kordylewski H, "A large memory storage and retrieval neural network for browsing and medical diagnosis applications", *Intelligent Engineering Systems through Artificial Neural Networks*, eds. Dagli C H *et al.*, Vol. 6 (ASME Press, 1996), 711–716.

Hubel D H, Wiesel T N, "Receptive fields of single neurons in the cat's striate cortex", *J Physiol* **148**(3):574–591 (1959).

Ji S, Xu W, Yang M, Yu K, "3D Convolutional neural networks for human action recognition", *IEEE Transactions on Pattern Analysis and Machine Intelligence* **35**(1):221–231. doi:10.1109/TPAMI.2012.59. ISSN 0162-8828. PMID 22392705, 2013.

Karpathy A, Toderici G, Shetty S, Leung T, Sukthankar R, Fei-Fei L, "Large-scale video classification with convolutional neural networks", *IEEE Conference on Computer Vision and Pattern Recognitio*n (CVPR), 2014.

Karpathy A, *et al.*, GITHUB- Stanford University, http://cs231n.github.io/convolutional-networks/, retrieved Feb 20, 2016.

Krizhevsky A, Sutskever I , Hinton GE, "Imagenet classification with deep convolutional neural networks", *Advances in Neural Information Processing System*s 25 (NIPS 2012), papers.nips.cc, 2012

LeCun Y, Boser B, Denker J S, Henderson D, Howard R E, Hubbard W, Jackel L D, "Backpropagation applied to handwritten zip code recognition". *Neural Computation* **1**(4):541–551 (1989).

LeCun Y, Bottou L, Bengio Y, Haffner P, "Gradient-based learning applied to document recognition", *Proceedings of the IEEE* **86**(11):2278–2324 (1998). doi:10.1109/5.726791.

Matusugu M, Mori K, Mitar Yi, Kaneda Y, "Subject independent facial expression recognition with robust face detection using a convolutional neural network" (PDF). *Neural Networks* **16**(5):555–559 (2013).

Rios A, Kavuluru, R, "Convolutional neural networks for biomedical text classification: application in indexing biomedical article", *Proc. 6th ACM Conf. on Bioinformatics, Computational Biology and Health Informatics* (2015), pp. 258–267.

Scherer D, Muller A, Behnke S, "Evaluation of pooling operations in convolutional architectures for object recognition", http://www.ais.uni-bonn.de, *20th International Conference on Artificial Neural Networks (ICANN)*, Thessaloniki, 2010.

Simonyan, K, Zisserman, A, "Two-stream convolutional networks for action recognition in videos", *arXiv:1406.2199* [*cs.CV*], 2014.

Siripurapu A, "Convolutional networks for stock trading", http://cs231n.stanford.edu/reports/ashwin_final_paper.pdf

Srivastava N, Hinton G, Krizhevsky A, Sutskever I, Salakhutdinov R, "Dropout: A simple way to prevent neural networks from overfitting". *Journal of Machine Learning Research* **15**:1929–1958 (2014).

Wallach I, Dzamba M, Heifets A, "AtomNet: A deep convolutional neural network for bioactivity prediction in structure-based drug discovery", *arXiv:1510.02855* [cs.LG], 2015.

CHAPTER 6

LAMSTAR-1 and LAMSTAR-2 Neural Networks

6.1. LAMSTAR Principles

6.1.1. Introduction

The neural network discussed in the present section is a deep learning artificial neural network for fast large-scale memory storage and retrieval of information [Graupe and Kordylewski, 1996a,b]. This network attempts to imitate, in a gross manner, processes of the human central nervous system (CNS), concerning storage and retrieval of patterns, impressions and sensed observations, including processes of forgetting and of recall. It attempts to achieve this without contradicting findings from physiological and psychological observations, at least in an input/output sense. Furthermore, the LAMSTAR (LArge Memory STorage And Retrieval) network attempts to do so in a computationally-efficient manner, using tools of neural networks from the previous sections. Hence, it employs SOM (Self-Organizing-Map) based layers [Kohonen, 1977, 1984] and combines these with Kohonen's Winner-Take-All [Kohonen, 1984], as in Chapter 2 of the present text, it also employs Hebbian weights [Hebb, 1949] in its architecture.

However, the LAMSTAR differs from all other neural networks in the way in which it uses weights, since it distinguishes between **storage weights**, which are essentially Associative Memory weights (AM) as in Chapter 2 above [Kohonen, 1977, 1984] with inter-cortex **link weights**, that are its learning engine and which provide it with its deep learning capability through easy, fast and intelligent **integration** of as many co-processors as may be needed for a given problem.

The Link Weights (LW) are conceptually based on the Kantian concept of "Verbindungen", namely, "Interconnections" introduced in his famous "Critique of Pure Reason" (Kant, 1781) — also see: [Ewing, 1938]. According to Kant, the process of Understanding is based on two fundamental concepts, namely, on memory elements ("things", atoms of memory) and on the interconnections between the memory elements ("things"). Without either of these, understanding is not possible. In artificial neural networks (ANN's), memory storage is facilitated via, say Associative Memory weights, as in the Kohonen SOM layers [Kohonen, 1984], while "Verbindungen" are facilitated via Hebb's principle [Hebb, 1949], which is only implicit in most designs, as in the previous in the chapters. In the LAMSTAR NN, the "Verbindungen" are introduced in a purely **Hebbian** and even **Pavlovian** manner [Pavlov, 1927], through the use of Link-Weights [Graupe and Lynn, 1969], [Graupe and Kordylewski, 1996b], [Graupe, 1997].

These link weights are those observed by functional MRI as connections (flow) of neural information from one section of the Central Nervous System (CNS) to another. They are the address-correlation gates (links) in [Graupe and Lynn, 1969], and their use was suggested for machine learning and relate to Minsky's K-Lines (Knowledge-Lines), as in [Minsky, 1980]. The use of Link-Weights makes the LAMSTAR ANN a **transparent** network, in contrast to other ANN's, noting that the lack of transparency was one of the very main criticisms of ANN.

The link weights are biologically motivated in their structure and operation, they follow the basic Hebbian rules [Hebb, 1949] as discussed in Section 2.1 above, in the sense of the 1901 Pavlovian Dog experiment [Pavlov, 1927] — also discussed in Section 2.1 of this text, and as verified by functional MRI observation. Such MRI observation also verify inter-cortex links in the brain. This Hebbian-Pavlovian structure also supports the count-up/down and punishment/reward mechanism used in the LAMSTAR for the link weights, which gives the network its speed by avoiding complex mathematical computations in its basic structure.

Still, integration of nonlinear functions is also not at all alien to biology. The central nervous system (CNS) integrates external sensors, such as retina, cochlea, taste buds, smell buds, which perform functions resembling wavelet transforms (cochlea), color separation (retina), and complex but sensitive chemical analysis of odor and taste — all being integrated and further processed in the CNS in an inter-cortex manner and all in parallel processing.

Among the other features of the LAMSTAR network are the **forgetting** feature, which is biologically essential for learning in **non-stationary** environments, and the **inhibition** feature that is also essential in the CNS. The LAMSTAR can also compensate for unbalanced datasets (see Section 6.5 below) and it incorporates inhibition. Furthermore, it is insensitive to **initialization** problems and, above all, it never stops learning (training) — thus again imitating the CNS. This also avoids getting stuck at local minima. The above features and especially forgetting and non-ending learning, also help the network to avoid overfitting.

6.1.2. Versions of LAMSTAR

In this chapter we discuss two versions of the LAMSTAR, denoted as **LAMSTAR- 1**, which is the original version, and **LAMSTAR-2** (also referred to as the Modified or Normalized LAMSTAR), which is a newer (2008) version, based on [Schneider and Graupe, 2008]. Both versions share the same basic principles. The differences between the two versions are minor. Therefore, all but Section 6.3 of the present Chapter 6 applies to both versions. However, since the performance of the Modified LAMSTAR, is practically always superior and theoretically never inferior to the original version, we term the original version as LAMSTAR-1 and the modified version as LAMSTAR 2. When LAMSTAR is mentioned in the literature prior to 2008, it relates to LAMSTAR-1, while after 2008, when Modified-LAMSTAR is mentioned, this usually relates to LAMSTAR-2 [Graupe, 2013]. Still, when this text discusses LAMSTAR alone, the discussion applies to both versions.

Any discussion in this text that uses the term LAMSTAR alone, applies to both versions. Otherwise, the text refers to the two versions as **LNN-1** or **LNN-2**. The Case Studies of Chapter 8 and the subsequent Appendices to this text illustrate the differences in performance between the two versions, to explain the need to refer to each version separately and to allow selecting the right version when needed.

Core algorithms presented in Section 6.2.1 for LAMSTAR-1 and in Section 6.3.3 for LAMSTR-2, to clarify the differences between the two versions. Indeed, the core program for LAMSTAR-1 can be extracted from that of LAMSTAR-2, but not vice versa.

6.1.3. Basic principles of the LAMSTAR neural network

The LAMSTAR neural network in its two versions is specifically designed for application to **information** retrieval, diagnosis, classification, prediction and decision problems which involve a very large number of categories. The resulting LAMSTAR neural network [Graupe, 1997], [Graupe and Kordylewski, 1998] is designed to store and retrieve patterns in a computationally efficient manner, using tools of neural networks, especially Kohonen's SOM (Self Organizing Map)-based network modules [Kohonen, 1988], combined with statistical decision tools.

By its structure as described in Section 6.1.4, the LAMSTAR network is uniquely suited to deal with analytical and non-analytical problems where data are of many vastly different categories and vector-dimensions, where some categories may be occasionally partly or totally **missing**, where data are both exact and fuzzy and where the vastness of data requires very fast algorithms [Graupe and Kordylewsky, 1996], [Graupe, 1997]. Missing data requires no re-programming or interruption in operation. These features are rare to find, especially when coming together, in other neural networks.

The LAMSTAR can be viewed as in intelligent expert system, where expert information is continuously being ranked for each case through learning and correlation. These characteristics are facilitated by the network's features of forgetting, interpolation and extrapolation. These allow the network to zoom out of stored information via forgetting and still being able to approximate forgotten information by extrapolation or interpolation. The full transparency of the LAMSTAR is due to its unique weight structure, since link weights provide clear information on what is going on inside the network at any time and in any points of the network.

As mentioned earlier, the LAMSTAR's computational power concerning deep learning, lies to a great extent in its ability to easily integrate and rank any external co-processor's input, mathematical, analytical or other, to its input-layer array. Consequently, the network has been successfully applied to many decision, diagnosis and recognition problems in various fields.

The major principles of neural networks (NN's) are common to practically all NN approaches. Its elementary neural unit or cell (neuron) is the one employed in all NN's, as described in Chapter 2 of this text. Accordingly, if the p inputs into a given neuron (from other neurons or from sensors or transducers at the input to the whole or part of the whole network) at the j'th SOM layer are denoted as $x(ij)$; $i = 1, 2, \dots, p$, and if the (single) output of that neuron is denoted as y, then the neuron's output y satisfies;

$$y = f\left[p \sum_{i=1} w_{ij} x_{ij} \right] \tag{6.1}$$

where f [.] is a nonlinear function denoted as Activation Function, that can be considered as a (hard or soft) binary (or bipolar) switch, as in Section 2.2 above. The weights w_{ij} of Eq. (6.1) are the Associative Memory weights assigned to the neuron's inputs and whose setting is the learning action of the NN. Also, neural firing (producing of an output) is of all-or-nothing nature [McCulloch and Pitts, 1943]. For details of the setting of the storage weights (w_{ij}), see Sections. 6.1.5 and 6.1.6 below.

The WTA (Winner-Take-All) principle, as in Section 2.4, is employed [Kohonen, 1984], such that an output (firing) is produced only at the winning neuron, namely, at the output of the neuron whose storage weights w_{ij} are closest to vector $x(j)$ when a best-matching memory is sought at the j'th SOM module.

By using a link-weights structure for its decision and browsing, the LAMSTAR network considers not just the stored memory values $w(ij)$ as in other neural networks, but also the interrelations (the Kantian Verbindungen discussed above) between these memories and the decision modules and between the memories themselves. These relations (link weights) are fundamental to its operation. As mentioned above, by Hebb's Law of Section 2.1 [Hebb, 1949], interconnecting inter-cortex weights (link weights) adjust and serve to establish flow of neuronal-signal traffic between groups of neurons, such that when a certain neuron fires very often in close time regarding a given situation/task, then the interconnecting link-weights (not the memory-storage weights) increase as compared to other interconnections Indeed, link weights serve as Hebbian inter-synaptic or inter-cortex weights and adjust accordingly. These weights and their method of adjustment (based on flow of traffic in the interconnections), are in principle in line with the organization of the CNS [Levitan *et al.*, 1997]. They are also responsible to the LAMSTAR's ability to interpolate/extrapolate and operate without re-programming or retraining in cases of incomplete data sets, as was stated earlier.

6.1.4. Basic structural elements

The basic storage modules of the LAMSTAR network are modified Kohonen SOM modules that are Associative-Memory-based WTA [Kohonen, 1984]. They are set in accordance with the resolution required (Section 6.1.6 below) and the degree of proximity of storage weights in the AM-sense to any input sub-word that is being considered per any given input word to the NN. In the LAMSTAR network the information is stored and processed via correlation links between individual neurons in separate SOM modules. The LAMSTAR's ability to deal with a large number of categories is partly due to its use of simple calculation of link weights and by its use of forgetting features and features of recovery from forgetting. The link weights are the main engine of the network, connecting many layers of SOM modules such that the emphasis is on (co)relation of link weights between atoms of memory, not on the memory atoms (BAM weights of the SOM modules) themselves. In this manner, the design becomes closer to knowledge processing in the biological CNS than is the practice in most conventional artificial neural networks. The forgetting feature too, is a basic feature of biological networks whose efficiency depends on it (see Section 6.1.10), as is the ability to deal with incomplete data sets (Section 6.1.13).

The input word is a coded real matrix X given by:

$$X = [x_1 \, x_2 \, ... \, x_N] \tag{6.2}$$

x_i being sub-vectors (sub-words describing categories or attributes of the input word). Each sub-word x_i is channeled to a corresponding i'th SOM module that stores data concerning the i'th category of the input word.

Many input sub-words, and similarly, many inputs to practically any other neural network architecture, can be derived only after pre-processing. This is the case in signal/image-processing problems, where only autoregressive or discrete spectral/wavelet parameters can serve as a sub-word rather than the signal itself.

Whereas in most SOM networks [Kohonen, 1984] all neurons of an SOM module are checked for proximity to a given input vector, in the LAMSTAR network only a maller sub-group of q neurons may be checked at a time, due to the huge number of neurons that may be involved. The finite set of p neurons is determined by link-weights (N) as shown in Fig. 6.1. However, if a given problem requires, by considerations of its quantization, only a small number of neurons in a given SOM storage module, namely, of possible states of an input sub-word, then all neurons in a given SOM module will be checked for possible storage and for subsequent selection of a winning neuron in that SOM module (layer) and N_i weights are not

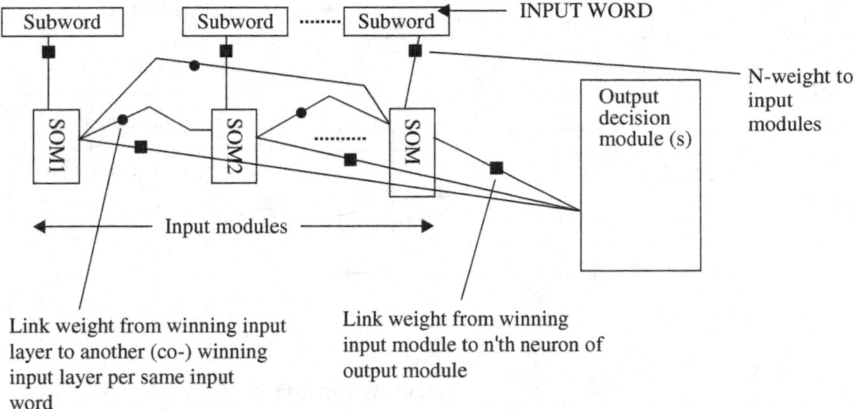

Fig. 6.1. A generalized LAMSTAR block-diagram.

used. Consequently, if the number of quantization levels in an input sub-word is small, then the sub-word is channeled directly to all neurons in a predetermined SOM module (layer). For further details of storing input data, see Section 6.1.5 below.

The main element of the LAMSTAR, which forms its decision engine, is the array of **link weights** that interconnect neurons between all input-storage neurons of the input SOM layers and the neurons at the output (decision) layers. These input-layer link weights are updated in accordance with traffic volume. The link weights to the output layers are updated by a reward/punishment process in accordance to success or failure of any decision, thus forming a learning process that is not limited to training data but continuous throughout running the LAMSTAR for a given problem. Weight-initialization is simple and unproblematic as all weight are initially set to **zero**. The LAMSTAR's feed-forward structure guarantees its stability, since feedback is provided at the end of each cycle, namely at one-step delay. Details on the link weight adjustments, its reinforcement (punishment/reward) feedback policy and related topics are discussed in the sections below.

Figure 6.1 gives a block-diagram of the complete and generalized of the LAMSTAR network. A more basic diagram, to be employed in most applications where the number of neurons per SOM layer is not huge, is given in Fig. 6.2. This design is a slight simplification of the generalized architecture, since each input sub-word is pre-assigned to a specific input SOM layer. It is also employed in the case studies of Appendices below. Only large browsing/retrieval cases, with little

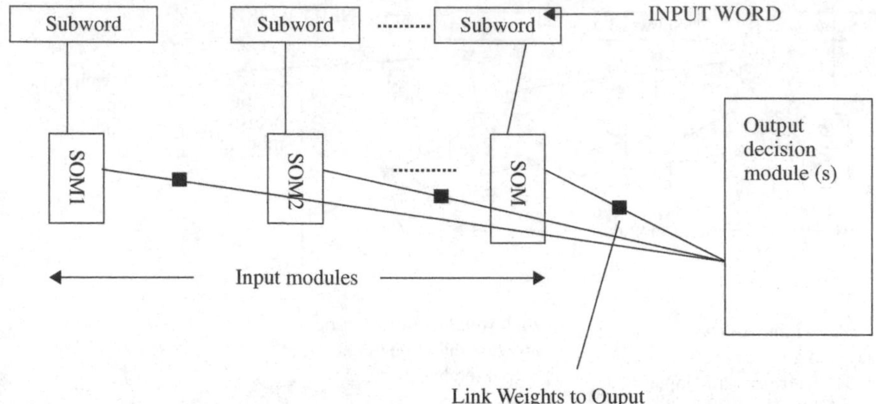

Fig. 6.2. The basic LAMSTAR architecture: Simplified version for most applications.

case studies of Appendices below. Only large browsing/retrieval cases, with little prior information on what kind of input is expected, should employ the complete design of Fig. 6.1. In the design of Fig. 6.2, the internal weights from one input layer to other input layers are omitted, as are the N_{ij} weights. Since they are usually not implemented (except for very specific retrieval and search-engine problems from huge databases. Hence, Fig. 6.2 represents the preferred LAMSTAR architecture.

6.1.5. Setting of input storage-weights and determination of winning neurons

When a new input word is presented to the system during the training phase, the LAMSTAR network inspects all storage-weight vectors (w_j) in SOM module i that corresponds to an input sub-word x_i that is to be stored. If any storedpattern matches the input sub-word x_i within a preset tolerance, it is declared as the winning neuron for that particularly observed input sub-word. A winning neuron is thus determined for each input based on the similarity between the input (vector x in Figs. 6.1 and 6.2) and a storage-weight vector w (stored information). For an input sub-word x_i, the winning neuron is thus determined by minimizing a distance norm $||*||$, as follows:

$$d(j, \mathbf{j}) = \left\| x_j - w_j \right\| \leq \left\| x_j - w_{k \neq j} \right\| = d(j, k) \qquad \forall k \tag{6.3}$$

As was already stated, in many applications where storage of numerical input-sub-words is concerned, the storage of such sub-words into SOM modules **can be**

simplified by directly channeling each such sub-word into a pre-set range of values, via pre-assigning statements or inequalities for each input-SOM layer. In that case, each range of values will correspond to a given input layer at that SOM. Hence, an input sub-word whose value is 0.41 will be stored in an input neuron corresponding to a range 0.25 to 0.50, etc… at the given SOM layer, rather than using the algorithm of Eq. (6.3) above.

6.1.6. Adjustmenting resolution in SOM modules

Equation (6.3), which serves to determine the winning neuron, does not deal effectively with the resolution of close clusters/patterns. This may lead to degraded accuracy in the decision making process when decision depends on local and closely related patterns/clusters which lead to different diagnosis/decision. The local sensitivity of neuron in SOM modules can be adjusted by incorporating an adjustable maximal Hamming distance function d_{max} as in Eq. (6.4):

$$d_{max} = \max[d(x_i\ w_i)]. \quad (6.4)$$

Consequently, if the number of sub-words stored in a given neuron of the appropriate module exceeds a threshold value, then storage is divided into two adjacent storage neurons (i.e. a new-neighbor neuron is set) and d_{max} is reduced accordingly. For fast adjustment of **resolution**, link weight to the output layer (as discussed in Section 6.3.4 below) can serve to adjust the resolution, such that storage in cells that yield a relatively high N_{ij} weights can be divided (say into 2 cells), while cells with low output link weights can be merged into the neighboring cells. This adjustment can be automatically or periodically changed when certain link weights increase or decrease relative to others over time, and considering the networks forgetting capability as in Section 6.1.10 below.

6.1.7. Links between SOM modules and from SOM modules to output modules

Information in the LAMSTAR system is mapped via link weights $L_{i,j}$ (Figs. 6.1, 6.2) between individual neurons in different SOM modules. The LAMSTAR system does not create neurons for an entire input word. Instead, only selected sub-words are stored in Associative-Memory-like manner in SOM modules (w weights), and correlations between sub-words are stored in terms of creating/adjusting L-links ($L_{i,j}$ in Fig. 6.1) that connect neurons in different

SOM modules. This allows the LAMSTAR network to be trained with partially incomplete data sets. The L-links are fundamental to allow interpolation and extrapolation of patterns, when a neuron in an SOM model does not correspond to an input sub-word but is highly linked to other modules serves as an interpolated estimate. We comment that the setting (updating) of Link Weights, as considered in this sub-section, applies to both link weights between input-storage (internal) SOM modules AND also link-weights from any storage SOM module and an output module (layer). In most applications **it is advisable** and economical to consider **only** links to output (decision) module. All applications, as in the case studies in the appendix to this text, do so.

Specifically, link weight values L are set (updated) such that for a given input word, after determining a winning i'th neuron in input module j and a winning k'th neuron in any output or in a different input module m, then the link $L(i, j/k, m)$ is counted up by a reward increment ΔL, whereas, all other links $L(s, j/k, m)$ may be reduced by a punishment increment ΔM.

The values of L-link weights are modified according to:

$$L_{i,j/k,m}(t+1) = L_{i,j/k,m}(t) + \Delta L \tag{6.5a}$$

$$L_{s,j\,k,m}(t+1) = L_{s,j/k,m}(t+1) - \Delta M,\ s \neq i \tag{6.5b}$$

$$L(0) = 0 \tag{6.5c}$$

where:

$L_{i,j/k,m}$ denotes links between winning neuron i in the j'th input module and winning neuron k in m'th input or output module.

ΔL, ΔM being reward/punishment increment values (predetermined fixed values). It is sometimes desirable to set M (either for all LAMSTAR decisions or only when the decision is correct) as:

$$\Delta M = 0 \tag{6.6}$$

The values of L are unbounded. However, they can be limited via forgetting to avoid unreasonable high or low values.

The link weights thus serve as address correlations [Graupe and Lynn, 1970] to evaluate traffic rates between neurons [Graupe, 1997, Minsky, 1980]. See Fig. 6.1. The L link weights above thus serve to integrate the various sub-words by intelligent ranking and to speed it up in problems involving very many sub-words (patterns) and huge memory in each such pattern. They also serves to exclude patterns that totally overlap, such that one or more of them are redundant and need be omitted. In most applications, the only link weights considered and updated are those between the SOM storage layers (modules) and the output layers, as in Fig. 6.2, while link-weights between the various SOM input-storage layers (namely, internal link-weights) are not considered or updated, unless they are required for decisions related to Section 6.1.12a below.

6.1.8. N_j weights (not implemented in most applications)

The N_j weights of Fig. 6.1 [Graupe and Kordylewski, 1998] are updated by the amount of traffic to a given neuron at a given input SOM module, namely by the accumulative number of sub-words stored at a given neuron, subject to adjustments due to forgetting as in Section 6.1.10 below, as determined by Eq. (6.7):

$$\begin{gathered} \left\| x_i - w_{i,m} \right\| = \min \left\| x_i - w_{i,k} \right\|, \\ \forall k \in \langle l, l+p \rangle; \qquad l \sim \{N_{i,j}\} \end{gathered} \tag{6.7}$$

where m is the winning unit in i'th SOM module (WTA), ($N_{i,j}$) denoting of the weights to determine the neighborhood of top priority neurons in SOM module i, for the purpose of storage search. In most applications, k covers all neurons in a module and both N_{ij} and l are disregarded, as in Fig. 6.2. l: denoting the first neuron to be scanned (determined by weights $N_{i,j}$); ~ denoting proportionality.

The N_j weights of Fig. 6.1 above are only used in huge retrieval/browsing problems. They are initialized at some small random non-zero value selected from a uniforms distribution, and increase linearly each time the appropriate neuron is chosen as winner.

We note that in most applications N-weights are not used at all, since selection of SOM modules is pre-set according to the number of features required for solving a given problem. Elimination of unused SOM modules is discussed in Section 6.4 below.

6.1.9. Initialization and local minima

In contrast to most other networks, the LAMSTAR neural network is not sensitive to initialization and will not converge to local minima. All link weights should be initialized as **zero**.

Again, in contrast to most other neural networks, the LAMSTAR will not get stuck at a local minimum, due to its link-weight punishment/reward structure since punishments will continue at local minima to move beyond it.

6.1.10. Forgetting and inhibition

Forgetting is introduced by a forgetting factor F, such that $L(k)$ is reset at every $k = sK$, $s = 0, 1, 2, 3, \ldots$, and where K is an integer predetermined constant (say, $K = 100$) as follows:

$$L(k+1) = FL(k) \tag{6.8a}$$

$0 > F > 1$ being the preset forgetting factor.

Subsequently, continue with the LAMSTAR computations as usual, including applying reinforcement (punishments/ rewards) to $L(k + 1)$.

In certain realizations one may set

$$F = 0 \tag{6.8b}$$

To fully delete old data after a certain number of datasets.

Alternatively, a stepwise Forgetting algorithm can be implemented, where, $L(k)$ is resent at every $k = sK$, $s = 0, 1, 2, 3, \ldots$, as:

$$L(k+1) = F(i)\, L(k) \tag{6.9}$$

where:

$$F(i) = (1 - \varepsilon)^i\, L(k) \tag{6.10a}$$

$$i = (k - sK) \tag{6.10b}$$

and where s in Eq. (6.10b) denotes the highest integer to yield $Ks < k$, such that i is restarted from zero and increasing with k every K runs.

Subsequently, continue with the LAMSTAR computation as usual, including applying reinforcement (punishment/reward) to $L(k + 1)$.

Inhibition must be pre-programmed. It is incorporated in the LAMSTAR by pre-assigning one or more neurons in a given input layer as an inhibitory neuron. Its inhibitory function must also be pre-programmed, since they will not follow the regular link weight format.

Simple applications of the LAMSTAR neural network do not always require the implementation of the forgetting feature. If in doubt about using the forgetting property, it may be advisable to compare performance "with forgetting" against "without forgetting" (when continuing the training throughout the testing period).

6.1.11. Setup of input layers from pre and co-processors

A major aspect of the LAMSTAR network, especially in complex problems that require deep-learning, is its ability to integrate and rank any co-processing or preprocessing algorithm of any kind that may help in solving the given problem. Obviously, difficult problems need all the help they can get. By its ranking ability which is due to the use of link weight, it can also eliminate or rank lowly any co/preprocessing algorithm that is redundant, as is explained later in this Chapter, in Section 6.4. Furthermore, the LAMSTAR (both LNN-1 and LNN-2) can do this by parallel processing, so that speed is not affected.

To integrate such processors into the LAMSTAR, the output of such a processor will be considered as one or more sub-words of the input word (matrix/tensor). Hence it will be assigned to one or more input (SOM) layers.

Similarly, different data sets related to a given problem, will also be sub-words of their own and therefore separate input layers.

To illustrate this capability of LAMSTAR, the reader is advised to look into the references, such as [Waxman *et al.*, 2010, 2014] or into the many case studies of Chapter 8 below.

Concrete examples for such situation are the following:

In predicting onset of apnea events in patients [Waxman *et al*., 2014], data comes from several non-invasive sensors, including pressure on the nose, blood pressure and more. All are taken simultaneously, and each serves as one or more input layers. Also the correlation between them forms separate layers, especially if cross correlation is of interest at several time delays. Similarly, in financial analysis, price of a stock is of interest over several days, and so is volume, or trends of the market as a whole and of sectors of the market that relate to a given stock. Each of these will serve as one or more separate input layers.

Similarly, in predicting onset of tremor in Parkinson patients in the author's lab [Basu *et al*., 2010}, one must note that symptoms in the Parkinson disease are associated with synchronization in the firing of neurons in the sub-thalamic nucleus (STN) in the brain. Also, the effect of deep-brain stimulation (DBS) is desynchronization of the firing. A convenient mathematical tool for detecting such synchronization is Sample Entropy analysis. Hence, one of the sub-words for a LALSTAR-based prediction is using sample entropy as a sub-word. Other sub-words used are peak frequency and power in certain frequency bands. Each of these is another sub-word for the LAMSTAR, so are correlations between them. Any over-kill due to using redundant information is taken care by the transparency of LAMSTAR, using analysis as in Section 6.4 below.

6.1.12. Training vs. operational runs

There is no reason to stop training at any point, since the first n sets (input words) of data serve only to establish initial weights for the testing set of input words, which are, indeed, normal-run situations. However, in the LAMSTAR, we can still, and should continue training, in a set- by-set (input-word by input-word) manner. Thus, the network continues adapting itself during testing and regular operational runs. The network's performance benefits significantly from continued training while the network does not slow down and no additional complexity is involved. In fact, this does slightly simplify the network's design. Still, in scoring network performance, a number of initial runs should not be considered, since the network has not "learnt" sufficiently and is too far from convergence. However, if decision is still needed early on, then even "untrained" outputs can be used, though at the risk of being wrong".

6.1.13. Operation in face of missing data

The operation of the LAMSTAR network and its decision process, in both its LAA-1 and LNN-2 versions, (to be discussed in detail in Sections 6.2 and 6.3) are fully applicable even when some data sub-words are missing from any given input word, since the summation over k is still valid when some k are missing. In that case, the summation over k just ignores some values just as a physician can make a diagnostic decision, if need be, even when one result item did not come back from the lab. The LAMSTAR ANN is therefore fully operational in case of missing data or data set. In that case, of course, the decision may not be as good as when all sub-words were available, just as the physician's decision when one or a few lab tests are missing. But, if decision must be made (say, to save a critical patient) the physician may still go ahead with the best assessment of the information that is available.

6.1.14. The decision process of LAMSTAR

The structure of the LAMSTAR network and its settings as described in the previous sections, are common to both LAMSTAR-1 (LNN-1) and LAMSTAR-2 (LNN-2). These two versions also share the same decision philosophy. However, the decision algorithms differ slightly. The decision algorithm of LNN-1 (the original version of LAMSTAR) is described in Section 6.2.1 below. This 1996 version [Graupe and Kordylewski, 1996a] [Graupe, 1997] was modified in 2008 [Schneider and Graupe, 2008] and is referred to as LAMSTAR-2. Its decision process is described in Section 6.3.2.

6.2. LAMSTAR-1 (LNN-1)

6.2.1. Determination of winning decision via link weights

The diagnosis/decision at the output SOM modules is found by analyzing correlation links L between diagnosis/decision neurons in the output SOM modules and the winning neurons in all input SOM modules selected and accepted by the process outlined in Section 6.1.7. Furthermore, all L-weight values are set (updated) as discussed in Section 6.1.7 above (Eqs. (6.5) and (6.6)).

The winning neuron (diagnosis/decision) from the output SOM module is a neuron with the highest cumulative value of L-links connecting to the selected (winning) input neurons in the input modules. The output decision equation for output SOM module (i) is given by:

$$\sum_{k(w)}^{M} L_{k(w)}^{i,n} \geq \sum_{k(w)}^{M} L_{k(w)}^{i,j} \ \forall\, i, j, k, n, \qquad j \neq n \tag{6.11}$$

where

i: i'th output module.
n: winning neuron in the i'th output module $k(w)$: winning neuron in the k'th input module. M number of input modules.
L_{kw}^{ij}: link weight between winning neuron in input module k and neuron j in i'th output.

Link weights may be either positive or negative. They are preferably initiated at zero though initialization of all weights at some other fixed value poses no difficulty. If two or more weights are equal then a certain decision must be pre-programmed to be given a priority.

Note that in every input SOM layer there is ONLY one winning neuron, if at all — by the Winner-Takes-All principle.

6.2.2. LAMSTAR-1 core algorithm (dynamic LAMSTAR version)

The algorithm consists only of operations as in the 21 numbered programming instructions (or sets of expressions) entered in Italics — below. All else serves as comments. Furthermore, two of the instructions are used only when forgetting is practiced. Also, three instructions are "PRINT" instructions while three more are for setup and initialization. Therefore, only 13 instructions are carried out in each iteration (dynamic dataset).

The program assumes DIRECT INPUT STORAGE rather than using Eq. (6.3) of Section 6.1.5 above. However, Direct Storage can still be used in this program if desired or needed. The program also assumes a single output (decision) layer having two decision neurons denoted as A and B.

THE PROGRAM IS DYNAMIC AND **MUST BE EXECUTED IN THE SEQUENCE GIVEN BY STEPS** #1, #2.... (BELOW), IN THAT ORDER

#1. DATA SETUP

SET each of the F features (sub-words) of the input word into N_k *(*$k = 1, 2, \ldots F$*) ranges (neighborhoods).*

The arrangement of the **input data sets** in these ranges may require pre-setting the data into dividing it into neighborhoods or ranges by value or by other understanding of the contents of the data, for the purpose of storing it in a reasonable number of neurons in a given SOM layer. In many applications this may call for normalizing the data, say in percentage form.

For example, dealing with financial data we must convert changes in value into percentage-changes from some past value (say, from the past day's closing of the market). In medical data, again, we may be interested in percentage-change or in percentage deviation from some value that in medically important. Scaling need not be linear. In an investment policy, results above a certain percentage gain or percentage loss can be lumped together if the network is to make a buy/don't-buy decision, or if the physician must continue or discontinue using a certain medication.

#2. INPUTS

$BIAS = \ldots\ ;\ THRESHOLD = \ldots\ ;\ M = \ldots\ ;\ R = \ldots\ ;\ P = \ldots$ (1*-a, b, c, d, e)

F = *max. number of layers (max. # of sub-words/features in an input-word),* (1-f)

N = *max. number of neurons in a layer;* N_k = *max. number of neurons in layer k* (1-g)

$j = 1, 2, 3, \ldots N_k;\ k = 1, 2, 3, \ldots F,$

j denoting j'th input neuron, k denoting k'th input layer, R denoting Reward and P denoting Punishment.

Note that not all layers (SOM modules) must have the same number of neurons, namely the SOM matrix V needs not to be square. Alternatively, neurons with zero input can be filled in to make V a square matrix.

#3. INITIALIZATION

All link weights are initialized as 0, namely (for possible outcomes *A*, *B*),

$$LA_{i,k}(0) = LB_{i,k}(0) = 0;\ TLA(0) = TLB(0) = 0;\ w(j,\ k) = 0\ \textit{for all}\ j,\ k,\ n = 0 \qquad (2^*)$$

n denoting the iteration number.

#4. STORAGE in individual neurons of INPUT-MATRIX (iteration *n*)

Sequencing starts here:

SET

$$n = n + 1 \qquad (3^*)$$

INPUT: STORAGE MATRIX V with elements $W_{i.k}$ (as in the Data Setup paragraph #1 above):

(4*)

At iteration n:

$W_{j=k(w),k} = 1$ for all input layers k; Else: $W_{j,i} = 0$

for all i, k; $j = 1, 2, \ldots N(k)$; $k = 1, 2, \ldots F$, $k(w)$ *denoting the* ***winning*** *neuron in layer k*

(5*)

Set:

$$W_{j=k(w),k} = W_{k(w)}(n) \qquad (6^*)$$

noting that every column (vector) of W has **only one** element (neuron) = 1, while **all other** elements of that vector are = 0.

#5. COMPUTATION OF LINK-WEIGHTS

Let weights from individual input-layer neurons to Winner-Takes-All decision-layers (say, to decision-neurons $\{A\}$ and $\{B\}$ for a case of two neurons in a single output layer) be denoted $LA_{i,k}(n)$ and $LB_{i,k}(n)$, respectively, and let:

ALWAYS:

$$LA_{i,k}(n) = LA_{i,k}(n-1) + W_{i,k}(n);\ LB_{i,k}(n) = LB_{i,k}(n-1) + W_{i,k}(n) \tag{7*}$$

Such that for every tuplet $\{i, k\}$ for which $w_{i,k}(n) = 0$, the value of $LA_{i,k}(n)$ remains unchanged, namely: $LA_{i,k}(n) = LA_{i,k}(n-1)$.

Consequently,

For all i, k where $w_{i,k}(n) = 1$:

$$TLA(n) = \Sigma_k^F[LA_{i,k}^*(n)];\ TLB(n) = \Sigma_k^F[LB_{i,k}^*(n)],$$
$$else\ TLA(n) = TLB(n) = 0 \tag{8*}$$

such that one **CONSIDERS ONLY** those $LA_{i,k}(n)$ and $LB_{i,k}(n)$ for which $w_{i,k}(n) = 1$.

#6. DECISION

Let $\{BIAS\}$ be given by:

BIAS = ... *(enter value, say*: 0) (9*)

HENCE:

If $TLA(n) > [1 + BIAS][TLB(n)]$, *then output decision "A",*
else, output "B" (10*)

such that one considers **ONLY** those $LA_{ij}(n)$

and $LB_{ij}(n)$, for which $W_{i,j}(n) = 1$

LET

$$DTL(n) = TLA(n) - TLB(n) \tag{11*}$$

PRINT DTL(n) (12*)

At this point of running the program, we await OUTCOME INFORMATION that is still UNKNOWN and will be entered at step #7 below.

#7. REWARD/PUNISHMENT OF LINK-WEIGHTS (a-posteriori update of Link-Weights)

INPUT: OUTCOME(n) = ... (13*)

from system's information on outcome (or, in a prediction problem, of what next iteration of input is, once it became available).

PRINT OUTCOME(n) (14*)

Also:

Set:

R = ... *(enter value (say:* 1) *of reward* (15*-a)

P = ... *(enter value (say:* 1 *or* 0) *of punishment,* (15*-b)

HENCE:

LET

CORRECT = outcome(n) >/= outcome(n − 1) + THRESHOLD (16*-a)

INCORRECT = outcome(n) < outcome(n − 1) + THRESHOLD (16*-b)

Subsequently,

FOR ALL TUPLETS {ij} WHERE $W_{i,j}(n) = 1$:

$LA_{ij}(n) = LA_{ij}(n-1) + R;\ LB_{ij}(n) = LB_{ij}(n-1) - P$ *(12a)*

Else, if decision {A} will eventually be ***incorrect****, then:*

$LA_{ij}(n) = LA_{ij}(n-1) - P;\ LB_{ij}(n) = LB_{ij}(n-1) + R$ (17*)

Subsequently,

save $LA_{ij}(n)$; $LB_{ij}(n)$ for all ij (18*)

and:

GO TO NEXT INPUT WORD n + 1, as in #3 above. (19*)

Note: The updated *LA* and *LB* of Eq. (16*) are the ones used for the $(n + 1)$'th run (iteration). Hence they must be saved at this point.

#8. FORGETTING

After every M iterations (say, $M = 50$ or $M = 100$, etc... — see Eq. 1-c):

Reset *{n} to zero*

and initialize LA(n), LB(n), TLB(n), TLO(n) to become the previous LA(n), LB(n), TLA(n), TLB(n) ***when multiplied*** *by a factor of*

"FACTOR" (20*)

where FACTOR is to be set at ***initialization*** *if forgetting is employed.*

Then:

RESET (n = 51, *or* n = 101, ... *etc...*) *to be* $n = 1$ *and continue as above* (*steps #3 to #8*).

(21*)

6.3. LAMSTAR-2 (LNN-2)

6.3.1. Motivation

In many applications of the LAMSTAR (LAMSTAR-1) neural network, certain input neurons of the input word in a given layer may only rarely be winners, since their form (say, value or shape) is rarely met with respect to the feature (sub-word) represented by that layer. Yet, this rare situation, when it occurs, may be very important and even critical relative to the decision to be taken on the problem at hand. However, the decision Eq. (6.11) for the original LAMSTAR (LAMSTAR-1), as in Section 6.2.1 is solely concerned with comparing link weights. Hence, the rarely occurring input neuron $\{i, j\}$, even though when it is the winner (namely, its situation occurs in its particular layer), then the correct outcome is (almost) ALWAYS decision A. However, since this neuron occurs so seldom that its link weight is low. In contrast, a certain often-occurring (winning) neuron will always have a relatively high link weight, even if it rarely occurs when decision A turns out to be correct. Hence, this "popular" neuron may nullify the effect of the rarely occurring (winning) neuron $\{i, j\}$ in terms of link weight, even with respect to decision A above. Therefore, it is logical that the mere number of times that a neuron being winner is not sufficient in doing justice to the rarely occurring neuron that may represent important information relative to decision A.

The modification as in the coming sub-section [Schneider and Graupe, 2008] was formulated to avoid this kind of situation. As is shown in the various case studies appended below. It appears to be helpful very often, while it hardly ever has a negative effect on either performance or computational speed.

6.3.2. LAMSTAR-2: The modified LAMSTAR algorithm

The situation described in Section 6.3.1 gave rise to a somewhat modified version of the LAMSTAR, as proposed in [Schneider and Graupe, 2008]. By this modification, the link weights $L_{i,j}(m, k)$ from neuron m in the k'th SOM input layer to any output layer j in the i'th output (decision) layer is replaced by a normalized link weight denoted as $L^*_{i,j}(m, k)$ where

$$L^*_{i,j}(m,k) = L_{i,j}(m,k)/n(m,k) \tag{6.12}$$

$n(m, k)$ denoting the count of the number of times when neuron m in input layer k is the winning input neuron in that layer.

Consequently, the winning decision, as in Eq. (6.11) of Section 6.2.1 will employ L^* rather than L throughout. Similarly, L^* will replace L in weight links between any two different input layers, if applicable, to yield the following revised decision equation:

$$\sum_{k(w)}^{M} \boldsymbol{L}_{k(w)}^{i,n,*} \geq \sum_{k(w)}^{M} \boldsymbol{L}_{k(w)}^{i,j,*} \quad \forall\ i, j, k, n, \qquad j \neq n \tag{6.13}$$

This modification is important when certain input neurons are significant even though the occur (become "winners") only rarely. It proved important in several applications, such as [Waxman *et al.*, 2010], where it greatly outperformed the original (un-normalized) version of the LAMSTAR network.

Still, punishments and rewards will be unchanged from the original version of the LAMSTAR (LAMSTAR 1).

Thus, LAMSAR-2 still maintains all the beneficial aspects of the original LAMSTAR, differing only in the interpretation of the network's link-weights with respect to the final decision process.

6.3.3. LAMSTAR-2 core algorithm (Dynamic LAMSTAR version)

Since there is yet no detailed source available elsewhere for LAMSTAR-2 in the open literature, and noting its performance, a detailed core program is described here, with comment on its steps. This may help to understand the ease of programming the network. Any filters that feed the various layers are, as in LAMSTAR-1, the choice of the programmer with respect to the specific problem (application) in question. These can, in most cases, be taken from their corresponding mathematical program libraries and handles totally outside the LAMSTAR which serves to integrate them. Hence, they can be easily computed in parallel devices.

The Core Algorithm for LAMSTAR-2 is very similar to that for LAMSTAR-1. The changes affect only three sections of the program:

(a) At initialization, in paragraph #3, the counting the number of times any neuron is the winning neuron is not part of LAMSTAR-1.

(b) Paragraph #5, on normalizing the link weights according to the counting the number of times is winner, is unique for LAMSTAR-2.

(c) In paragraph #7, the normalization is implemented in the decision part of the network.

The algorithm consists of only 24 numbered program instructions (or sets of expressions) entered in Italics — below. All else serves as comments.

The program assumes DIRECT INPUT STORAGE rather than using Eq. (6.3) of Section 6.1.5 above. However, Direct Storage can still be used in this program if desired or needed. The program also assumes a single output (decision) layer having two decision neurons denoted as A and B.

#1. DATA SETUP

SET each of the F features (sub-words) of the input word into N_k ($k = 1, 2, \ldots F$) *ranges (neighborhoods).*

See also paragraph on DATA SETUP in Section 6.2.1. (#1 in Core Algorithm).

#2. INPUTS

$BIAS = \ldots.\ ; THRESHOLD = \ldots\ ; M = \ldots\ ; R = \ldots\ ; P = \ldots$ (1**a, b, c, d, e)

F = *max. number of layers (max. # of sub-words / features in an input-word)* (1**f)

N = *max. number of neurons in a layer;* N_k = *max. number of neurons in layer k* (1**g)

$i = 1, 2, 3, \ldots N_k;\ k = 1, 2, 3, \ldots F$ (1**h)

j denoting j'th input neuron, k denoting k'th input layer, R denoting Reward and P denoting Punishment.

Note that not all layers (SOM modules) must have the same number of neurons, namely the SOM matrix V must not to be square. Alternatively, neurons with zero input can be filled in to make V a square matrix.

Input data is allocated to be stored in the neurons of the input (SOM) layers as in Sections 6.1.5 and 6.1.6 above. Storage may be direct, which is the fastest way. Alternatively, it may follow Eq. (6.3) of Section 6.1.4.

#3. INITIALIZATION

All link weights are initialized as 0, namely (for possible outcomes A),

$LA_{j,k}(0) = LB_{j,k}(0) = 0$; $TLA(0) = TLB(0) = 0$; $w(j, k) = 0$ *for all j, k,*
$n = 0$; $q(j, k) = 0$ *for all j, k* (2**)

n denoting iteration number (namely, $n = 0, 1, 2, 3, \ldots$) and q denoting number of times a given neuron is a winner in a given layer (SOM module).

#4. STORAGE IN individual neurons of INPUT-MATRIX (iteration *n*)

Sequencing starts here:

SET

$$n = n + 1 \tag{3**}$$

If a sub-word of Feature $\{i\}$ fits sub-range $\{i, k\}$, which is the sub-range allocated to neuron $[j, k\}$, as in the provided the Data Setup paragraph #1 above, for feature k, then execute:

INPUT: STORAGE MATRIX $V(N)$ with elements $V_{i.k}$ (as in the pre-Dara Setup)

$W_{j=k(w),k} = 1$ *for all k, Else:* $W_{j,i} = 0$ *for all i, k;* $j = 1, 2, \ldots N$; $k = 1, 2, \ldots F$, $k(w)$ *denoting winning neuron in layer k*

(4**)

by the Winner-Takes-All principle. Now:

Set:

$$W_{j=k(w),k} = W_{k(w)}(n) \tag{5**}$$

noting that every column (vector) of V has only one element (neuron) with an output of 1, while all other elements of that vector output a zero.

#5. Counting number of wins for a given neuron

For all i, k where $W_{i,k} = 1$*:*

$$q_{j,k}(n) = q_{j,k}(n) + 1 \tag{6**}$$

#6. COMPUTATION OF LINK-WEIGHTS

Let weights from individual input-layer neurons to Winner-Takes-All decision-layers (say, to decision-neuron $\{A\}$ and $\{B\}$ for case of 2 neurons in a single output layer) be denoted $LA_{i,k}(n)$ and $LB_{i,k}(n)$, respectively, and let:

ALWAYS:

$$LA_{i,k}(n) = LA_{i,k}(n-1) + W_{k(w)}(n);\ LB_{i,k}(n) = LB_{i,k}(n-1) + W_{k(w)}(n) \qquad (7^{**})$$

such that, for every tuplet $\{i, k\}$ for which $W_{i,k}(n) = 0$, the value of $LA_{i,k}(n)$ remains unchanged, namely: $LA_{i,k}(n) = LA_{i,k}(n-1)$.

Consequently,

For all i, k where $w_{i,k}(n) = 1$:

$$TLA(n) = \Sigma_k^F [LA^*_{i,k}(n)];\quad TLB(n) = \Sigma_k^F [LB^*_{i,k}(n)],$$
$$else\ TLA(n) = TLB(n) = 0 \qquad (8^{**})$$

such that one **CONSIDERS ONLY** those $LA_{i,k}(n)$ and $LB_{i,k}(n)$ for which $w_{i,k}(n) = 1$.

#7. NORMALIZATION OF LINK WEIGHTS

Let

$$[LA_{i,k}(n)]/q_{j,k}(n) = LA^*_{i,k}(n);\ q > 1 \qquad (9^{**})$$

and let:

$$[LB_{i,k}(n)]/q_{j,k}(n) = LB^*_{i,k}(n);\ q > 1 \qquad (10^{**})$$

Then:

For all i, k where $w_{i,k}(n) = 1$:

$TLA^*(n) = \sum_k^F [LA^*_{i,k}(n)]$; $TLB^*(n) = \sum_k^F [LB^*_{i,k}(n)]$,
else $TLA^*(n) = TLB^*(n) = 0$ (11**)

which were derived from **ONLY** those values of $LA_{i,k}(n)$ and of $LB_{i,k}(n)$ for which $W_{k(w)}(n) = 1$.

#8. DECISION

Let {BIAS} be given by

BIAS = ... (enter value, say: 0) (12**)

HENCE, the decision is:

If $TLA^*(n) > [1 + BIAS]\,[TLB^*(n)]$, *then output decision "A",*
else, output is "B" (13**)

such that one **CONSIDERS ONLY** those $LA_{ij}(n)$ and $LB_{ij}(n)$, for which $w_{i,j}(n) = 1$.

LET

$DTL(n) = TLA(n) - TLB(n)$ (14**)

PRINT DTL(n) (15**)

AT THIS POINT WE still AWAIT TO FIND IF THE DECISION WAS CORRECT OR NOT by the OUTCOME THAT IS STILL UNKNOWN AND WILL BE ENTERED AT STEP #6 BELOW

#9. REWARD/PUNISHMENT OF LINK-WEIGHTS (a-posteriori update of Link-Weights)

INPUT: OUTCOME(n) = ... (16**)

from system's information on outcome (or, in a prediction problem, of what next iteration of input is, once it became available).

PRINT OUTCOME(n) (17**)

Enter:

$R = \ldots$ (enter reward value, **say: 1**), **and** *enter:* $P = \ldots$ (enter punishment value, say: 1 or 0), as in Eq. (1d, e) above.

HENCE:

LET

$$CORRECT = outcome(n) >/= outcome(n-1) + THRESHOLD \qquad (18^{**}\text{-a})$$

$$INCORRECT = outcome(n) < outcome(n-1) + THRESHOLD \qquad (18^{**}\text{-b})$$

Subsequently,

ONLY:

FOR ALL TUPLETS $\{ij\}$ *WHERE* $w_{i,j}(n) = 1$:

If actually (a-posteriori, i.e. by the OUTCOME) *decision* $\{A\}$ **will turn out to** *be* ***correct****, then:*

$$LA_{ij}(n) = LA_{ij}(n-1) + R;\ LB_{ij}(n) = LB_{ij}(n-1) - P \qquad (19^{**})$$

Else, if decision $\{A\}$ will eventually *be* ***incorrect****, then:*

$$LA_{ij}(n) = LA_{ij}(n-1) - P;\ LB_{ij}(n) = LB_{ij}(n-1) + R \qquad (20^{**})$$

save

$$LA_{ij}(n);\ LB_{ij}(n) \text{ for all } ij \qquad (21^{**})$$

and:

GO TO NEXT INPUT WORD $n + 1$**, as in #3 above.** (22**)

Note: The updated *LA* and *LB* of Eq. (16) are the ones used for the next $(n + 1)$ run (iteration). Hence they must be saved at this point.

#10. FORGETTING

At every M iterations (say, M = 50 *or M* = 100, *etc... — see Eq. 1c*):

Reset {n} to zero and initialize LA(n), LB(n), TLB(n), TLO(n) to become the last previous LA(n), LB(n), TLA(n), TLB(n) when multiplied by a factor of "FACTOR".

(23)**

where FACTOR is to be set at initialization if forgetting is employed.

Then:

RESET (*n* = 51, or *n* = 101, … etc...) *to be n* = 1 *and continue as above* (*steps #3 to #10).*

(24**)

6.4. Data Analysis with LAMSTAR-1 and LAMSTAR-2

6.4.1. Data analysis capabilities based on link-weight information

Since all information in the LAMSTAR network is embodied in the link weights, the LAMSTAR can be utilized as a data analysis tool. In this case the system provides analysis of input data such as evaluating the importance of input layers and their respective sub-words, of the strengths of correlation between categories, or of the strengths of correlation of between individual neurons.

The system's analysis of the input data involves two phases:

(1) Setup of the system (as outlined in Section 6.1.1)

(2) Analysis of the values of correlation links as discussed below.

The purpose of the analysis is to provide insight into the problem at hand. Furthermore, performance and speed may be enhanced by the information that is derived from the analysis concerning if and where to add or remove layers or neurons at given layers, say, according to the significance of a layer or of a neuron, as indicated below.

Clusters connected by the links with the highest values determine the trends in the input data and facilitate calibrating the network's resolution.

The analysis phase can be exercised at any point during normal operation. It is a phase that serves to improve the network's performance, namely, to train the network, while normal operation continues. In this it is training on the job.

In this training phase, the LAMSTAR system finds the highest correlation links (link weights) and retrieves information associated with the clusters in SOM modules connected by these links. The links can be chosen by two methods: (1) links with value exceeding a pre-defined threshold, (2) a pre-defined number of links with the highest value.

6.4.2. Link-weight situation map of input of the LAMSTER neural network

The structure of the LAMSTAR neural network displays in itself important information on the state of the data and hence on the status of the problem that is considered by the LAMSTAR.

First, the winning neurons in each layer (the neurons whose output is 1, since all others are at 0) give a condition map (matrix). More importantly, the map of the values of the link-weights from all these winning neurons is a matrix $A(i, j)$ that is a status map which displays the importance of each sub-word (memory, neuron) with respect to the problem at hand. This illustrates both the transparency of the LAMSTAR and its power. This map can be used, if so desired, as an input-feature map for a CNN network.

6.4.3. Feature extraction and removal in the LAMSTAR *NN*

Features can be extracted or removed in the LAMSTAR network according to the derivations leading to the properties of certain elements of the LAMSTAR network as follows:

Definition I: **Most/Least Significant memory/Layer**: A most (least) significant layer (feature, SOM-module) can be extracted by the matrix $A(i, j)$ where i denotes a winning neuron in SOM storage module j. By the Winner-Takes-All principle, all winning entries (neurons) are 1 while the rest are 0. Furthermore, $A(i, j)$ can be reduced via considering properties (b) to (e) below.

(a) The **most (least) significant sub-word** (winning memory neuron) $\{i\}$ over all SOM modules (i.e., over the whole *NN*) with respect to a given output decision $\{dk\}$ and over all input words, denoted as $[i^*, s^*/dk]$, is given by:

$$[i^*, s^*/dk]: L(i, s/dk) \geq L(j, p/dk) \text{ for any winning neuron } \{j\} \text{ in any module } \{p\} \quad (6.14)$$

where p is not equal to s, $L(j, p/dk)$ denoting the link weight between the j'th (winning) neuron in layer p and the winning output-layer neuron dk. Note that for determining the least significant neuron, the inequality as above is reversed.

(b) The **most (least) significant SOM module** $\{s^{**}\}$ per a given winning output decision {dk} over all input words, is given by:

$$s^{**}(dk): \sum_i (\{L(i, s/dk)\}) \geqq \sum_j (\{L(j, p/dk)\}) \text{ for any module } p \quad (6.15)$$

Note that for determining the least significant module, the inequality above is reversed.

(c) The neuron $\{i^{**}(dk)\}$ that is **most (least) significant neuron in a particular SOM module** (s) per a given output decision (dk), over all input words per a given class of problems, is given by $i^*(s, dk)$ such that:

$$L(i, s/dk) \geq L(j, s/dk) \text{ for any neuron } (j) \text{ in same module } (s) \quad (6.16)$$

Note that for determining the least significant neuron in module (s), the inequality above is reversed.

(d) **Definition II**: **REDUNDANCY**: If **whenever** a particular neuron (i) in SOM input layer (s) is the winner for any input word considered by the LAMSTAR (for a given class of problems assigned to it) with respect to decision dk, **then also** neuron (j) in layer (t) is a winner for its particular sub-word of the same input word, **and when** such unique pairing holds for all and every neurons in both layers (s) and (t), then one of these two layers (s and t) is REDUNDANT.

Definition III: If the number of $\{q(p)\}$ neurons is less than the number of $\{p\}$ neurons, then layer $\{b\}$ is called an INFERIOR LAYER to $\{a\}$.

Also see Property (h) below on redundancy determination via correlation-layers.

(e) **Definition IV**: ZERO-INFORMATION REDUNDANCY: If only one neuron is ALWAYS the winner in layer (k), regardless of the output decision, then the layer contains no information and is redundant.

The above definitions and properties can serve to reduce number of features or memories by considering only a reduced number of most-significant modules or memories or by eliminating the least significant ones.

We comment that the information that is provided by this simple analysis may serve to construct or to re-construct a more efficient and faster network by removing least important or redundant layers or neurons if so desired.

6.4.4. Correlation and interpolation

(f) Correlation feature

Consider the (m) most significant layers (modules) with respect to output decision (dk) and the (n) most significant neurons in each of these (m) layers, with respect to the same output decision. (Example: Let $m = n = 4$). We comment that correlation between sub-words can also be accommodated in the network by assigning a specific input sub-word of that correlation, this sub-word being formed by pre-processing.

Correlation-Layer Set-Up Rule: Establish additional SOM layers denoted as CORRELATION-LAYERS $\lambda(p/q, dk)$, such that the number of these additional correlation-layers is:

$$\sum_{i=1}^{m-1} i \text{ (per output decision } dk) \tag{6.17}$$

(Example: The correlation-layers for the case of $n = m = 4$ are: $\lambda(1/2, dk)$; $\lambda(1/3, dk)$; $\lambda(1/4, dk)$; $\lambda(2/3, dk)$; $\lambda(2/4, dk)$; $\lambda(3/4, dk)$.)

Subsequently, **WHENEVER** neurons $N(i, p)$ and $N(j, q)$ are simultaneously (namely, for the same given input word) winners at layers (p) and (q) respectively, and when both these neurons also belong to the subset of 'most significant' neurons in 'most significant' layers (such that p and q are 'most significant' layers), THEN we declare a neuron $N(i, p/j, q)$ in Correlation-Layer $\lambda(p/q, dk)$ to be the winning neuron in that correlation-layer and we reward/punish its output link-weight $L(i, p/j, q - dk)$ as need be for any winning neuron in any other input SOM layer.

(Example: The neurons in correlation-layer $\lambda(p/q)$ are: $N(1, p/1, q)$; $N(1, p/2, q)$; $N(1, p/3, q)$; $N(1, p/4, q)$, $N(2, p/1, q)$; … $N(2, p/4, q)$; $N(3, p/1, q)$; … $N(4, p/1, q)$; … $N(4, p/4, q)$, to total $m \times m$ neurons in the correlation-layer).

Any winning neuron in a correlation layer is treated and weighted as any winning neuron in another (input-SOM) layer as far as its weights to any output layer neuron are concerned and updated. Obviously, a winning neuron (per a given input word), if any, in a correlation layer p/q is a neuron $N(i, p/j, q)$ in that layer where both neuron $N(i, p)$ in input layer (p) and neuron $N(j, q)$ in layer (q) were winners for the given input word.

It must be noted that both auto-correlations and cross-correlation at any delay (interval) can also be entered into the LAMSTAR neural network as input SOM-layers (for given delays) from appropriate per-processor that compute these functions.

(g) **Interpolation/Extrapolation by means of Correlation Layers:**

Let p be a 'most significant' layer and let i be a 'most significant neuron with respect to output decision dk in layer p, where no input subword exists in a given input word relating to layer p. Thus, neuron $N(i, p)$ is considered as the interpolation/extrapolation neuron for layer p if it satisfies:

$$\sum_q \{L(i, p/w, q-dk)\} \geqq \sum_q \{L(v, p/w, q-dk)\} \tag{6.18}$$

where v are different from i and where $L(i, p/j, q \rightarrow dk)$ denote link weights from correlation-layer $\lambda(p/q)$. Note that in every layer q there is only one winning neuron for the given input word, denoted as $N(w, q)$, whichever w may be at any q'th, layer.

(Example: Let $p = 3$. Thus consider correlation-layers $\lambda(1/3, dk)$; $\lambda(2/3, dk)$; $\lambda(3/4, dk)$ such that: $q = 1, 2, 4$).

Obviously, no punishment/reward is applied to a neuron that is considered to be the interpolation/extrapolation of another neuron not actually arising from the input word itself.

(h) **Redundancy Detection via Correlation-Layers:**

Let p be a 'most significant' layer and let i be a 'most significant' neuron in that layer. Layer p is redundant if for all input words there is there is another 'most significant' layer q such that, for any output decision and for any neuron $N(i, p)$, only one correlation neuron $i, p/j, q$ (i.e., for only one j per each such i, p) has non-zero output-link weights to any output decision dk, such that every neuron $N(j, p)$ is always associated with only one neuron $N(j, p)$ in some layer p.

(Example: Neuron $N(1, p)$ is always associated with neuron $N(3, q)$ and never with $N(1, q)$ or $N(2, q)$ or $N(4, q)$, while neuron $N(2, p)$ is always associated with $N(4, q)$ and never with other neurons in layer q).

Also, see property (d) above.

6.4.5. Innovation detection in the LAMSTAR *NN*

(i) If link-weights from a given input SOM layer to the output layer output change considerably and repeatedly (beyond a threshold level) within a certain time interval (a certain specified number of successive input words that are being applied), relatively to link weights from other input SOM layers, then innovation is detected with respect to that input layer (category).

(j) Innovation is also detected if weights between neurons from one input SOM layer to another input SOM layer similarly change.

6.5. LAMSTAR Data-Balancing Pre-Setting Procedure

6.5.1. Solution for data imbalance

The preprocessing algorithm for LAMSTAR neural networks is applicable to classification situations where there is an imbalance between classes, such that certain classes have (far) more data than others. This data-imbalance happens also in dynamic situations where over may time intervals (input words) data belongs to a state of undetected events and only then an event is detected (at one or a few successive time intervals or datasets). It thus applies to situations, such as detection or prediction of a particular event, such as the start of tremor (in Parkinson disease), of seizure (in epilepsy) or of intrusion (in the Web). This is especially important when prediction must be accomplished as close as possible to a given event, say, for fast warning.

This preprocessor can be used with both LAMSTAR-1 or LAMSTAR-2. It differs from LAMSTAR-1 andLAMSTAR-2 only in that it uses an initial training algorithm given below that serves to modify LAMSTAR's reward/punishment terms. All else remains unchanged.

In recent results computed by Nivedita Khobragade of the University of Illinois at Chicago concerning prediction of onset of tremor in Parkinson Patients [Khobragade, 2016], performance more than 50% when using the present pre-training procedure, in comparison to ignoring this imbalance, for exactly the same LNN-2 algorithm. (Comment: in this case performance was in terms of success rate in prediction within a time interval close to the occurrence of tremor, noting that the clinically important parameter is that success-rate which also maximizes the period of no tremor without stimulation).

6.5.2. Preprocessing training core algorithm — LAMSTAR preprocessor *P*

The core algorithm is outlined as follows:

(A) Network SET-UP

Use the setup of LAMSTAR [1], having 2 output neurons in its output layer, denoted as "*d*" (event in question is "detected") and "*nd*" ("not detected"), such that each input neuron (i) in each input layer (j) has two *LWs*, denoted as $L(i, j/d)$, $L(i, j/nd)$, respectively.

As in the regular LAMSTAR *NN*, if the event in question is not observed, then all link-weights (*LW*'s) from winning input neurons of the given step (sub-word) n to output "*nd*" are rewarded by $R(nd)$ and all LW's of the same winning input neuron to output neuron "d" are punished by $P(nd)$.

Similarly, if the event is actually observed, all *LW*'s to output neuron "*d*" are rewarded by $R(d)$ and the *LW*'s to output neuron "*nd*" are punished by $P(d)$.

Note that $R(d)$ and $R(nd)$ above are not be similar in LAMSTAR-P. Neither are $P(d)$ and $P(nd)$. The successive sub-words relate to two states (situations): "*DT*" and "*UDT*" which are a-priori unknown and are to be learnt by the neural network.

Input words are numbered [PER EACH INPUT NEURON] in the order (time) that they are entered the WINNING input neurons, this time is denoted as n (= 1, 2, 3, …). They are also ordered as $n(DT)$ and as $n(UDT)$ according to the (time-) order, if they belong to states (situations) when the event has been or has not yet been observed), respectively, where:

$$n(DT) = 1, 2, 3, \ldots, \tag{1^a}$$

$$n(UDT) = 1, 2, 3, \ldots. \tag{1^b}$$

(B) Initial Neural Network training

In contrast to the regular LAMSTAR, initial training is necessary, as follows:

Enter 1st input sub-word of 1st dataset.

All Link-Weights (*LWs*) start as

$$LW(0) = 0 \tag{2^}$$

Subsequently: Count (time-) step:

$$k = 1, 2. 3, \ldots. \tag{3^}$$

and count:

$$N(i,j) = 1, 2, 3\ldots \tag{4^}$$

per each input layer (only) when that neuron is the winning neuron.

We assume that each dataset starts in state "*UDT*" and stays in that state for a relatively large number of runs (considerably larger). Hence, count:

$$n(i,j, UDT) = 1, 2, 3\ldots \tag{5^}$$

per each input layer (only) when that neuron is the winning neuron until an event (say, tremor) is observed:

As in LAMSTAR-1 and LAMSTAR-2, reward and punishment are also executed in state D as follows:

$$LW\{(i, j/d), N\} = LW\{(i, j/d), N-1) + P(UDT) \quad (6^\wedge)$$

where $LW\{(iw, j/d), N\}$ denotes the link weight from neuron i in layer j (whichever it happens to be) to output neuron d at dataset (time-frame) $N-1$ (and where "$/d$" refers to a link-weight connected to output neuron d, not to be confused with state DT or state UDT)

$$LW\{(i, j/nd), N\} = LW\{(i, j/nd), N-1) + R(UDT) \quad (7^\wedge)$$

where neuron (iw, j) denotes the WINNING input neuron in layer j (whichever it is), by the Winner-Takes-All nature of LAMSTAR). $R(UDT)$ and $P(UDT)$ may be set as a constant , say (+1) and (−1) respectively.

Subsequently: Once the event in question has been observed for the FIRST time:

Let:

$$k = K \quad (8^\wedge)$$

and define at that (exact) point:

$$N(i, j, UDT) = n(i, j, UDT) \quad (9^\wedge)$$

$$N(i, j, UDT) = n(i, j, DT) \quad (10^\wedge)$$

Furthermore, define the ratio:

$$p'(i, j, UDT) = [N(i, j, UDT)]/K \quad (11^\wedge)$$

Once the event to be detected has been observed, the program is considered to be in state D and is to stay in this state for a number (Q) of datasets (say, time-frames) to allow some more data to be collected and processed for better learning. Usually Q will be 1 to 3, but it can be higher if so desired.

We now count the datasets where neuron i in layer j is winner as

$$m(i, j, DT) = 1, 2, \ldots \tag{12^}$$

We therefore define

$$M(i, j, DT) = m(i, j, DT) \text{ at dataset (time frame) } q \tag{13^}$$

$$p'(i, j, DT) = [M(i, j, DT)]/Q \tag{14^}$$

p' above is to serve as estimates of the probability that any particular neuron (i, j) is a winner in a given state, assuming (local-) ergodicity of the data for the given problem in the given datasets.

In order to improve the estimates of p' (Eqs. 9^, 11^), several databases must be used. This will necessitate to update Q and K from one dataset to another. Furthermore, usually, not all neurons have information on computing p' in one dataset. Hence, several data sets will be also need to cover all neuron with respect to p'. If no sufficient datasets are available for training purposes, one should employ as many as are available.

Hence, and using V datasets in this training algorithm rather than one, we define:

$$v = 1, 2, \ldots V \tag{15^}$$

and replace Eqs. for p' of (11) and (14) with p as follows:

$$p(i, j, UDT) = \sum [N(i, j, UDT)]_v / \sum K_v \tag{16^}$$

$$p(i, j, DT)) = \sum [M(i, j, DT)] / \sum Q_v \tag{17^}$$

respectively, where summations ($\sum$) are over $v = 1, 2, \ldots V$.

Note that Q and V need not be equal for all datasets. Hence, they are denoted as functions of the given dataset (v). We now defined a ratio B, as follows:

$$B(i,j) = [p(i,j,DT)]/[p(i,j,UDT)] \quad (18\text{^})$$

B being the ratio between the relative weight of the given neuron in determining that a data set is in the state that is free of a given event ("state 1") and its being in the state of the given event ("state 2"), regardless of the fact that only few datasets are within the state of that event whereas many datasets are event-free.

Consequently, when running LAMSTAR-1 or LAMSTAR-2, when state "*d*" is observed (or predicted, if one does not wait for it to happen, as is the case in problems of predicting an event rather than of its detection), reward will be computed as follows:

$$R(i,j,DT) = B(i,j) \times R(UDT) \quad (19\text{^})$$

and punishment will be:

$$P(i,j,DT) = B(i,j) \times P(UDT) \quad (20\text{^})$$

Note that reward and punishment now differ from one neuron to another. But for the change in reward and punishment in state DT, LAMSTAR-1 and LAMSTAR-2 remain unchanged. The training above is needed only to derive the ratio B.

Also, note that the LAMSTAR already has the information on getting into state DT from its own punishment/reward system.

6.6. Comments and Applications

6.6.1. Concluding comments

The LAMSTAR neural network utilizes the basic features of many other neural network, and adopts Kohonen's SOM modules [Kohonen, 1977, 1988] with their associative-memory-based setting of storage weights (w_{ij} in this Chapter) and its WTA (Winner-Take-All) feature.

It differs in its neuronal structure in that every neuron has not only storage weights w_{ij}), but also the link weights L_{ij}. This feature directly follows Hebb's Law [Hebb, 1949] and its relation to Pavlov's Dog experiment, as discussed in Section 2.1. It follows the concept of Verbindungen [Kant, 1781] and its role in "understanding" in a neural-network/machine-intelligence setting. Hence, not only does LAMSTAR deal with two kinds of neuronal weights (for storage and for linkage to other layers), but in the LAMSTAR, the link weights are the ones that count for decision purposes. The storage weights form "atoms of memory" in the Kantian sense [Ewing, 1938], while the link weights provide the "understanding" as Kant calls them.

The LAMSTAR's decisions are solely based on the **link weights** — see Sections 6.2.2 and 6.3.3 below. The link weights are the ones that facilitate integrating and ranking any number of pre-processors (filters) and therefore, great processing power, when necessary. Thus they are responsible for the computational power to this network. Straight Hebbian learning within simple arithmetics of reward/ punishment is what gives it computational speed. The CNS itself uses a superb system of organization, but not of advanced calculus. It appears to keep the mathematics simpler rather than too complex, in its clever binary way.

A common criticism of neural networks, and especially of BP-based networks is their lack of transparency. The weights in BP do not yield direct information on what their values mean. In LAMSTAR the link weights directly indicate the significance of a given feature and of a particular sub-word relative to the particular decision, as indicated in Sections 6.2 and 6.3 below. The LAMSTAR, unlike most neural networks, attempts to provide a transparent representation of the problem it must solve (Rosenblatt, 1961). This representation, regarding the networks decision, can be formulated in terms of a nonlinear mapping L of the weights between the inputs (input vector) and the outputs, that is arranged in a matrix form. Therefore, L is a nonlinear mapping function whose entries are the weights between inputs and the outputs, which map the inputs to the output decision. Considering the Back-Propagation (BP) network, the weights in each layer are the columns of L. The same holds for the link weights L_{ij} of L to a winning output decision in the LAMSTAR network. Obviously, in both BP and LAMSTAR, the matrix L is not a square matrix-like function, nor are all its columns of same length. However, in BP, the matrix L has many entries (weights) in each column per any output decision. In contrast, in the LAMSTAR, each column of L has only one non-zero entry at a given time. This accounts both for its **transparency**.

LAMSTAR-1 requires the computation of only Eqs. (6.5) and (6.11) per iteration. These involve only addition/subtraction and thresholding operations while no multiplication is involved, to contribute to the LAMSTAR's computational speed.

Most important for taking full advantage the LAMTAR unique structure in complex deep learning problems, is the use of any coprocessor or preprocessor or related dataset for the problem of interest and the integrating of it intelligently into the LAMSTAR, in terms of separate sub-words, This is discussed in detail in Section 6.1.11 above.

6.6.2. Applications

Applications of the LAMSTAR, as reported in the literature, cover a broad range of topics, including:

Medical diagnosis [Kordylewski and Graupe, 2001], [Nigam and Graupe, 2004], [Muralidharan and Rousche, 2005], [Sivaramakrishnan and Graupe, 2004], [Isola *et al.*, 2012]; **Finance**: [Schneider and Graupe, 2008], [Dong *et al.*, 2012]; **Fault Diagnosis**: [Yoon *et al.*, 2013]; **Data mining and Information Retrieval**: [Chang *et al.*, 1998], [Malhorta and Nair, 2015], [Isola *et al.*, 2012]; **Video Processing**: [Girado *et al.*, 2004]; **Prediction**: [Waxman *et al.*, 2010]; **Speech Processing**: [Graupe and Abon, 2007]; **Adaptive Filtering**: [Graupe *et al.*, 2008], [Graupe and Abon, 2002]; **Computer Security** (Intrusion Detection): [Venkatachalam, 2007]; **Browsing** [Malhorta and Nair, 2015], **Nonlinear Control** [Graupe and Smollack, 2007], and more.

The **Case Studies**, as in Chapter 8 (see also: Appendices below) give details of several applications of the LANSTAR, some of which compare the performance of the LAMSTAR with CNN and Back Propagation. Certain applications given in these Case Studies also give comparisons with RBF (Radial Basis Function) and SVM (Support Vector Machine), which lies outside the field of neural networks.

The applications covered in these Case Studies are in the fields of **Medicine** (predicting epileptic seizures, cancer detection), **Finance** (microtrading — also compared with BP, SVM and RBF), **Speech** in heavy noise (blind adaptive filtering of unknown high-level noise from speech — comparison with BP), **Prediction** related to sports events, **Oil Drilling** site selection, Estimating **3D from 2D images** (compared with CNN), **Security**: (Credit card fraud detection), **Human Activities** classification (compared with CNN), and beyond.

References

Basu I, Graupe D, Tuninetti D, Shukla P, Slavin K V, Metman L V, Corcos D, “Pathological tremor prediction using surface electromyogram and acceleration: Potential use in ‘ON–OFF’ demand driven deep brain stimulator design”.

Dong F, Shatz SM, Xu H, Majumdar D, "Price comparison: A reliable approach to identifying shill bidding in online auctions", *Electronic Commerce Research and Applications* **11**(2):171–179 (2012).

Ewing A C, *A Sort Commentary on Kant's Critique of Pure Reason* (Univ. of Chicago Press, 1938).

Girado J I, Sandin D J , DeFanti T A, Wolf L K, “Real-time camera-based face detection using modified LAMSTAR neural network system”, *Proc. IS&T/SPIE 15th Annual Symp. on Electronic Imaging* (2003).

Graupe D, *Principles of Artificial Neural Networks* (World Scientific Publishers, 1st edition 1997, 3rd edition 2013).

Graupe D, Abon J, “Neural network for blind adaptive *filtering* of unknown noise from speech”, *Proc. ANNIE Conf.*, Paper WP2.1A (2002).

Graupe D, Kordylewski H, “Network based on SOM modules combined with statistical decision tools”, *Proc. IEEE 29*th *Midwest Symp. on Circuits and Systems*, Ames. IO (1996).

Graupe D, Kordylewski H, “A large memory storage and retrieval neural network for browsing and medical diagnosis applications”, *Intelligent Engineering Systems through Artificial Neural Networks*, eds. Dagli C H *et al.*, Vol. 6 (ASME Press, 1996), pp. 711–716.

Graupe D, Lynn J W, “Some aspects regarding mechanistic modelling of recognition and memory”, *Cybernetica* **3**:119 (1969).

Graupe D, Smollack M, “Control of unstable nonlinear and nonstationary systems using LAMSTAR neural networks”, *Proc. IASTED 10th Conf. on Intelligent Systems and Control* (2007), pp. 50–53.

Graupe D, Zhong Y, Graupe M H, Jackson R, “Blind adaptive filtering for non-invasive diagnosis of the fetal ECG and its non-stationarities”, *ASME Transactions Part H: Jour. Eng. in Medicine* **222**(8):1221–1234 (2008).

Hebb D, *The Organization of Behavior* (John Wiley, 1949).

Isola R, Carvalho R, Tripathy A K, "Knowledge discovery in medical systems using differential diagnosis, LAMSTAR, and *k-NN*", *IEEE Trans. on Info Theory and Biomed* **16**(6):1287–1295, 2012.

Kant E, *Critique of Pure Reason* (Koenigsbarg, Germany, 1781).

Khobragade, N, P_Lamstar_Results_033/016, (unpublished), Apr. 4, 2016.

Kohonen T, *Associated Memory: A system Theoretical Approach* (Springer Verlag, 1977).

Kohonen T, *Self-Optimizing and Associative Memory* (Springer Verlag, 1984, 1988).

Levitan L B, Kaszmarek L K, *The Neuron* (2nd edition), (Oxford University Press, 1997).

Malhotra M, Nair T R G, "Evolution of knowledge representation and retrieval techniques", *Int J. Intelligent Systems and Applications*, 2015, 07, 18–28 June 2015, 07, 18-2, 2015.

McCulloch W S, Pitts W, "A logical calculus of the ideas imminent in nervous activity", *Bull. Math. Biophysics* **5**:115–133 (1943).

Minsky M, Papert S, *Perceptrons* (MIT Press, 1969).

Muralidharan A, Rousche P J, "Decoding of auditory cortex signals with a LAMSTAR neural network, *Neurological Research* **27**(1):4–10 (2005).

Nigam P V, Graupe D, "A neural-network-based detection of epilepsy, *Neurological Research* **26**(1):55–60 (2004).

Pavlov I P, *Conditional Reflexes*, (in Russian), 1927. English translation: Oxford University Press, 1927, Dover Press, 1962.

Rosenblatt F, "The perceptron, a probabilistic model for information storage and organization in the brain", *Psychol. Rev.* **65**:386–408 (1958).

Schneider N A, Graupe D, "A modified LAMSTAR neural network and its applications", *International Jour. Neural Systems* **18**(4):331–337 (2008).

Sivaramakrishnan A, Graupe D, "Brain tumor demarcation by applying a LAMSTAR neural network to spectroscopy data", *Neurol. Research* **26**(6):613–621 (2004).

Venkatachalam V, Selvan S, "Intrusion detection using an improved competitive learning Lamstar neural network", *IJCSNS, International Journal of Computer Science and Network Security* 7(2):255–263 (2007).

Waxman J A, Graupe D, Carley D W, "Prediction of Apnea and Hypopnea using LAMSTAR artificial neural network", *Amer. Jour. Respiratory and Critical Care Medicine* **181**(7):727–733 (2010).

Waxman J A , Graupe D, Carley D W, "Real-time prediction of disordered breathing events in people with obstructive sleep apnea", *Sleep and Breathing* **19**(1):205–212 (2015).

Yoon J M, He D, Qiu B, "Full ceramic bearing fault diagnosis using LAMSTAR neural network", *IEEE Conf. on Prognostics and Health Management* (*PHM*), 24–27 June. Pages 1–9 (2013).

CHAPTER 7

Other Neural Networks for Deep Learning

7.1. Deep Boltzmann Machines (DBM)

Deep Boltzmann Machines (DBM) serve as stochastic neural networks. They evolved from Ackley and Hinton's 1985 derivation of the Boltzmann Machine [Ackley, 1985] and the subsequent from the Restricted Boltzmann Machine. These machines are essentially unsupervised, in contract to CNN or LAMSTAR.

The **Boltzmann Machine (BM)** is a stochastic neural network having 2 layers stochastic neurons, one layer consisting of visible neuron v_j and the other consisting of hidden neurons h_i where v_j and $h_i \in \{0, 1\}$, and of a symmetric weight matrices W, L, J which are the matrices of weights connecting visible-hidden, visible-visible and hidden-hidden neurons, respectively, noting that all the BM neurons are interconnected, both within a layer and between layers. [Haykin, 1999].

Also

$$W_{ii} = L_{jj} = J_{ii} = 0 \text{ for all } I \tag{7.1}$$

Furthermore, in the BM networks, the hidden and the visible neurons are binary, namely

$$v_j, h_i \in \{0, 1\} \tag{7.2}$$

The learning process of neural network is designed such that the network converges at a thermodynamic equilibrium that fits the network's input pattern according to a Gibbs-Boltzmann distribution.

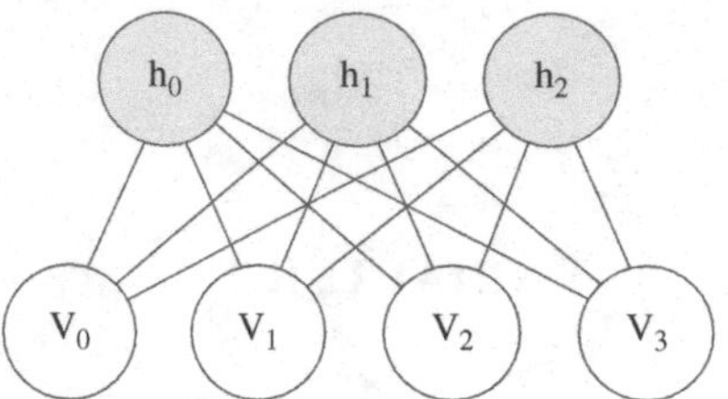

Fig. 7.1. An RBM neural network.

Learning is performed through gradient maximization of the Log-Likelihood of the error-energy of the network, considering errors between data and model.

The **Restricted Boltzmann Machine (RBM)** (Hinton, 2002] is a Boltzmann Machine where no interconnections exist between neurons of the same layer (visible-visible and hidden-hidden). See Fig. 7.1.

Deep Boltzmann Machines (DBM) where proposed by Salakhutdinov and Hinton to enhance the efficiency of RBM [Salakhutdinov, 2009]. The need for the DBM network arose from the difficulty in the need for learning all weights of the fully connected BM, especially when attempting to design a deep multi-layer network based on the BM approach. The DBM design can be viewed as the stacking of several RBM networks, while simplifying the resultant multi-layer by pre-training, as shown in Fig. 7.2 (according to [Salakhutdinov, 2009]).

The pre-training method used to compose a DBM network from stacked RBM, as in Fig. 7.2 was introduced by Hinton in 2006 [Hinton, 2006] and named as greedy layer-wise pre-training. It serves to initialize the parameter of the resultant DBM. In this re-training the RBM is slightly modified to avoid double-counting, where the lower RB's input is doubled while tying the *v*-to-*h* weights. Also, the number of the RBM hidden neurons is doubled. When composing the two modified RBMs, the total input entered into the first hidden layer is halved to result in a modified conditional distribution. The resulting DBM (Fig. 7.3) thus achieves initialization of weights to reasonable values and yields fast performance in a single path [Salakhutdinov, 2009].

Due to the long computation time involved in using DBM, its applicability to complex problems is limited (Vincent *et al*., 2010]. A Random Markov Field method (RMF) on which DBM is based, is compared (indirectly) in one

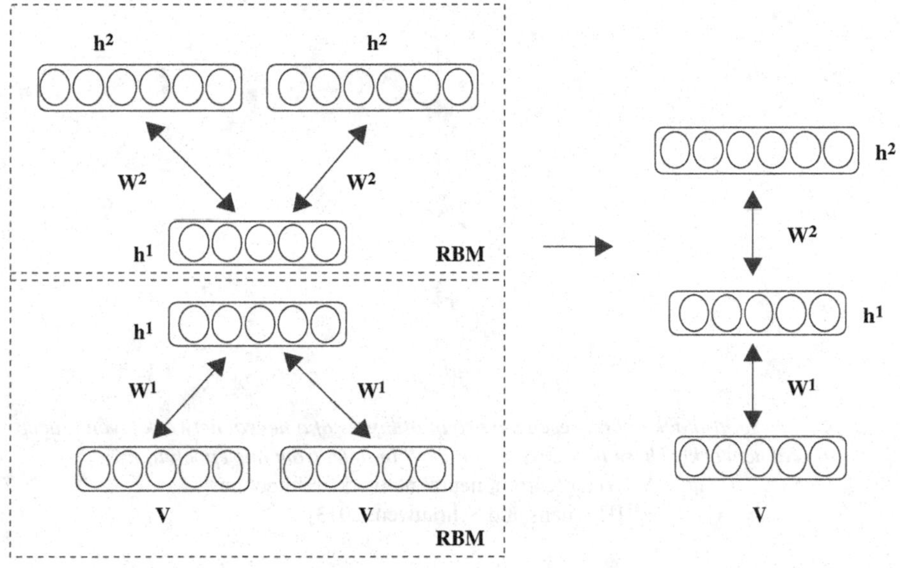

Fig. 7.2. Composing of two-layer DBM from 2 RBM networks.

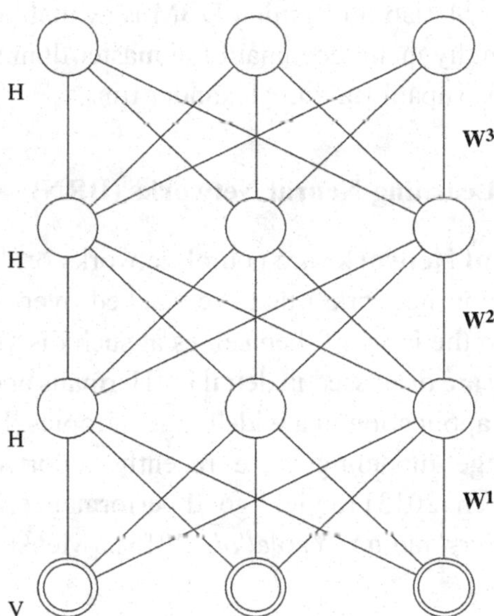

Fig. 7.3. Three-layer deep Boltzmann machine.

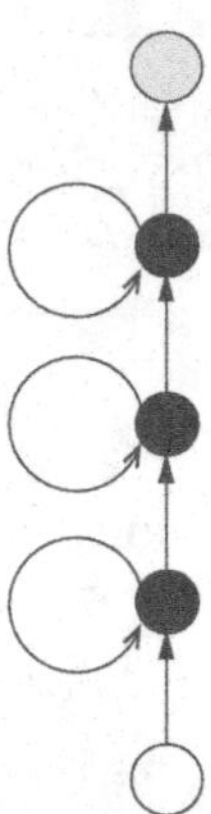

Notation: Each solid-black dot represents a group of layers of a neural network (even a deep neural network). These networks are stacked in time, from one epoch to next.
Fig. 7.4. Deep recurrent neural network architecture.
[Hermans and Schrauwen, 2013]

Case Study below, in Section 8.4, which concerns depth information retrieval from 2D images. Few applications of DBS appeared in the literature, such as [Salakhutdinov, Hinton, 2009] and [Saxena *et al.*, 2009].

An open-access code in Matlab for training DBM is available at: https://github.com/kyunghyuncho/deepmat/blob/master/dbm.m (Copyright © 2011, KyungHyun Cho, Tapani Raiko, Alexander Ilin).

7.2. Deep Recurrent Learning Neural Networks (DRN)

Deep Recurrent Neural Networks are neural networks or deep neural networks (mostly Back propagation networks) that are stacked over time at discrete time interval and feed also to the input of themselves at such discrete time intervals, as shown in Fig. 7.4. They are discussed in detail in [Hermans and Schrauwen, 2013]. They are very slow for application in a wide range of topics. However, successful, applications to language modeling were recently reported [Mikolov, 2010], [Hermans and Schrauwen, 2013] to yield good performance, as were applications to spoken language understanding [Yao *et al.*, 2013], [Mensil *et al.*, 2013].

7.3. Deconvolution/Wavelet Neural Networks

In 1988, an **Inverse-Convolution** design of a neural network was proposed by Graupe *et al.*, for the deconvolution of surface EMG signals in order to retrieve single-motor-neuron action-potentials, which satisfy a convolution-integral model [Graupe *et al.*, 1988] — see Section 2.1. The design was extended [Huang *et al.*, 1989], [Graupe and Liu, 1989], [Graupe *et al.*, 1989] to other neural network architectures. In contrast to CNN, these networks employed de-convolution to decompose convolution parameters (amplitude, duration and time-delay) of neuronal action-potentials, thus localizing convolution-based events embedded in the surface-EMG input signal. These designs were not initially intended to serve as a deep-learning networks, since they were originally used for extracting the location (timing) and the parameters (K_i, delay t_i and σ_i) of a function of the form of:

$$x(t) = \sum_{i=1}^{3} K_i \exp\left[-\left(\frac{t-t_i}{\sigma_i}\right)^2\right] \tag{7.3}$$

However, noting that this function can also be considered to describe a mother wavelet, these networks were termed in [Zhang and Benvenisti, 1992] as **Wavelet Neural Networks**. Neural networks arose, which is only justified subject to the limitation to the functions (shapes) considered above.

The EMG decomposition problem above, which, by the nature of the neuronal action-potential as in Eq. (7.3) is a deconvolution problem. To solve this problem, and noting that (action-potential) signals $h(t)$, with many different values of K_i, t_i and σ_i, composes the measured EMG signal, namely, the input data, we first generalize Eq. (7.3) such that

$$h(t) = \sum_{i=1}^{N} K_i G(w_i t + \theta_i) \tag{7.4}$$

$h(t)$ being a finite sequence of $x(t)$ signals (action potentials).

For solving this problem, we now design a neural network in order to iteratively estimate the parameters K_i, w_i and σ_i of $h(t)$ for as finite N to be as close as possible to an input $f(t)$, which is, in this case, the measured (input) surface EMG signal where:

$$z_i(k) = G[w_i(k)t(k) + \theta_i(k)] \tag{7.5}$$

and

$$G(t) = \exp(-t^2), \qquad t \in R \tag{7.6}$$

$z_i(k)$ above is therefore the output of the i'th node of the neural network (say, a back propagation network) at the k'th iteration step. Separability is assumed and is proven in [Huang *et al.*, 1989].

Consequently, let the measure of the error between

$$J(k) = \frac{1}{2}\|h_k(t(k)) - f(t(k))\|^2 \tag{7.7}$$

The gradient of Eq. (7.7) yields [Huang *et al.*, 1989]:

$$\begin{aligned} \frac{\partial J(k)}{\partial K_i(k)} &= e(k)z_i(k) \\ \frac{\partial J(k)}{\partial w_i(k)} &= -2e(k)\delta_i(k)t(k) \\ \frac{\partial J(k)}{\partial \theta_i(k)} &= -2e(k)\delta_i(k) \end{aligned} \tag{7.8}$$

where $i = 1, 2. \ldots, N$ and:

$$\delta_i(k) = K_i(k)z_i(k)[w_i(k)t(k) + \theta_i(k)] \tag{7.9}$$

and

$$e(k) = h_k(t(k)) - f(t(k)) \tag{7.10}$$

Such that

$$\begin{aligned} K_i(k+1) &= K_i(h) + \alpha e(k)z_i(k) \\ w_i(k+1) &= w_i(k) - 2\alpha e(k)\delta_i(k)t(t) \\ \theta_i(k+1) &= \theta_i(k) - 2\alpha e(k)\delta_i(k) \end{aligned} \tag{7.11}$$

where $\alpha \in [0, 1]$ denotes step-size [Huang *et al.*, 1989]. Obviously, this design can apply to any other convolution-type signal or to a mother wavelet [Rao and Bopardikar, 1998]. It is not restricted to a Backpropagation neural network. Indeed, [Graupe *et al.*, 1988] and [Graupe *et al.*, 1989] considered a Hopfield Neural Network to solve this problem. Furthermore, the design can be extended to 2D and 3D functions.

Figures 7.5 and 7.6 show the neural network's design

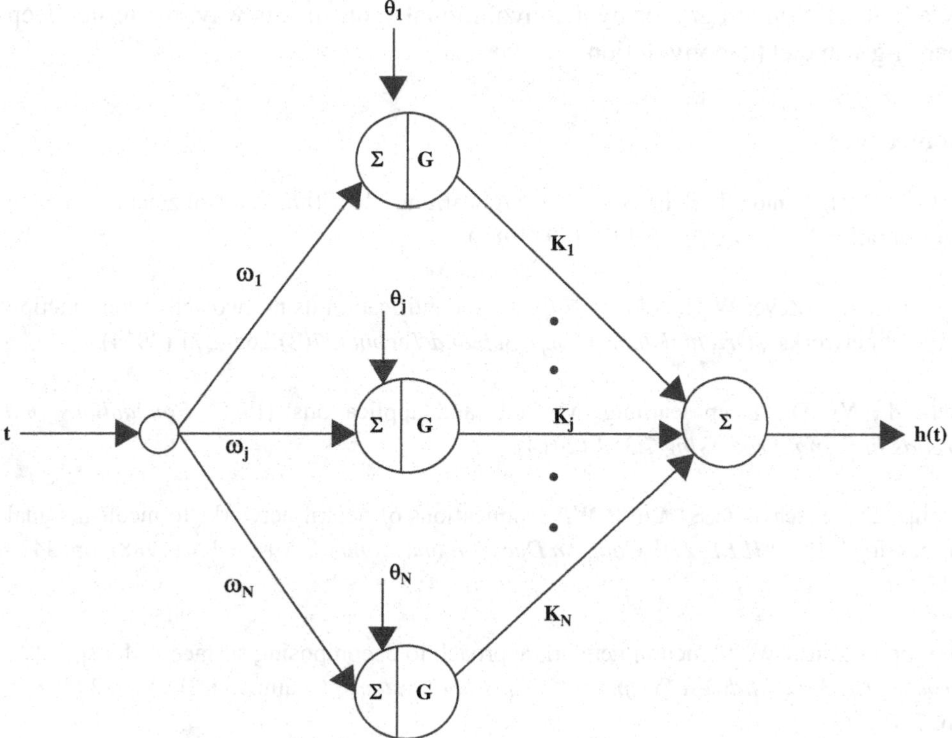

Fig. 7.5. Deconvolutional/wavelet neural network design.

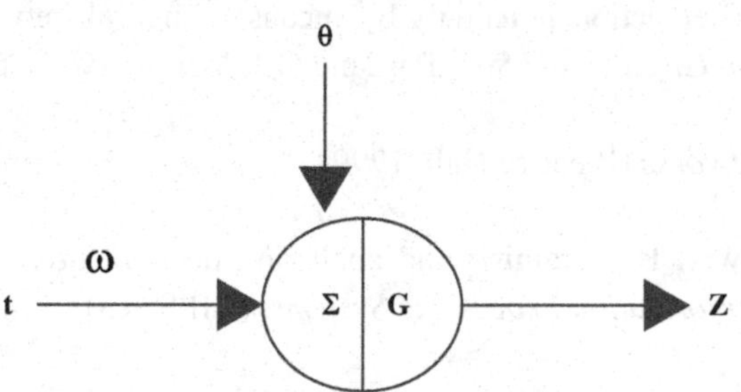

Notation: $\sum$ *denoting summation of neuron's inputs, G is as in Eq. (7.4)*
Fig. 7.6. Neural activation function *G* (Eq. 7.4) in neuronal model.

The **Deconvolution/Wavelet NN** was applied (with certain modifications) to other problems but for its application to EMG signals in **neurology** mentioned above, such as **Iris Recognition** [Almallah *et al.*], **Robot Control** [Moraud, 2014], **Finance** [Tan, 2009], etc., to serve for deep learning as long as the learning aimed at finding "shapes" that can be transformed into wavelets or otherwise be described by a convolution integral or by a convolutional sum. In this way, the term "deep learning wavelet (deconvolution).

References

Ackley D H, Hinton J, Seinowski T J, "A learning algorithm for Boltzmann Machine configuration", *Cognit. Sci.* 7:147–169 (1985).

Almallah A S, Zayer W H, Alkaam N O, "Iris identification using two activation function wavelet networks", *Oriental Jour. Comp. Sci. and Technol.* 7(2):265–271 (2014).

Deng L, Yu D, "Deep learning: Methods and applications" (PDF), *Foundations and Trends in Signal Processing* 7:3–4 (2014).

Graupe D, Moschytz G S , Liu R W, "Applications of neural networks to medical signal processing", *Proc. IEEE 27th Conf. on Decision and Control*, Austin TX (1988), pp. 343–347.

Graupe D, Liu R W, "A neural network approach to decomposing surface EMG signals", *Proc. IEEE 32nd Midwest Symp. on Circuits and Systems,* Champaign IL, Vol. 2 (1989), pp. 740–743.

Graupe D, Vern B, Gruener G, Field A S, Huang Q, "Decomposition of surface EMG signals into single fiber action potentials by means of neural networks", *Proc. IEEE International Conf. on Circuits and Sys.*, Portland OR, Vol. 2 (1989), pp 1008–1011.

Haykin S, *Neural Networks* (Prentice Hall, 1999).

Hermans M, Schrauwen B, "Training and analyzing deep recurrent neural networks", *Advances in Neural Information Processing Systems*, (NIPS '13), Vol. 26 (2013).

Hinton G E, "Training products of experts by minimizing contrastive divergence", *Neural Computation* **14**(8):1711–1800 (2002).

Huang Q, Graupe D, Liu R W, Huang Y F, "Identification of firing patterns of beuronal signals", *Proc. IEEE Conf. on Decision and Control*, Vol. 1 (1989), pp. 266–271.

Mesnil G, He X, Deng L, Bengio Y. "Investigation of recurrent neural network architectures and learning methods for spoken language understanding", *Proc. Interspeech* (2013).

Mikolov T *et al.*, "Recurrent neural network based language model," *Interspeech* (2010).

Moraud E M, "Wavelet Networks", http://homepages.inf.ed.ac.uk/rbf/CVonline/LOCAL_COPIES/AV0809/martinmoraud.pdf, 2009.

Rao R M, Pobardikar A S, *Wavelet Transforms* (Addison-Welseley, 1998).

Salakhutdinov R, Hinton G, "Deep Boltzmann Machines", http://machinelearning.wustl.edu/mlpapers/paper_files/AISTATS09_SalakhutdinovH.pdf, AISTAS, 2009.

Saxena A, Sun M, Ng A Y, "Make3d: Learning 3d scene structure from a single still image", *IEEE Transactions of Pattern Analysis and Machine Intelligence* (PAMI) **30**(5):824–840 (2009).

Sutskever I, *Training Recurrent Neural Networks*, Ph. Thesis, University of Toronto, (2013).

Tan C, "Financial time series forecasting using improved wavelet neural network", http://www.cs.au.dk/~cstorm/students/Chong_Jul2009.pdf, MS Thesis, CS Dept., Aarhus University, Denmark, (2009).

Vincent P, Larochelle H, Lajoie I, Bengio Y, Manzagol P A, "Stacked denoising autoencoders: Learning useful representations in a deep network with a local denoising criterion", *The Journal of Machine Learning Research* **11**:3371–3408 (2010).

Yao K, Zweig G, Hwang M, Shi Y, Yu D, "Recurrent neural networks for language understanding", *Proc. Interspeech* (2013).

Zhang Q, Benveniste A, "Wavelet networks", *IEEE Transactions on Neural Networks* **3**(6):889–898 (1992).

CHAPTER 8

Case Studies

Comment: In the discussions concerning the LNN-1 and LNN-2 deep learning networks in the Case Studies below, learning never stops after training but is carried out for all samples, and at all iterations from the first sample on. However, an initial number of datasets in these 2 networks is named as the training sets whereas all later datasets are considered as testing sets and performance statistics are computed only for later datasets. In this way, the number of data sets for training and for testing is the same for all neural networks considered in a given case study. Only when a pre-training algorithm such as the data-balancing pre-training algorithm of Section 6.5 above is employed, will this pre-training be considered in the training-mode statistics of comparing neural networks. Still, in none of the case studies in this text was this kind of pre-training employed.

This aspect of LAMSTAR must be taken into account when it is compared with other networks, where the meaning of training is different.

8.1. Human Activities Recognition (A Bose)

The goal of this Case Study is to apply CNN, LNN-1 and LNN-2 deep learning neural networks to the problem of recognizing human activities Classification problem and to compare the performance of these three networks and their respective computational times. All 3 networks considered in this study share the same input data and the same preprocessing. Comparison is also made with results from 18 other recently published (2012–2015) studies on the same problem and for the same database (see the Results tabulations of the present study, below).

DATA: The data for this Case Study comes from 2 human activities datasets: (1) the MSRDailyActivity3D [Microsoft. MRSDaily] from the Microsoft Research Laboratory, and (2) CAD-60 from Computer Science Department, Cornell University [Cornell. CAD60, 2009]. The data is of RGBD (RGB and Depth) images from Kincet sensors. Of 16 daily activities in MRSDaily, six were selected (Eating, Talking on cellphone, Standing up, Sitting still, Standing still, Walking). In these 6 activities 7590 different poses served for training and 600 for testing. Of 12 activities in CAD-60, 5 were selected for this study ((Brushing teeth, talking on phone, drinking water, cooking/chopping, working on computer).

PREPROCESSING: Our data is in terms of 3D images. Hence we must consider 3D Euclidean coordinates of 20 joints (see Fig. 8.1): 1. Hip Center, 2. Spine, 3. Shoulder Center, 4. Head, 5. Shoulder Right, 6. Elbow Right, 7. Wrist Right, 8. Hand Right, 9. Shoulder Left, 10. Elbow Left, 11. Wrist Left, 12. Hand Left, 13. Hip Right, 14. Knee Right, 15. Ankle Right, 16. Foot Right, 17. Hip Left, 18. Knee Left, 19. Ankle Left, 20. Foot Left. Therefore, the body orientation must be preprocessed (computed) to achieve a view-invariant activity recognition. After normalization of the above, we obtain 60 coordinates from 20 body-joints for each frame (pose of human activity). By adding zeros, we then get a 1×64 input vector that is arranged as an 8×8 input matrix and which serves as input to the neural networks considered in this Case Study.

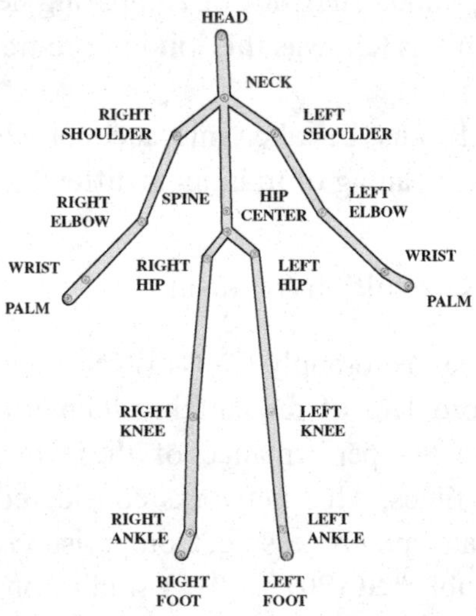

Fig. 8.1. Skeleton body joints given by Kincet.

Table 8.1a. Precision and recall of present and previous results on MRSDaily database — Human activity classification.

Method	Accuracy (%)
LOP [Wang J, 2012]	42.5
Depth motion maps [Yang X, 2012]	43.13
Joint position [Wang J, 2012]	68
Moving pose [Zanfir, 2013	73.8
Local HOV 4D [Oreifej, 2013]	80
Actionlet ensemble [Wang J, 2012]	85.75
SNV [Yang X, 2014]	86.25
HDMM+3ConvNets [Wang P, 2015]	81.88
CNN (present study)	93
LNN-1 (present study)	95.33
LNN-2 (present study)	99.67

Table 8.1b. Precision and recall of present and previous results on CD-60 database — Human activity classification.

Method	Precision	Recall
MEMM [Sung, 2011], [Sung, 2012]	67.9	55.5
SSVM [Koppula, 2013]	80.8	71.4
Structure-Motion Features [Zhang C, 2012]	86	84
NBNN [Yang X, 2013]	71.9	66.6
Image Fusion [Ni B, 2013]	75.9	69.5
Spatial-based Clustering [Gupta R, 2013]	78.1	75.4
K-means Clusterings+SVM+HMM [Gaglio, 2014]	77.3	76.7
S-ONI [Parisi, 2015]	91.9	90.2
SI Point Feature [Zhu Y, 2014]	93.2	84.6
Pose Kinetic Energy [Shan J, 2014]	93.8	94.5
CNN (present study)	92.33	93
LNN-1 (present study)	96.67	95.33
LNN-2 (present study)	100	100

Table 8.1c. Summarized comparison MRSDaily database human activity classification.

Parameter	CNN	LAMSTAR-I	LAMSTAR-II
Training time (sec)	507.30*	378.63†	429.425†
Training accuracy (%)	94.33‡	98.67‡	100‡
Testing time (sec)	172.36§	151.23§	153.365§

*Training time of 7590 training samples for 50 epochs
†Training time of 7590 training samples for threshold 0.9999
‡Testing with the same input used as training set
§Testing time of 600 test samples on trained network
¶For a trained CNN for 50 epochs
ΔFor a trained LAMSTAR/LAMSTAR II with threshold 0.9999

COMPUTATION: The CNN network receives an 8×8 input vector of the coordinate image above. The CNN program used in this study is the DeepLearnToolbox [Rasmus, 2012] for CNN written in MATLAB. DeepLearnToolbox is a MATLAB/Octave toolbox for deep learning — see Part 1 of Appendix A.8.1. The code for LNN-1 is in Part 2 of the same appendix, while Preprocessing is as in Part 3 of that Appendix.

RESULTS: Table 8.1a compare performances of present study (bottom 3) for poses from the MRSDaily database , while Table 8.1b compare performances of present study (bottom 3) for poses from the CD-60 database. Table 8.1c compares Computing Time and Accuracy for the 3 networks of the Present Case Study. Observe the perfect recognition by LNN-2 in the results of Table 8.1c.

References

[Cornell. CAD60, 2009] http://pr.cs.cornell.edu/humanactivities/data.php. Copyright (c) Cornell University, (2009).

[Gaglio, 2014] Gaglio S, Lo Re G, Morana M, "Human activity recognition process using 3-D posture data", in *IEEE Transactions on Human-Machine Systems* (2014).

[Gupta R, 2013] Gupta R, Chia A Y S, Rajan D, "Human activities recognition using depth images", in *Proc. of the 21st ACM International Conference on Multimedia* (2013).

[Koppula 2013] Koppula H S, Gupta R, Saxena A, "Learning human activities and object affordances from RGB-D videos", arXiv:1210.1207v2, May 2013.

[Microsoft, MRSDaily]
http://research.microsoft.com/en-us/um/people/zliu/actionrecorsrc/

[Ni B, 2013] Ni B, Pei Y, Moulin P, Yan S, "Multilevel depth and image fusion for human activity detection", *IEEE Trans. Cybernetics* (2013).

[Oreifej, 2013] Oreifej O, Liu Z, "Hon4d: Histogram of oriented 4d normals for activity recognition from depth sequences", in *CVPR* (2013).

[Parisi, 2015] Parisi G I, Weber C, Wermter S, "Self-organizing neural integration of pose-motion features for human action recognition", in *Frontier in Neurobotics* (2015).

[Rasmus, 2012] https://github.com/rasmusbergpalm/DeepLearnToolbox. Copyright (c) 2012.

[Shan J, 2014] Shan J, Akella S, "3D Human action segmentation and recognition using pose kinetic energy", in *IEEE Workshop on Advanced Robotics and its Social Impacts* (ARSO), 2014.

[Sung J, 2011] Sung J, Ponce C, Selman B, Saxena A, "Human activity detection from RGBD images", in *Proc. AAAI Workshop on Pattern, Activity and Intent Recognition* (PAIR), 2011.

[Sung J, 2012] Sung J, Ponce C, Selman B, Saxena A, "Unstructured human activity detection from RGBD images," in *Proc. ICRA* (2012).

[Wang J, 2012] Wang J, Liu Z, Wu Y, Yuan J, "Mining action let ensemble for action recognition with depth cameras", in *Proc. CVPR* (2012), Providence, Rhode Island, June 16–21, 2012.

[Wang P, 2015] Wang P, Li W, Gao Z, Zhang J, Tang C, Ogunbona P, "Deep convolutional neural networks for action recognition using depth map sequences," arXiv, preprint arXiv:1501.04686, 2015.

[Yang X, 2012] Yang X, Zhang C, Tian Y, "Recognizing actions using depth motion maps-based histograms of oriented gradient", in *ACMMM* (2012).

[Yang X, 2013] Yang X, Tian Y, "Effective 3D action recognition using eigenjoints", *Journal of Visual Communication and Image Representation (JVCIR), Special Issue on Visual Understanding and Applications with RGBD Cameras* (2013).

[Yang X, 2014] Yang X, Tian Y, "Super normal vector for activity recognition using depth sequences," in *CVPR* (2014).

[Zafir, 2013] Zanfir M, Leordeanu M, Sminchisescu C, "The moving pose: An efficient 3d kinematics descriptor for low-latency action recognition and detection", in *ICCV* (2013).

[Zhang C, 2012] Zhang C, Tian Y, "RGB-D camera-based daily living activity recognition", *Journal of Computer Vision and Image Processing* Vol. 2, No. 4, December 2012.

[Zhu Y, 2014] Zhu Y, Chen W, Guo G, "Evaluating spatiotemporal interest point features for depth-based action recognition", in *Image and Vision Computing* (2014).

8.2. Medicine: Predicting Onset of Seizures in Epilepsy (J Tran)

The goal of this Case Study is to predict onset of epileptic seizures in Epilepsy patients from Intracranial EEG (iEEG) data by using 3 deep learning neural networks, Back Propagation (BP), LNN-1 and LNN-2 and comparing performance and computational speed of these 3 networks. Prediction is carried out by detecting the 20–30 minutes Pre-ictal (pre-seizure) phase as compared with the inter-ictal phase (of no seizures) that usually lasts for days or even for a few weeks, and which precedes the ictal phase of a few minutes. Obviously, computational speed is almost as critical as accurate prediction (oncoming seizures being missed).

DATASET: The data for this case study was downloaded from https://www.kaggle.com/c/seizure-prediction/data [epilepsy soc., 2014]. Both the inter-ictal (no seizures) and the pre-ictal sections used as data were of same duration (10 minutes). The pre-ictal data was taken between 15 and 5 minutes BEFORE start of seizures. Each data window is of 30 seconds duration. All inter-ictal data were randomly chosen at least a week before or after a seizure occurred.

PREPROCESSING: For both LNN-1 and LNN-2, the input data includes the dominant frequency of the in each 1 sec. time window.

COMPUTING: The convolutional program used was a Python Lasagne version of CNN. The data was entered into the CNN network using https://lasagne.readthedocs,org/, see Appendix A.8.2 below. The LAMSTAR LNN-1 and LNNN-2 programs were both based on the Core code in Chapter 6. Both LNN-1 and LNN-2 use five SOM input layers.

RESULTS: See Table 8.2 below. Results with CNN of 71% sensitivity were reported in [Mirowski, 2009], though for a different data source (University of Freiburg, Germany) and with different preprocessing.

Table 8.2. Comparison of results — Seizure prediction.

Method	Accuracy	Training Time	Testing Time
CNN	70%	170 sec	3 sec
LNN-1	81.25%	< 1 sec	< 1 sec
LNN-2	81.25%	< 1 sec	< 1 sec

References

[epilepsy soc., 2014] American Epilepsy Society Seizure Prediction Challenge https://www.kaggle.com/c/seizure-prediction/data, 2014.

[Mirowski, 2009] Mirowski P, Madhavan D, LeCun Y, Kuzniecky R, "Classification of patterns of EEG synchronization for seizure prediction" (https://epilepsy.uni-freiburg.de/freiburg-seizureprediction-project/eeg-database/), *Clinical Neurophysiology* **120**(11): 1927–1940 (2009).

8.3. Medicine: Image Processing: Cancer Detection (D Bose)

The goal is to build a classifier that can distinguish between cancer and control patients from the mass spectrometry data. The classifiers used were BP, CNN, LNN-1, and LNN-2 deep learning neural networks. The same data and the same preprocessing was used in all neural networks used for this Case Study.

DATASET: The data in this example is from the FDA-NCI Clinical Proteomics Program Databank [1]. Specifically, the data used was of High Resolution SELDI-TOF Study Sets from the databank's link -

http://home.ccr.cancer.gov/ncifdaproteomics/OvarianCD_PostQAQC.zip under "High Resolution SELDI-TOF Study Sets". This link contains two sets of data, one for "cancer" and the other for "normal". It has having 121(cancer) and 95 (normal) text files (.txt files) of individual patients.

PREPROCESSING: The methodology followed in this project is to select a reduced set of measurements or "features" that can be used to distinguish between cancer and control patients using a classifier. These features will be ion intensity-levels at specific mass/charge values. The raw mass-spectrometry data, that was obtained from the text files of the dataset above, was extracted to create the OvarianCancerQAQCdataset.mat file in program #3 named MSSEQPROCESSING.

The MSSEQPROCESSING file contains 3 variables named:

1. "grp", a 216 × 1 matrix having either "cancer" or "normal" label,
2. "MZ", a 15000 × 1 matrix having 15000 mass-charge values
3. "Y", a 15000 × 216 matrix having 15000 ion intensity levels at each of the corresponding 15000 Mass-Charge values of MZ, of 216 patients.

The Ranking Key Feature of this program was used to choose a feature vector having 100 points from 15000 points previously discussed and which forms a 100 × 216 matrix. The resulting 100 × 216 matrix, was ultimately taken as the input for both Lamstar and CNN i.e. 100 feature point for each 216 patients. But for CNN the 100 feature point was converted into a 10 × 10 matrix for each 216 patients. The data.mat in the CNN loads two variables, namely, x in (100 × 216 matrix) and t in 2 × 216 (for labeling of "cancer" or "normal").

COMPUTATION:

CNN: For the Convolution Neural Network, ConvNet for CNN, which is a MATLAB/Octave toolbox, was used. The source code is available in: https://github.com/sdemyanov/ConvNet. Copyright (c) 2014 Sergey Demyanov. Its 100 × 216 input is as discussed in the Preprocessing paragraph above. Also, see program in part 1 of Appendix A.8.3. LAMSTAR uses 100 layers to correspond to the features resulting from the preprocessing above. Also see Part 1 of Appendix A.8.3. BP — Matlab Toolbox was used.

RESULTS: See Table 8.3 below:

Table 8.3. Comparison of performance and computation time — Cancer detection.

Parameter	BP	CNN	LAMSTAR-I	LAMSTAR-II
Training time (sec)	3.984	4.1190	0.8019	0.7998
Training accuracy (%)	88.8	86.768	98.67	100
Testing time (sec)	1.728	0.7068	0.142	0.1605
Recognition rate (%)	84.4	88	92.00	94.00

8.4. Image Processing: From 2D Images to 3D (J C Somasundaram)

The goal of this Case Study is to apply CNN and LNN-1 deep learning neural networks to extract depth information from 2D images and to compare the performance of these three networks and their respective computational times. All 3 networks considered in this study share the same input data. Comparison is also made with results from 2 other recently published studies on the same problem (see the Results tabulation of the present study, below)

DATABASE: The data for this study is taken from the B3DO: Berkeley 3-D Object Dataset [7]. The Berkley dataset is mainly intended for object recognition and labelling, but it also serves well for the present study. The dataset has 849 RGB images and 849 corresponding ground truth depth maps of size 640 × 480. These were captured only in indoor environments using the Microsoft Kinect depth camera. In this study the indoor dataset is used to eliminate the need for infinite depth condition.

PREPROCESSING: Three pre-processing steps are employed namely (1) Segmentation of the image into super-pixels; (2) Quantization and log-scaling of the depth data; and (3) Patch creation around the superpixel centroid. These led to a final training set comprises 319,200 unique patches, each being labeled with an integer depth from 1 to 18.

PROGRAMMING: The CNN grogram used is ConvNet, by Sergey Demyanov. The codes can be found on the following link: https://github.com/sdemyanov/ConvNet. The CNN network uses 5 convolutional and 4 fully-connected layers (see Part 1 of Appendix A.8.4). The CNN parameters are shared across all *n* superpixels. The LNN-1 network employs 22 SOM layers and 18 output neurons in the decision layer, as in Part 2 of the same Appendix.

RESULTS: The results, as tabulated below, are compared with those by Eigen *et al.* [Eigen, 2014] which is CNN-based and the Make3D method [Saxena, 2009], which is RMF (Random Markov Field)-based (see Chapter 5 above).

Table 8.4. Comparison of performance (RMS error) – 3D from 2D image.

	RMSE Train	RMSE Test
CNN	19.14%	21.82%
LNN-1	15.83%	22.46%
Eigen *et al.* – CNN-based	17.51%	24.92%
Make3D – RMF-based	20.06%	26.73%

References

[Saxena *et al.*, 2009] Saxena A, Sun M, Ng A Y, "Make3d: Learning 3d scene structure from a single still image", *IEEE Transactions of Pattern Analysis and Machine Intelligence (PAMI)*, **30**(5): 824–840 (2009).

[Eigen, 2014] Eigen D, Puhrsch C, Fergus R, "Depth map prediction from a single image using a multi-scale deep network", CoRR, abs/1406.2283, 2014.

8.5. Image Analysis: Scene Classification (N Koundinya)

The goal of this Case Study is to apply CNN, LNN-1 and LNN-2 deep learning neural networks to a Scene Classification problem and to compare the performance of these three networks and their respective computational times. All three networks considered in this study share the same input data and the same preprocessing.

DATASET: The dataset considered are those concentrating on mini-places. Specifically: Places2 dataset ILSVRC2015 [Russakovsky, 2015]. The Mini–Places dataset covers 400 scene categories, while this Case Study is limited to 100 categories. Each image is RGB 128 × 128.

PREPROCESSING: In the preprocessing step the images are resampled to 64 × 64 resolution.

COMPUTATION: The Keras framework in Python is used [Murphy, 2015] in coding the CNN network (see Appendix 8.5). Its input is 128 × 128 × 3 and its output is 1 × 100. It employs 10 convolution layers with 3 × 3 filters, 5 Max-Pooling layers and 3 fully connected layers. The LAMSTAR-1 code follows the core code of Section 6.3. It employs 128 layers and uses 100 neurons in the decision layer (module).

RESULTS: The results are summarized in Tables 8.5a and 8.5b below.

Table 8.5a. Computation time — Scene classification.

Network	Train Time (128 × 128) Min.	Test Time (10,000 images) Min.
CNN	954 (30 epochs)	5.83
LNN-1	734.6 (27 epochs)	62.5
LNN-2	581.7 (21 epochs)	64.17

Table 8.5b. Comparison of performance – Scene classification.

Network	Accuracy (128 × 128)	Accuracy (64 × 64)
CNN	69.24%	47.53%
LNN-1	71.04%	49.54%
LNN-2	73.04%	47.23%

Observe that even for 10.000 images, the training time is vastly longer than the testing time. The smaller number of epochs for LNN-1 and LNN-2 is due to their faster convergence than CNN. Observe also that parallel computing in LLN such that there are only 2 neurons in the decision layer and employment of 30 parallel processors (1 per category) will speed up the testing with each of the LNN networks by a factor of 15 (since the number of link-weights is reduced by a factor of 15).

References

[Russakovsky, 2015] Russakovsky O, *et al.*, ImageNet large scale visual recognition challenge. *IJCV* (2015). paper | bibtex | paper content on arxiv

[Murphy, 2015] Murphy J, https://www.microway.com/hpc-tech-tips/keras-theano-deep-learning-frameworks/, 2015.

8.6. Image Recognition: Fingerprint Recognition 1 (A Daggubati)

The goal of this Case Study is to apply CNN, LNN-1 and LNN-2 deep learning neural networks to a Fingerprint Recognition problem and to compare the performance of these three networks and their respective computational times. All three networks considered in this study share the same input data and the same preprocessing.

DATASET: The dataset used in this study is taken from the fingerprint dataset of [FVC, 2002]. It contains 8 black/white fingerprints taken from each of 10 different persons. Six of the fingerprints per person are used for testing (60 fingerprints total), while two per person (20 total) are used for testing.

METHOD: The basic patterns used in the present fingerprint recognition study are three ridge patterns, namely, Arch, loop and whorl, as in Fig. 8.6a

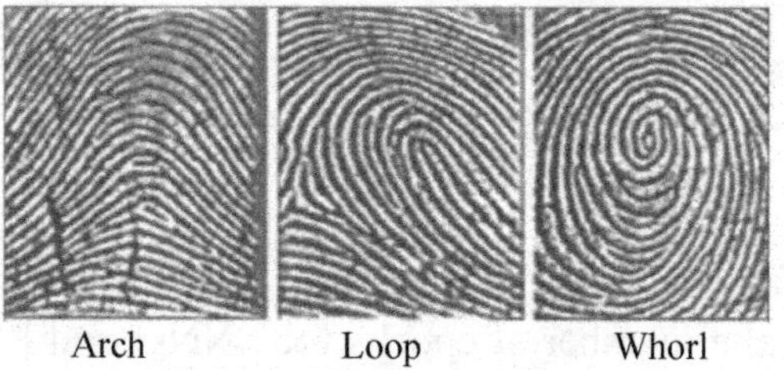

Fig. 8.6a. Fingerprint ridge patterns.

PREPROCESSING: Certain unique features in the patterns are called Minutiae. The major Minutiae in fingerprint ridges are ridge endings and bifurcations (Fig. 8.6.b). These Minutiae are extracted in a preprocessing, using the Matlab algorithm of [Matlab, Fingerprint Minutiae] — See Appendix A.8.6. This algorithm also includes ridge thinning.

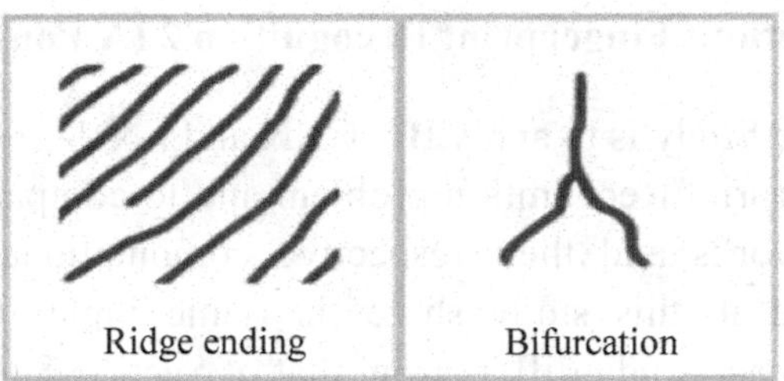

Figure 8.6b. Fingerprint minutiae.

The preprocessing program is as in [FVC, 2002], it consists of 3 parts, Thinning, Ridge-end Fining and Bifurcation Finding. Its outputs are entered into the 3 deep-learning neural networks of this Case Study.

COMPUTATION:
Computation is performed using 4 program, Preprocessing (see above), NN, LNN-1 and LNN-2. The CNN algorithm is a Python Theano.tensor program, whose utilization for this Case Study is outlined in Part 1 of Appendix A.8.6. Both LNN-1 and LNN-2 have a 16 × 16 input matrix, namely 16 layers with 16 inputs per layer. The LNN-1 program is given in full in Part 2 of the same Appendix. Noting the Core Program of LNN-2 in Section 6.3, the adaptation of the LNN-1 code to an LNN-2 code should be straightforward.

RESULTS: The summary of the results for this case study is tabulated below.

Table 8.6. Summary of results — Fingerprint recognition.

Network	Success-Rate	Computation Time
CNN	90%	1.3 sec
LNN-1	92%	0.9 sec
LNN-2	96.3%	0.7 sec

References

[FVC, 2002] FVC, 2nd Fingerprint Verification Competition, University of Bologna, bias.csr.unibo.it/fvc2002/databases.asp, 2002

[Matlab, fingerprint minutiae]
http://www.mathworks.com/matlabcentral/fileexchange/31926fingerprint-minutiae-extraction/content/Fingerprint_Minutiae_Extraction/Minutuae_Extraction.m

8.7. Image Recognition: Fingerprint Recognition 2 (A Ponguru)

The goal of this Case Study is to apply BP, CNN and LNN-1 deep learning neural networks to a Fingerprint Recognition problem and to compare the performance of these three networks and their respective computational times. All three networks considered in this study share the same input data and the same preprocessing. This case study differs from that of Section 8.6 in database and in the processing of minutiae. It uses BP but not LNN-2, in contrast to Section 8.6.

DATABASE: The dataset in this study is from [4] which is CASIA Fingerprint Image Database Version 5.0 (http://biometrics.idealtest.org/). The database contains 20,000 fingerprints of 500 people. The fingerprint images were captured using URU4000. There are 40 fingerprint images of 8 fingers (left and right thumb/second/third/fourth finger), i.e. 5 images per finger. All fingerprint images are 8 bit gray-level BMP files and the image resolution is 328 × 356.

PREPROCESSING: The preprocessing procedure of in this study for preprocessing involves the steps of image enhancement, binarization, thinning and feature extraction. In general, this procedure is similar to that followed in the case of Section 8.6, but it differs in several details. Preprocessing is as in Appendix A.8.6.

COMPUTATION: The BP program was enhanced by postprocessing as in [Kaur, 2008], which involves removal of false minutiae (where it differs from case study of Section 8.6). The CNN code uses Python's Lasagne (http://lasagne.readthedocs.org/en/latest/user/installation.html). — see Appendix A.8.7: The LNN-1 code requires no modification from that of Chapter 6.

RESULTS: The results are given in Table 8.7.

Table 8.7. Comparison of results — Fingerprint recognition 2.

Method	Accuracy	Computation Time
BP	92.2%	38.6 sec
BP (with postprocessing)	94.5%	28.9 sec (faster convergence)
CNN	92.3%	2.4 sec
LNN-1	95.1%	1.1 sec

References

[Kaur, 2008] Kaur M, Singh M, Girdhar A, Sandhu P S, "Fingerprint verification system using minutiae extraction technique", *International Journal of Computer, Electrical, Automation, Control and Information Engineering* Vol. 2, No. 10 (2008).

8.8. Face Recognition (S Gangineni)

The goal of this Case Study is to apply CNN, LNN-1 and LNN-2 deep learning neural networks to a Face Recognition problem and to compare the performance of these three networks and their respective computational times. All three networks considered in this study share the same input data and the same preprocessing.

DATABASE: In this Case Study 45 RGB face images belonging to 15 individuals, taken from the Yale University Face Database [yale face-database] are used.

PREPROCESSING: The data above is first being preprocessed in 4 stages, as follows:

(1 Converting RGB to Grayscale;
(2) Cropping;
(3) Binarization;
(4) Feature Extraction via Principal Components Analysis (PCA).

The PCA output of 20 eigenvectors per face, which represent the characteristic features of a face, serve as input to the LNN-1 and LNN-2 neural networks of this study. CPA preprocessing in CNN is incorporated in the network's input via Python's PIL image library (See Part 1 of Appendix A.8.8).

COMPUTATION: The CNN network is a CaffeeNetConv code. It consists of (1) Input layer (accepts 64 × 64 images); Convolution Layer 1 (filter size 5 × 5, stride: 1); Max Pool Layer 1 (pool size 2 × 2); Conv. Layer 2 (filter size 5 × 5, stride: 1); Max Pool 2 Layer (size 2 × 2); ReLu Layer; Output Layer (uses Python Softmax Regression, 15 output neurons). See also Part 1 of Appendix 8.8, for the initial section of the CNN program. Both LNN-1 and LNN-2 employ 20 layers (same as number of eigenfaces/eigenvectotrs with 10 neurons per layer The LNN-1 program is given in Part 2 of Appendix 8.8.

RESULTS: See Table 8.8 below:

Table 8.8. Performance comparison — Face recognition

	Success Rate	Computational Time
LAMSTAR-2	97.78%	0.914a
LAMSTAR-1	95.56%	1.286a
CNN	91.12%	1.405a

References

[yale face-database] http://vision.ucsd.edu/content/yale-face-database

8.9. Image Recognition — Butterfly Species Classification (V N S Kadi)

The goal of this Case Study is to apply CNN, LNN-1 and LNN-2 deep learning neural networks to Butterfly Species Classification and to compare the performance of these three networks and their respective computational times. All three networks considered in this study share the same input data.

DATABASE: The data for this Case Study was taken from the Leeds Butterfly Dataset [Wang *et al.*, 2009]. The Dataset includes 832 RGB images for 10 butterfly categories, which are sorted by their scientific names. 80% of the images were used for training and 20% for testing.

PREPROCESSING: The preprocessing steps that were employed include background removal, grayscale conversion, removing noise, segmented mask using contour and feature extraction. Feature extraction involves establishing 3 vectors, namely, color, geometry and texture. A normalized histogram was used to derive the color vector, while geometric area, perimeter and distance equations were used for the geometry vector and discrete wavelet transforms for the texture vector [Siddique, 2002]. Thus, a total of 16 features were obtained to represent one image. See Part 1 of Appendix A.8.9.

PROGRAMMING: A Keras (Python Library) Theano code [Keras Python] was used for the CNN network (see description in Part 2 of Appendix A.8.9). The CNN input is a 150 × 150 raw image. The CNN output size is 1 × 10. The LNN-1 code is I given in Part 3 of the same Appendix. LNN-1 and LNN-2 employ 16 layers and receive their input from the preprocessor algorithm of Part 1 of the Appendix.

RESULTS: Performance results are given in Table 8.9 below. Observe that no preprocessing is performed in the CNN program. This may affect CNN Accuracy and also further increase CNN computation time, since the preprocessing time is included in the results for LNN-1 and LNN-2.

Table 8.9. Comparing training performance — Butterfly classification.

Network	Accuracy	Training Time (sec)
CNN (1 epoch)	91.2%	20.3
LAMSTAR-1	92.1%	2.1
LAMSTAR-2	94.4%	1.07
State of the art-MLP-BP	81.57%	
State of the art (3-layer feed forward) BP	86%	

References

[Siddique, 2002] Siddique S, "A wavelet based technique for analysis and classification of TextureImages", Carleton University, Ottawa, Canada, Proj. Rep. 70.593, April 2002.

[Keras, Python] Keras 0.1.0, Python Software Foundation https://testpypi.python.org/pypi/Keras/0.1.0

[Wang *et al.*, 2009] Wang J, Markert K, Everingham M, "Leeds Butterfly Dataset", http://www.comp.leeds.ac.uk/scs6jwks/dataset/leedsbutterfly/, in: *Learning Models for Object Recognition from Natural Language Descriptions, Proceedings 20th British Machine Vision Conference* (*BMVC*), 2009.

8.10. Image Recognition: Leaf Classification (P Bondili)

The goal of this Case Study is to apply CNN, LNN-1 and LNN-2 deep learning neural networks to an Image Classification problem and to compare the performance of these three networks and their respective computational times. All 3 networks considered in this study share the same input data.

DATASET: RGB images of 32 plant species, totaling 50 images per species were downloaded from the Flavia database [Flavia, Leaf].

PREPROCESSING: All images were converted to grayscale. Subsequently Feature Extraction was performed [Chaki and Parekh, 2010] to extract five Geometric feature vectors (area, perimeter, diameter, compatibility and compactness) feature vectors and six Textural (median, variance, uniformity, entropy homogeneity and inertia) feature vectors. The resulting total of 11 feature vectors was then used to represent each image. This preprocessing is not used in CNN.

PROGRAMMING: The Lasagne (Python Library) Theano code [Lasagne, Python] was used for the CNN network (see Part 1 of Appendix A.8.10). The CNN input is a 200 × 200 raw image. The CNN output size is 1 × 32. The LNN-1 code is given in Part 2 of the same Appendix. LNN-1 and LNN-2 employ 11 layers and receive their input from the preprocessor algorithm that is included in the LNN-1 algorithm of this Appendix.

RESULTS: See Table 8.10. Note that the CNN algorithm uses the Preprocessing as above, while CNN uses the raw data. This may affect performance.

Table 8.10. Comparison of performance — Leaf classification (CNN does not use preprocessing).

Network	Accuracy	Training Time (sec)
CNN	91.7%	100.3
LAMSTAR-1	92.5%	5.6
LAMSTAR-2	94.2%	3.48
State of the art using (MLP) BP	90%	

References

[Flavia, Leaf] Flavia Database, http://flavia-plant-leaf-recognition-system.soft112.com/

[Chaki and Parekh, 2010] Chaki J, Parekh R, "Plant leaf recognition using shape based features and neural network classifiers", *International Journal of Advanced Computer Science and Applications* (*IJACSA*), **2**(10), 2011.

[Lasagne, Python] https://pypi.python.org/pypi/Lasagne

8.11. Image Recognition: Traffic Sign Recognition (D Somasundaram)

The goal of this Case Study is to apply CNN, LNN-1 and LNN-2 deep learning neural networks and SVM to traffic sign recognition. The goal of this Case Study is to apply CNN, LNN-1 and LNN-2 deep learning neural networks and SVM to a text Classification problem for data visualization and to compare the performance of these three networks and their respective computational times. All three networks and SVM considered in this study share the same input data and the same preprocessing.

DATASET: The data for this Case Study was taken from http://benchmark.ini.rub.de/?section=gtsrb&subsection=dataset. The images are in PPM (Portable Pixmap P6) format. Image sizes vary between 15 × 15 and 250 × 250.

PREPROCESSING: Traffic sins are of different colors, shapes and sizes. They are rectangle, circular, triangular etc., and may be connected with other signs. Hence preprocessing is essential. The major preprocessing steps are: Converting to greyscale, noise filtering, thresholding, filling region holes, finding boundaries and separating connected signs, cropping, resizing.

COMPUTATION: The LNN codes consist of 20 input layers, with 10 neurons per layer. The LNN code follows the Core code of Chapter 6. Its setup part of the code is given in Appendix A.8.11. The CNN code is from the MatConvLibrary. The following packages are used: Python-dev, python-numpy, python-spicy, python-magic, python-matplotlib, Libatlas-base-dev, libjpeg and libopencv-dev. The CNN network consists of 2 convolutional layers. Softmax regression is used for classification in the CNN output layer. The codes themselves are not appended to this text.

RESULTS: The results are given in Table 8.11 below.

Table 8.11. Comparison of results — Traffic sign recognition

Method	Success Rate	Computation Time
CNN	94.23%	12.64 sec
LNN-1	86.93%	18.54 sec
LNN-2	92.23%	15.29 sec

8.12. Information Retrieval: Programming Language Classification (E Wolfson)

The goal of this Case Study is to classify programming languages used in an entered computer program that was written in an unknown language by using 3 deep learning neural networks, Back Propagation (BP), LNN-1 and LNN-2 and comparing performance and computational speed of these 3 networks. The present study considers a 4-way classification, to detect programs written in Python, C, Ruby or in "other" languages.

DATASET: The data for this Case Study is from a GENERATOR that generates snippets of codes from C, Python, Ruby, or from other randomly selected languages. Each snippet represents an object oriented function passed in local variables declared (and/or assigned) as well as one of these parameters or local variables returned. The types may be either an integer, or a floating point value. The lines of code may either be raw operations, ***if*** statements, ***while*** loops, or ***for*** loops. The code snippet size is always 600.

PREPROCESSING: All code snippets will be represented in ASCII, to allow the mapping in values from 0 to 63, after appropriate subtraction. In BP all values are multiplied by 0.015873 to uniformly distribute each of the possible 64 values to a range from 0 to 1. In LNN1 and LNN2, the values of the input are normalized to vectors of length 1.

COMPUTATION: The coding of the Backpropagation network employs the Matlab BP Library code, while the LAMSTAR coding follows the Core Code of Chapter 6. The main part of the GENERATOR code is given in Appendix A.8.12 below.

RESULTS: The comparative results for performance and computational time are given in Table 8.12.

Table 8.12. Comparison of results – Programming language classification.

Method	Accuracy	Training Time	Test Time
BP	44.6%	1.34–11.11 sec	0.036–0.038 sec
LNN-1	72.76%	0.34–1.25 sec	0.35–0.46 sec
LNN-2	83.15%	0.13–0.975 sec	0.27–0.525 sec

8.13. Information Retrieval: Data Classification from Transcribed Spoken Conversation (A Kumar)

The goal of this Case Study is to apply CNN, LNN-1 and LNN-2 deep learning neural networks and SVM to the classification of information from transcribed natural language conversation for data visualization and to compare the performance of these three networks and their respective computational times. All three networks and SVM considered in this study share the same input data and the same preprocessing.

In this problem a user provides spoken natural language queries which is subsequently transcribed and applied to retrieving data for three possible response types as follows:

(1) new data visualization based on the data of interest described by the user request;
(2) visualization based on an existing one based on the data of interest described by the user request;
(3) moving existing data visualizations on the screen.

DATASET: The data used was obtained from the Chicago crime data (https://data.cityofchicago.org/Public-Safety/Crimes-2001-to-present/ijzp-q8t2). It includes crime types, location types, and time types. As an example, the user may ask the query "Show me homicides that happen in restaurants by month". In this case, "homicides" is a crime type, "restaurants" is a location type, and "month" is a time type. Below is a tabular description of the Chicago crime data that is available to the user (see Table 8.13a).

Of the data above, this Case Study considers 40 user requests for training and 60 requests for testing.

PREPROCESSING: In this Case Study, Preprocessing was applied to the data so that non-important words do not remain in each user request. In order that only discriminating features (i.e., words) to be included. The various preprocessing steps are tabulated below. Note that while stop-word removal does not require any special API since we are just removing from a list of stop-words, however lemmatization is accomplished with the Stanford Parser in Java [stanford, Lemmatization], and the Part-of-Speech step is accomplished with OpenNLP in Java [apache, OpenLNP] — see Table 8.13b.

Table 8.13a. Types of Chicago crime data.

Crime Types		
Homicide	Criminal Damage	Criminal Trespass
Theft	Battery	Deceptive Practice
Location Types		
Alley	Apartment	Street
Gas Station	Parking Lot	Residence
Small Retail Store	Restaurant	Grocery Food Store
Time Types		
Day of Month	Day of Year	Month of Year
Time of Day	Year	Month of Year

Table 8.13b. Preprocessing steps.

Stop-word Removal	Remove common words (“the”, “because”, “for”, …).
Lemmatization	Provide lemma of each word (“meet” is lemma of “meeting”)
Part-of-Speech	Remove word if not noun, Verb, or adjective

COMPUTATION: The main LNN code follows the Core code of Chapter 6. It is followed by a LAMSTAR Text Classification. Java code as in Part 1 of Appendix A.8.13. The SVM code is in Part 2 of the same Appendix.

RESULTS: See Table 8.13c.

Table 8.13c. Comparison of performances — Natural language text classification.

Method	Accuracy	Computation Time
BP	60%	1268 m sec
SVM	67%	345 m sec
LNN-1	78%	322 m sec
LNN-2	78%	680 m sec

References

[stanford, Lemmatization] Stanford Parser Java API used for Lemmatization preprocessing (http://nlp.stanford.edu/software/lex-parser.shtml).

[apache, OpenLNP] Apache OpenNLP Java API used for part-of-speech preprocessing (https://opennlp.apache.org/).

8.14. Speech Recognition (M Racha)

This goal of this Case Study is to apply CNN, LNN-1 and LNN-2 deep learning neural networks to a Speech Recognition problem and to compare the performance of these three networks and their respective computational times. All three networks considered in this study share the same input data and the same preprocessing.

DATABASE: The dataset for this study consists of 10 words ('Violet', 'Blue', 'Green', 'Yellow', 'Orange', 'Red', 'White', 'Black', 'Pink', 'Brown') recorded by 20 different speakers using microphones in different devices like mobiles and computers. Training dataset consists of 15 sets of words and testing dataset consists of 5 untrained sets where each set has 10 words mentioned above spoken by the same speaker.

PREPROCESSING: In this study there are 4 Preprocessing steps: (1) Pre-Emphasis — using a first order FIR filter H(z) where $H(z) = 1 - 0{,}95\ z^{-1}$ for enhancing high frequencies; (2) Frame Blocking; (3) Windowing; (4) Feature Extraction — Mel-frequency Cepstral Coefficients (MFCC). Consequently, each word will consist of 20 frame and 12 coefficients per frame.

COMPUTATION: The CNN (LeNet) code used in this case Study is a theano.tensor program [deep learning, lenet]/. See also Part 1 of Appendix A.8.14 (ReadData, cnn_ff, cnn_setup sections of the program).

LNN-1 and LNN-2 have 20 layers (sub-words) and 12 neurons per layer. See Part 2 of Appendix A.8.14 (lamstar.m section of the program).

RESULTS: See Table 8.14.

Table 8.14. Performance comparisons — Speech recognition.

Network	Success Rate	Computation Time
CNN	94%	1.4 sec
LNN-1	96%	1.0 sec
LNN-2	98%	0.93 sec

References

[deep learning, lenet] http://deeplearning.net/tutorial/lenet.html

8.15. Music Genre Classification (Y Fan, C Deshpande)

The goal of the Case Study conducted by Y Fan, was to apply CNN and BP networks to the classification of music genres and to compare the performance and speed of the networks used. The genres considered in the study are pop music, rock, folk songs and Chinese music.

DATASET: 500 songs at 20 seconds per song are used. Each song is sampled at 20 KHz. The songs are obtained from http://music.baidu.com, http://www.kuke.com.

PREPROCESSIMG: For CNN processing the data is first converted into a 2D spectrogram. The resulting 2D image shape serves as the CNN input.

COMPUTATION: The BP network is computed with the Matlab BP code. A CNN code in Matlab language is used, having a single convolutional layer.

RESULTS: Comparative results are given in Table 8.15a below. The CNN results are at 100 epochs. The computation time in this table refers to training time.

Table 8.15a. Comparison of results — Music genre classification.

Method	Accuracy	Computation Time
BP	81.91%	35.66 sec
CNN	92.52%	9.46 sec

A similar Case Study conducted by C Deshpande was limited to 3 genres (classical, rock, jazz). The dataset used was the Marsyas GTZAN dataset http://marsyasweb.appspot.com/download/data_sets/. It covered CNN, LNN-1 and LNN-2. The CNN code used was written in Python (see setup code in Appendix A.8.15) and its image-like spectrograms, that were used as input, were obtained using Marsyas Software (http://marsyas.info/). Its results are as in Table 8.15b, below:

Table 8.15b. Comparison of results — Music genre classification.

Method	Accuracy	Computation Time
CNN	90%	5.33 sec (train), 3.87 sec (test)
LNN-1	93.3%	4.965 sec (train), 2.11 sec (test)
LNN-2	96%	3.17 sec (train), 1.85 sec (test)

8.16. Security/Finance: Credit Card Fraud Detection (F Wang)

The goal of this Case Study is to employ BP, LNN-1, LNN-2 networks and SVM for detecting credit card fraud risk and to compare their performances and computational speeds.

DATASET: The dataset utilized for this Case Study is the German Credit dataset [Blake, 1998]. This dataset contains 1000 customers; each being classified with good/bad credit risk.

ATTRIBUTES: The German credit dataset contains 20 attributes. Among 20 attributes, 7 are numerical, while 13 are categorical. The numerical attributes include payment duration (months), credit amount, installment rate, age etc. The categorical attributes include status of existing checking account, credit history, purpose, savings account/bonds, etc. Qualitative attributes are of several categories; each category corresponds to a unique label. For example, attribute credit history is divided into 5 categories, no credits taken or all credits paid back duly, all credits at this bank paid back duly, existing credits paid back duly till now, delay in paying off in the past, and critical account/other credits existing (in other banks). The 20 attributes of the dataset are re-arranged (preprocessed) as 24 features/sub-words to be entered into all networks of this study.

Table 8.16. Comparison of results — Credit card fraud detection.

Method	Success Rate
BP	65.3%
LNN-1	70%
LNN-2	70%
SVM	68.6%

COMPUTATION: BP code is a standard Matlab program with 24 inputs and 1 hidden layer of 20 neurons. The LAMSTAR networks consist of 24 SOM input layers to correspond with the 24 features above. An LNN-2 code is given in Appendix A.8.16. The SVM (support Vector Machine) program that is utilized in this study is function fitcsvm in Matlab Statistical Toolbox.

RESULTS: See Table 8.16.

References

[Blake, 1998] Blake C, Merz C, "UCI repository of machine learning databases", in http://archive.ics.uci.edu/ml/index.html, 1998.

8.17. Predicting Location for Oil Drilling from Permeability Data in Test Drills (A S Hussain)

The present Case Study is on using deep learning neural networks for predicting suitable sites for crude oil production based on permeability data from well logs of expensive test drills. Crude oil production heavily depends on these few samples and correct estimates mean huge savings. The mathematical analysis of the permeability is a highly complex nonlinear problem which might be within the domain of deep learning neural networks. This study investigates and compares BP, LNN-1 and LNN-2 for this application.

DATABASE: The data for this Case Study is actual well logs data from 356 core data points of well logs at a reservoir area. The data used is: Microspherical focused resistivity log (MSFL — ohm-m), compressional wave travel time (DT — usec/m), neutron porosity (NPHI — fraction), total porosity

(PHIT — fraction), bulk density (RHOB — gm/cc), density (DRHO — gm/cc), un-flushed zone saturation (SWT — fraction), caliper log (CALI — inches), true formation conductivity (CT — micro-mhos/cm), gamma ray (GR — API unit), resistivity (RT — ohm-m) and permeability (PERM — Darcy).

PREPROCESSING: Correlation analysis was carried out on the data between the core permeability with individual logs. Log10 was applied to MSFL and CT Significant improvement was observed in including the correlation coefficients.

PROGRAMMIMG: The Matlab BP code consists of 2 hidden layers. The hidden layers have 5 neurons each, and the output layer had one neuron. The input to the network are the different well logs. The Matlab LAMSTAR (LNN-1 and LNN-2) codes (see Appendix A.8.17) consists of one SOM input layer per log variable (as listed in the Preprocessor paragraph of this Case Study).

RESULTS: See Table 8.17.

Table 8.17. Comparison of results — Drill site prediction.

Method	Success Rate	Computation Time (sec)
BP	50%	57.8 sec (to converging)
LNN-1	69.79%	0.865 sec
LNN-2	73.03%	0.8445 sec

8.18. Prediction of Forest Fires (S R K Muralidharan)

The goal of this Case Study is to predict forest fires by using CNN, LNN-1, LNN-2 deep learning neural networks and SVM and comparing their performance and computational speed.

DATASET: The data for this Case Study was obtained from the University of California, Irvine (UCI) Machine Learning Repository (http://archive.ics.uci.edu/ml/datasets/Forest+fires). It comprises of 13 input and one output variables (features). The input variables are XY coordinates, day, month, FFMC (fine fuel moisture code), DMC (Duff moisture code), DC (Drought code), ISI (initial spread index), temperature, humidity, wind speed rainfall. The output is in terms of 5 classes (0 to 4). Computation aims at correct classification of all 5 output classes.

PREPROCESSING: Of the 13 input features above, 8 are chosen for this study, namely, FFMC, DMC, DC, ICI, temp., humidity, wind speed and rainfall. This data is first normalized using grayscale normalization, and is subsequently binarized. To reduce the effect of class imbalance in the data under-sampling and over-sampling methods [Garcia, 2007], [Liu X Y, 2006] are used.

COMPUTING: The CNN source code https://github.com/rasmusbergpalm/DeepLearnToolbox was used. Its initial section is as in Part 1 of Appendix A.8.18 below. The LNN Core code of Chapter 6 was followed in the programming of LNN1 and LNN2. It consists of 8 layers to conform with the 8 features used in the dataset. The LNN setup section of the program is in Part 2 of Appendix A.8.18. Both linear and nonlinear SVM algorithm were used and compared in the SVM computation.

RESULTS: See Table 8.18 below:

Table 8.18. Performances and computational times — Forest fire prediction.

Method	Accuracy	Sensitivity	Computational Time (sec)
SVM (linear)	68.8%	60%	52
SVM (nonlinear)	70.6%	70%	53
CNN	85.71%	86%	21.3 (train), 0.23 (test)
LNN-1	90.47%	90.7%	12.6 (train), 1.5 (test)
LNN-2	92.86%	93%	13.2 (train), 1.6 (test)

References

[Garcia, 2007] Garcia V, Sanchez J S, Mollineda R A, Alejo R, Sotoca J M, "The class imbalance in Pattern Classification and Learning" in: F J Ferrer-Troyano (ed.) Cong Espanol de Informatica, pp. 283–291, Zaragoza (2007).

[Liu X Y, 2006] Liu X Y, Wu J, Zhou Z H, "Exploratory undersampling for class imbalance learning", *Proc. IEEE ICDM Conf.*, 965–969 (2006).

8.19. Predicting Price Movement in Market Microstructure (X Shi)

This Case Study was described in detail in Section 9.C of [Graupe, 2013].

The goal of this study was to predict price movements in market microstructure, where presently 90% of trading is done and where many stocks undergo over 100.0000 price movements daily. The Case Study was carried out with LNN-1 (LAMSTAR), BP, SVM and RBF (Radial Basis Function).

DATABASE: HFT (High Frequency Trading) data is public domain (Nasdaq HFT etc.).

PREPROCESSING: See Section 9.C.2.2 in [Graupe, 2013] for details.

PROGRAMMING: See Section 9.C.6 in [Graupe, 2013].

RESULTS: See Table 8.19 below.

Table 8.19. Comparison of performances — Market microstructure

Method	Accuracy	Computation Time
RBF	72.2%	126 sec
SVM	73.15%	206 sec
BP	73.15%	127 sec
LNN-1	73.35%	92 sec

8.20. Fault Detection: Bearing Fault Diagnosis via Acoustic Emission (M He)

The goal of this Case Study is to detect faults in machine bearings from acoustic emission (AE) data by using 3 deep learning neural networks, Back Propagation (BP), LNN-1 and LNN-2 and comparing performance and computational speed of these 3 networks.

DATASET: The data used in this Case Study is from AE measurement data provided by the Laboratory of Dr. David He, MIE Department, University of Illinois, Chicago (UIC). The AE measurements were performed on model 6025 full ceramic bearings manufactured by the Boca Bearings Company.

PREPROCESSING: The AE signal is preprocesses by using the Hilbert-Huang (HHT) transform [Huang N, 1971], to yield several Intrinsic Mode Functions (IMFs). Three IMF functions (RMS, Kurtosis and Peak-to-Peak) serve as features (Sub-words) for the LAMSTAR network and as inputs to the BP network of this Case Study.

COMPUTATION: The present Case Study was computed using BP, LNN-1 and LNN-2 neural networks. Appendix A.8.20 gives the preprocessing code used in this Case study.

RESULTS: See Table 8.20. Entries are given in terms of accuracy (%), while Training Time is in seconds, where the time given corresponds to the time when performance converges to the (maximal) accuracy given in the table. Observe the near perfect (99.56%) accuracy in detection by LNN-2 in the table below.

Table 8.20. Comparison of performance — Fault detection

	BP	LNN-1	LNN-2
Inner race	93.75	95.89	98.78
Outer race	100.00	100.00	100.00
Case	78.57	93.23	99.89
Bal	94.12	96.89	100.00
Healthy	100.00	100.00	99.14
Overall	93.75	97.20	99.56
Training time (s)	254	98	133

CHAPTER 9

Concluding Comments

This book discusses eight neural networks. The Cognitron and its offspring, the Neocognitron are presented (Chapter 3) mainly due to its historic value, in inspiring the design of the very important Convolutional neural network (CNN), which is most responsible to the rise in interest in deep learning neural networks. Indeed, the Neocognitron was designed to dig deeply into image recognition. However, in itself, it was not designed to do deep learning beyond vision.

Backpropagation (Chapter 4) was the first neural network whose range of applications was wide to be universally applicable. However, it suffers from the "curse of dimensionality". As is shown in the case studies of this book, it is both too slow and, relying on gradient optimization, its performance is usually weak, certainly, weaker than other deep learning networks.

Due to computational slowness and/or limited applicability, the Deep Boltzmann Machine (DBM — Section 7.1), the Deep Recurrent Neural Network (DRNN — Section 7.2) and the De-Convolutional Neural Network (including its related Wavelet Neural Network — Section 7.3) were given less detail that the two networks than CNN and the two version of LAMSTAR (LNN-1 and LNN-2). Therefore, this book concentrates on CNN, LNN-1 and LNN-2, whose performance, speed and universality in applications are well beyond what is accomplished with the other networks.

Several Case studies also compare performance with mathematical/computational methods that lie outside the field of neural networks. In this respect, five of the Case Studies compare SVM (Support Vector Machine) with both CNN and LAMSTAR (the Case Studies of Sections 1, 12, 15, 17 and 19 of Chapter 8), while

RBF (Radial Basis Function) is being compared once (Section 8.19). Also, several other non-NN architectures are being compared on Section 8.1.

This book uses specific comparative Case Studies (Chapter 8 and Appendices) to complement design theory of the various networks that are considered.

The Case Studies intend to illustrate and to stress the breadth of coverage of the major deep learning neural networks, which seems to be almost unlimited. It is felt that this is a major aspect in the understanding deep learning neural networks, and their role and significance. Furthermore, all Case Studies are comparative in the sense that they compare both performance and computational speed between deep learning networks for the exact same input data of the given case and using the same computer and computing language. The speed and performance results relate always to a specific dataset, specific code (within the codes for any given network at any given case) and specific preprocessing, and specific programming skill of its programmer. Hence, they may be biased. Still, they each use exactly the same data and therefore, they are considered to be worth presenting to give the reader insight on how to proceed in any application that the reader may face. Considering the Case Studies in this text, 11 of the 20 Case Studies are concerned with BP (Sections 3, 7, 9, 10, 12, 13, 15–17, 19, and 20 of Chapter 8). Fourteen of the Case Studies are concerned with CNN (all but Sections 12, 13, 16, 17, 19 and 20 of Chapter 8). Seventeen cases concern LNN-2 (all but Sections 4, 7 and 19 of Chapter 8) and all 20 cases are concerned with LNN-1

We comment that LNN-2 is very new, while most past literature on LAMSTAR was on the older version (the original LAMSTAR, referred to as LNN-1 in this text). Hence, the LAMSTAR-2 notation is used to distinguish between the old LAMSTAR design and its newer version.

To summarize the results of the 20 Case studies of this text, the generality of deep CNN, LNN-1, LNN-2 and also of BP, in their range of applicability, is obvious.

When considering performance and computational speed, and noting the reservation expressed above in this Chapter, we observe the following:

In the Case Studies considered, LNN-1 was always superior in performance to SVM (5 case studies — Sections 1, 13, 16, 18 and 19 of Chapter 8), though in one case (Section 8.19) the difference in accuracy is 0.2%. In the two cases where speed is also compared (Sections 8.13 and 8.19), LNN-1 was much faster than SVM. In one case (Section 8.13) SVM was slower than LNN-1 but faster than LNN-2, but its performance is vastly inferior compared with both LNN-1 and LNN-2. Five cases are of course, too few for any conclusion, but hopefully more cases of comparisons will be available in the future for better evaluation.

In all of the 11 Case Studies where BP is compared with LAMSTAR it was slower and its performance was poorer than LAMSTAR-1 or LAMSTAR-2, usually far slower and with far worse performance. In the 6 cases where BP was compared with CNN, the CNN network was ahead in performance in 4 cases (Section 8.3, 8.7 (without post-processing), 8.8, 8.9. and 8.16) and slightly behind in cases (8.3) and in the version of 8.7 where post-processing was involved. However, in all 6 cases CNN was far faster than BP.

The Case Study of Section 8.3 compares results quoted from the literature concerning DBM-related algorithm, that was applied to a similar problem as in that case study. The performance was significantly below that obtained with CNN or LNN-1 in that case study. The various algorithms were not compared together, and it was not a DBM network that was compared.

The performance of all other non-NN architectures considered in the Case Studies of Chapter 8 (in Sections 8.1, 8.19), was inferior to that of CNN, LNN-1 and LNN-2.

In 13 Case Studies CNN was compared with LNN-1 and LNN-2.

In 12 of these 13 cases, where LNN-2 was compared with CNN cases (see Sections 8.1–8.3, 8.5–8.10, 8.14, 8.15 and 8.18), LNN-2 performed better and was faster than CNN. In the case of Section 8.11 CNN yielded better performance, it was also faster than LNN-2. Furthermore, LNN-2 performed best and was fastest in all cases where it was considered in this text, but for case 8.11 above (where CNN also performed better). LNN-1 tied LNN-2 twice (Cases 8.2, 8.13), but was best in all comparisons with CNN where LNN-2 was not considered.

14 of 17 cases to which both LNN-1 and LNN-2 were applied, LNN-2 was ahead of LNN-1 in success-rate. The two networks tied in the other 3 cases. In computational speed there was hardly a difference between these two networks.

When analyzing the results of the Case Studies as above, one must keep in mind that the comparison of performances between LAMSTAR (LNN1 and LNN-2) with CNN must consider a fundamental difference between these two designs. The CNN setting is frozen at end of training. In contrast, LAMSTAR never stops training. Every new piece of data adds to its learning. Even forgetting part of its learning. Hence, for a data set of 10,000 samples, CNN may use 8,000 for training. LAMSTAR learns while it runs. Every new sample helps. Therefore, it implicitly has 10,000 samples for its learning. Actually, the 2,000 samples for testing in CNN may have some information for which CNN never trained and which cause, to somewhat spoil performance, as the results indicate (lower score for training than for testing with CNN results in the Case Studies of Chapter 8). If course, we may wish to re-train again and again with CNN. But this slows CNN down considerably, noting its BP-type learning. This consideration is illustrated by the Case Studies, regardless of the quality of their programming. Therefore, when data is mounting up over time, as is the case in most financial and medical applications, in weather prediction, in fault detection and in so many other on-line applications.

The LAMSTAR philosophy that the network never stops learning (and also forgets), and which imitates human learning, gives LAMSTAR an advantage (see Chapter 6) over a frozen setting at end of fixed-duration training. It also is advantageous in its ability to learn in face of missing data or imperfect data pieces, of missing attributes and in its ability to integrate and rank practically any processing method, ranking it low if useless. Parallel processing is a feature to be adopted in both CNN and LAMSTAR, noting that it can be easily and effortlessly implemented in both. Pre-training for data-balancing in LAMSTAR, as in Section 7.5 does not negate the above advantages, since it can be implemented by parallel processing and hence, repeated as necessary, if data structures change over time.

A blending of features from LAMSTAR and CNN should be explored in the future, regardless of other progress in the new and important field of deep learning neural network. The need and the promise in a simple computing architecture, as provided by biologically-inspired neural networks is with us. Results point to this approach to be superior to any ad-hoc approaches. Moreover, neural networks can or should eventually, be able to integrate almost any ad-hoc new or old technique into its architecture.

It is important to emphasize that CNN is considered the best network for complex 2D and 3D recognition and retrieval of still and video images. Presently, no information exists on applications of LNN-2 to such complex problems. Application of LAMSTAR to such applications and comparing it with CNN is greatly needed.

On the other hand, this author was involved in complex research problems, such as predicting onset of tremor from EMG data or predicting sleep apnea events, where we found the CNN or other deep learning methods (and non-NN methods, such as SVM) to be too difficult to apply. These problems involved data from very different sensors that often could not be used (even on same patients) often incomplete data to a degree that even on same patients. Here, LAMSTAR's ability of continuing to predict, even with missing very whole vectors (features) of the input matrix were missing, and without any interruption of the program, was essential. So was the need to use or try almost any mathematical preprocessing tool to squeeze out information to help prediction, even with little data, was essential. It was straightforward to integrate the parameters retrieved from these preprocessors into LAMSTAR while their integration into CNN seemed to be require considerable changes in the CNN setup and in its structure.

As mentioned earlier. DLNN is a very young discipline. It has already proven that it can do a lot. It is general in its range of applications. Its performance is as good or close to the best ad-hoc methods. It uses a standard architecture, not needing help from expert programmers. It is fast. It lends itself to be used in a miniaturized device on-line or as a laptop tool in the office of a graduate student. It certainly does not need a supercomputer. In short, it already has a lot to offer in every field of possible application and it presents great opportunities of further developments and of becoming more powerful in every aspect in the future.

Problems

CHAPTER 2

Problem 2.1:
Explain why a single-layer Perceptron cannot solve the logical XOR (Exlusive-Or) problem $[(x_1 \cup X_2) \cap (\neg x_1 \cup \neg X_2)]$ as in the Truth Table P.1 below. Use an x_1 vs. X_2 plot to show that a straight line cannot separate the XOR states.

Table 2.1. Truth table for XOR.

	Inputs		Output
State	X_1	X_2	Z
A	0	0	0
B	0	1	1
C	1	0	1
D	1	1	0

Problem 2.2:
Explain the Pavolovian dog experiment in terms of a plot between neurons and Hebbian weights.

CHAPTER 3

Problem 3.1:
(a) Explain why a 2-layer (including one hidden layer) suffices to solve the XOR problem.

(b) Design a BP neural network to solve the XNOR problem (same Truth Table as in Table 2.1 but the 0's in the output Z-column now become 1's and the 1's in that column become 0's).

Problem 3.2:
Explain with a simple BP schematic of one hidden layer why the BP network is not transparent.

Problem 3.3:
Design a BP neural network to recognize 3 characters/letters in a 8 × 8 grid where the symbols to be recognized are entered in Black/White (1/0) in each element of the grid. Your input database should consist of 6 sets of different 4 symbols. However, you train the network with ONLY 4 sets of 3 of the 4 symbols of the dataset, while you test with 2 untrained set of all 4 symbols. Stop computation when achieving at least 90% success rate. Present your full code and specify success rate (%), training time and testing time. Keep the code for further use. Results should be tabulated against all 4 symbols but specify which is the untrained symbol.

Problem 3.4:
Repeat problem 3.3 with the same symbols, but place randomly 1 bit of noise in each of the symbols and re-compute and store success rate and computational time. Repeat with 2, then 3, 4, ... bits of randomly placed noise. Tabulate performance & computational time against number of bits of noise A bit of noise is entered as a change of an element in the grid from 1 to 0 or vice versa.

CHAPTER 5

Problem 5.1:
Design a CNN network to recognize 3 characters/letters in a 8 × 8 grid where the symbols to be recognized are entered in Black/White (1/0) in each element of the grid. Your input database should consist of 6 sets of different 4 symbols. However, you train the network with ONLY 4 sets of 3 of the 4 symbols of the dataset, while you test with 2 untrained set of all 4 symbols. Stop computation when achieving at least 90% success rate. Present your full code and specify success rate (%), training time and testing time. Keep the code for further use. Results should be tabulated against all 4 symbols but specify which is the untrained symbol.

Problem 5.2:

Repeat problem 5.1 with the same symbols, but place randomly 1 bit of noise in each of the symbols and re-compute and store success rate and computational time. Repeat with 2, then 3, 4, ... bits of randomly placed noise. Tabulate performance & computational time against number of bits of noise A bit of noise is entered as a change of an element in the grid from 1 to 0 or vice versa.

Problem 5.3:

Explain the considerations in applying Sharing in CNN.

Problem 5.4:

Many problems in medicine involve non-stationary data (time varying parameters), say, in the evolution of a disease or disorder — with or without treatment. Nonstationarity also is dominant in financial markets and in many other problems (seasonal effect in weather, etc.). Explain how non-stationarity (time-varying parameters) of data may affect the performance and the speed of CNN when being applied to nonstationary problems. Be as specific as is possible.

Problem 5.5:

Explain the motivation for Dropout. Give an example.

Problem 6:

The Case Studies relating to CNN often show considerably faster computation than with BP (which is incorporated in CNN). Explain why it is so.

CHAPTER 6

Problem 6.1:

Explain why LAMSTAR networks are transparent. Be specific. Does this hold for LNN-1 and for LNN-2.

Problem 6.2:

Explain the motivation in the LNN-2 design as compared to LNN-1.

Problem 6.3:

Are LNN-1 and/or LNN-2 affected by local minima. Explain.

Problem 6.4:
Design an LNN-1 network to recognize 3 characters/letters in a 8 × 8 grid where the symbols to be recognized are entered in Black/White (1/0) in each element of the grid. Your input database should consist of 6 sets of different 4 symbols. However, you train the network with ONLY 4 sets of 3 of the 4 symbols of the dataset, while you test with 2 untrained set of all 4 symbols. Stop computation when achieving at least 90% success rate. Present your full code and specify success rate (%), training time and testing time. Keep the code for further use. Results should be tabulated against all 4 symbols but specify which is the untrained symbol.

Problem 6.5:
Repeat problem 3.3 with the same symbols, but place randomly 1 bit of noise in each of the symbols and re-compute and store success rate and computational time. Repeat with 2, then 3, 4, ... bits of randomly placed noise. Tabulate performance & computational time against number of bits of noise A bit of noise is entered as the change of an element in the grid from 1 to 0 or vice versa.

Problem 6.6:
Repeat problem 6.4 for LNN-2.

Problem 6.7:
Repeat problem 6.5 for LNN-2.

Problem 6.8:
Explain the role and need for rorgetting in LNN-1 and LNN-2.

Problem 6.9:
What elements in the LAMSTAR network contribute to its speed?

Problem 9: Can LNN-1 and LNN-2 solve the XOR problem? Design an LNN-1 network to do so (specify inputs, SOM-input layers, their number and their contents and the network's output layer/neurons.

CHAPTER 7

Problem 7.1:

Explain how the De-Convolution Network's design can handle discrete wavelet transforms.

Problem 7.2:

Explain how the De-Convolution network can de-convolute specific aspects in the image of a face. Be specific.

Problem 7.3:

Is it possible to use DBM in order to recognize 3 characters/letters in a 8×8 grid where the symbols to be recognized are entered in Black/White (1/0) in each element of the grid? Explain with details. See [Salakhutdinov, Hinton, 2009].

Reference

[Salakhutdinov, Hinton, 2009] Salakhutdinov R, Hinton G, Deep Boltzmann Machines: http://machinelearning.wustl.edu/mlpapers/paper_files/AISTATS09_SalakhutdinovH.pdf, AISTAS, 2009.

Appendices to Case Studies of Chapter 8

Introduction

Appendix numbers correspond to their respective subsection number in Chapter 8. It is important to note that none of these appendices is the complete code for any of the Case Studies. Their purpose is that together with the respective description in Chapter 8, the appendix may help the reader to solve the problem described in the case study. Full programs are far too long to fit a book with 20 case studies. Furthermore, the codes involve proprietary library codes that are accessible by license.

The appendices were selected, subject to the constrains mentioned, such that they give the reader insight into how to integrate data of the kind that is needed in a given study into the code described in Chapter 8 for that study. Certain appendices aim to help integrating specific preprocessing methods of a Case Study. The references given in Chapter 8 should also be consulted when attempting to reconstruct a Case Study.

For any specific application of deep learning neural networks, the reader should attempt to use library codes and integrate them, whenever possible. Selection of preprocessing algorithms requires first to understand the problem to be solved. Again, most preprocessing methods should serve to either reduce data or to add knowledge that is not built into the neural network. Again, mathematical methods for analyzing a given problem are often available in open-access library programs, say codes of spectral and wavelets analysis, for entropy analysis, DNA coding, market analysis, etc.

A.8.1. Human Activity — Codes (A Bose)

Part 1: CNN

1. *Code_CNN.m*

```
clear all; close all; clc;
load ('activity_dataset.mat');

[tsR, tsC] = size(testdata);
[trR, trC] = size(traindata);

for i = 1 : tsR
  testdata(i,3:62) = normalizeData(testdata(i,3:62));
end
for i = 1 : trR
  traindata(i,3:62) = normalizeData(traindata(i,3:62));
end
testdata = double(reshape(testdata',8,8,tsR));
traindata = double(reshape(traindata',8,8,trR));
testlabel = double(testlabel');
trainlabel = double(trainlabel');

rand('state',0)
ttr = [];
for i = 1:50
  cnn = [];
  cnn.layers = {
    struct('type', 'i') %input layer
    struct('type', 'c', 'outputmaps', 24, 'kernelsize', 5) %convolution layer
    struct('type', 's', 'scale', 2) %sub sampling layer
  };
  opts.numepochs = i;
  opts.alpha = 0.85;
  opts.batchsize = 30;

  cnn = cnnsetup(cnn, traindata, trainlabel);
  [cnn, ttr(i)] = cnntrain(cnn, traindata, trainlabel, opts);
  disp(['Total training time:' num2str(ttr(i))]);

  tic;
  [er(i), correct(i), decision{i}] = cnntest(cnn, testdata, testlabel);
  tts = toc;
  disp('--------------------------------');
end

save ttr ttr;
save er er;
save correct correct;
```

```
save decision decision;
generateConfusionMatrix(decision{50}');
figure; plot(er(1:50), 'LineWidth', 2);
xlabel('Number of epoch');
ylabel('Bit error (%)');

figure; plot(ttr(1:50), 'LineWidth', 2);
xlabel('Number of epoch');
ylabel('Training time (sec)');

figure; plot(correct(1:50)/600*100, 'LineWidth', 2);
('Number of epoch');
ylabel('Recognition rate (%)');
```

Part 2: LAMSTAR (LNN-1)

1. *Code_LAMSTAR.m*

```
clear all; close all; clc;
load ('activity_dataset.mat');

for i = 1 : size(traindata,1)
  traindata(i,3:62) = normalizeData(traindata(i,3:62));
end
disp('Training data acquisition done...');
X_train = traindata';
[row, col] = size(X_train);
numSubWords = 16;

nBit = 8;
alpha = 0.8;
tol = 1e-5;
thresh = 0.9999;

flag = zeros(1,numSubWords);
disp('Forming Sub Words');
for i = 1:size(X_train,2)
  tempX = reshape(X_train(:,i), nBit, nBit);
  for j = 1:numSubWords
    if j <= nBit
      X_in{i}(j,:) = tempX(j,:);
    else
      X_in{i}(j,:) = tempX(:,j - nBit)';
    end
  end

  check(1,:) = zeros(1, nBit);
  for k = 1:numSubWords
    for t = 1 : nBit
```

```
      if (X_in{i}(k,t) ~= check(1,t))
        X_norm{i}(k,:) = X_in{i}(k,:) / sqrt(sum(X_in{i}(k,:).^2));
      else
        X_norm{i}(k,:) = zeros(1,nBit);

      end
    end
  end
end

tic;
%%%%%%%%%%%%%%%%%%%%%%%%%%%%%
disp('Dynamic Building of neurons');
%%%%%%%%%%%%%%%%%%%%%%%%%%%%%
% Building of the first neuron is done as Kohonen Layer neuron
%(this is for all the subwords in the first input pattern for all SOM modules
i = 1;
ct = 1;
while (i <= numSubWords)
  cl = 0;
  for t = 1 : nBit
    if (X_norm{ct}(i,t)==0)
      cl = cl+1;
    end
  end
  if (cl == nBit)
    Z{ct}(i) = 0;
  elseif (flag(i) == 0)
    W{i}(:,ct) = rand(nBit, 1);
    flag(i) = ct;
    W_norm{i}(:,ct) = W{i}(:,ct)/sqrt(sum(W{i}(:,ct).^2));
    Z{ct}(i)= X_norm{ct}(i,:)*W_norm{i};
    while(Z{ct}(i) <= (1-tol)),
      W_norm{i}(:,ct) = W_norm{i}(:,ct) + alpha*(X_norm{ct}(i,:)' - W_norm{i}(:,ct));
      Z{ct}(i) = X_norm{ct}(i,:)*W_norm{i}(:,ct);
    end
  end
  r(ct,i) = 1;
  i = i+1;
end

r(ct,:) = 1;
ct = ct+1;
while (ct <= size(X_train,2))
  for i = 1 : numSubWords
    cl = 0;
    for t = 1 : nBit
      if (X_norm{ct}(i,t) == 0)
```

```
          cl = cl+1;
        end
      end
      if (cl == nBit)
        Z{ct}(i) = 0;
      else
        r(ct,i) = flag(i);
        r_new=0;
        for k = 1:max(r(ct,i)),
          Z{ct}(i) = X_norm{ct}(i,:)*W_norm{i}(:,k);
          if Z{ct}(i) >= thresh
            r_new = k;
           flag(i) = r_new;
           r(ct,i) = flag(i);
           break;
         end
        end
        if (r_new == 0)
          flag(i) = flag(i) + 1;
          r(ct,i) = flag(i);
          W{i}(:,r(ct,i)) = rand(nBit,1);
          %flag(i) = r
          W_norm{i}(:,r(ct,i)) = W{i}(:,r(ct,i))/sqrt(sum(W{i}(:,r(ct,i)).^2));
          Z{ct}(i) = X_norm{ct}(i,:)*W_norm{i}(:,r(ct,i));

          while(Z{ct}(i) <= (1-tol)),
            W_norm{i}(:,r(ct,i)) = W_norm{i}(:,r(ct,i)) + alpha*(X_norm{ct}(i,:)' -
            W_norm{i}(:,r(ct,i)));
           Z{ct}(i) = X_norm{ct}(i,:)*W_norm{i}(:,r(ct,i));
          end
        end
    end
  end
  ct = ct+1;
end

%%%%%%%%%%%%%%%%
% Link Weights
%%%%%%%%%%%%%%%%
outNum = size(trainlabel,2);
ct = 1;
m_r = max(r);
for i = 1:numSubWords,
  L_w{i} = zeros(m_r(i),outNum);
end

ct = 1;
disp('Link weights and output calculations');
```

```
Z_out = zeros(size(X_train,2), outNum);
while (ct <= size(X_train,2))
  L = zeros(size(X_train,2), outNum);
  for i = 1 : numSubWords
   count = size(find(r(:,i) == r(ct,i)) , 1);
    if (r(ct,i)~=0)
     for j = 1 : outNum
       if (trainlabel(ct,j)==0)
%          L_w{i}(r(ct,i),j) = L_w{i}(r(ct,i),j)- 5;
         L_w{i}(r(ct,i),j) = L_w{i}(r(ct,i),j)/count - 5;
       else
%          L_w{i}(r(ct,i),j) = L_w{i}(r(ct,i),j) + 5;
         L_w{i}(r(ct,i),j) = L_w{i}(r(ct,i),j)/count + 5;
       end
     end
%      L(i,:) = L_w{i}(r(ct,i),:);
      L(i,:) = L_w{i}(r(ct,i),:)/count;
    end
  end
  Z_out(ct,:) = sum(L);
  ct = ct+1;
end
toc;
save W_norm W_norm
save L_w L_w
LAMSTAR_test
```

2. generateConfusionMatrix.m

```
function generateConfusionMatrix(predicted)
classes = [1 0 0 0 0 0;
    0 1 0 0 0 0;
    0 0 1 0 0 0;
    0 0 0 1 0 0;
    0 0 0 0 1 0;
    0 0 0 0 0 1];
fprintf('+-------------+-------------------------------------------------------------------+-----------+\n');
fprintf('|       |Predicted Class                              |\n');
fprintf('+-----------+----------+-----------+-----------+-----------+----------+----------+---------+\n');
fprintf('|Actual Class |Class1  |Class2  |Class3  |Class4  |Class5  |Class6  |Other  |\n');
fprintf('+-----------+-----------+-----------+----------+----------+----------+----------+----------+\n');

for i = 1 : 6
  class1 = 0;
  class2 = 0;
  class3 = 0;
  class4 = 0;
  class5 = 0;
  class6 = 0;
```

```
  other = 0;
  for j = 1 : 100
    if (predicted((i-1)*100+j, :) == classes(1,:))
      class1 = class1 + 1;
    elseif (predicted((i-1)*100+j, :) == classes(2,:))
      class2 = class2 + 1;
    elseif (predicted((i-1)*100+j, :) == classes(3,:))
      class3 = class3 + 1;
    elseif (predicted((i-1)*100+j, :) == classes(4,:))
      class4 = class4 + 1;
    elseif (predicted((i-1)*100+j, :) == classes(5,:))
      class5 = class5 + 1;
    elseif (predicted((i-1)*100+j, :) == classes(6,:))
      class6 = class6 + 1;
    else
      other = other + 1;
    end
  end
  fprintf('|Class%d\t\t |%d \t\t |%d \t\t |%d \t\t |%d \t\t |%d \t\t |%d \t\t |%d \t\t |\n', i, class1,
class2, class3, class4, class5, class6, other);
  fprintf('+----------+----------+----------+-----------+----------+-----------+----------+----------+\n');
end
end
```

3. *LAMSTAR_test.m*

```
%% LAMSTAR_test.m
clear all;
load W_norm
load L_w
load ('activity_dataset.mat');
nBit = 8;

for i = 1 : size(testdata,1)
  testdata(i,3:62) = normalizeData(testdata(i,3:62));
end
X_test = testdata';
[row, col] = size(X_test);
numSubWords = 16;
% To make 12 subwords
correct = 0;
wrong = 0;
errPer = 0;
for i = 1:size(X_test,2)
  tempX = reshape(X_test(:,i), nBit, nBit);
  for j = 1 : numSubWords
    if j <= nBit
      X_in{i}(j,:) = tempX(j,:);
    else
```

```
      X_in{i}(j,:) = tempX(:,j - nBit)';
    end
  end

  check(1,:) = zeros(1, nBit);
  for k = 1 : numSubWords
    for t = 1 : nBit
      if (X_in{i}(k,t) ~= check(1,t))
        X_norm{i}(k,:) = X_in{i}(k,:) / sqrt(sum(X_in{i}(k,:).^2));
      else
        X_norm{i}(k,:) = zeros(1, nBit);
      end
    end
  end

  for k = 1 : numSubWords - 1
    if isempty(W_norm{k}),
      Z_out(k,:) = [0 0 0 0 0 0];
    else
      Z = X_norm{i}(k,:)*W_norm{k};
      index(k) = find((Z == max(Z)),1);
      L(k,:) = L_w{k}(index(k),:);
      Z_out(k,:) = L(k,:)*Z(index(k));
    end
  end
  final_Z(i,:) = sum(Z_out);
  sgm = sigmoid(final_Z(i,:));
  decision(i,:) = sgm >= max(sgm);
  err = xor(decision(i,:), testlabel(i,:));
  errPer = errPer + sum(err)/size(err,2);
  if (decision(i,:) == testlabel(i,:))
    out = 'Correct';
    correct = correct + 1;
  else
    out = 'Wrong';
    wrong = wrong + 1;
  end
  disp(['Test Pattern: ' num2str(i) ' |output: ' num2str(decision(i,:)) ' :' out]);
  if rem(i,100) == 0
    disp('----------------------------------------------------');
  end
end
disp(['Correct: ' num2str(correct)]);
disp(['Wrong: ' num2str(wrong)]);
disp(['Bit Error (%): ' num2str(errPer/size(X_test,2)*100) '%']);
generateConfusionMatrix(decision);
```

4. *normalizeData.m*
   % Code for normalizing MSR Daily Activity 3D Dataset & Cornell CAD-60
   % Dataset
   function [normalized_data] = normalizeData(Coordinates)

A.8.2. Predicting Seizures in Epilepsy (J Tran)

CNN: The code below uses Python's https://lasagne.readthedocs.org/

```
def cnn_preprocess(input, detect, predict):

  length = int(len(input)/23.6)
  dimension = 224
  padding = int((dimension - length)/2)
  result = []
  scaling = 0
  if detect is True:
    scaling = 1000
  if predict is True:
    scaling = 300

  while len(input) >= length:
    empty_array = create_empty_array(dimension)

    prev = -1
    for index in range(0, length):

      zero_axis = int(dimension/2)
      scale = int(scaling/zero_axis)

      if input[index] >= 0:
        row = index+padding
        col = int(input[index]/scale + zero_axis)
        if col >= dimension:
          col = dimension - 1
        if index != 0:
          if col < prev:
            for i in range(col + 1, prev):
              empty_array[row][i] = i
            prev = col
          if col > prev:
            for i in range(col - 1, prev, -1):
              empty_array[row][i] = i
            prev = col
        else:
          prev = col
        empty_array[row][col] = col
      elif input[index] < 0:
        row = index+padding
        scaled = int(input[index]/scale)
```

```
      if (zero_axis + scaled) < 0:
        col = 0;
      else:
        col = zero_axis + scaled

      if col >= dimension:
        col = dimension - 1

      if index != 0:
        if col < prev:
          for i in range(col + 1, prev):
            empty_array[row][i] = i
          prev = col
        if col > prev:
          for i in range(col - 1, prev, -1):
            empty_array[row][i] = i
          prev = col
      else:
        prev = col
      empty_array[row][col] = col
    result.append(empty_array)
    input = input[length:]
  return result

def get_variable(filename):
  new_name = filename[6:-4]
  while True:
    length = len(new_name) - 3
    if new_name[length] == '0':
      new_name = new_name[:length] + new_name[length+1:]
    else:
      break
  while True:
    length = len(new_name) - 2
    if new_name[length] == '0':
      new_name = new_name[:length] + new_name[length+1:]
    else:
      break
  return new_name

def load_cnn_dataset(detect, predict):
  training = '/Users/PycharmProjects/untitled/cnn_training_set/'
  validation = '/Users/PycharmProjects/untitled/cnn_validation_set/'
  testing = '/Users/PycharmProjects/untitled/cnn_test_set/'

  training_prediction_i = '/Users/PycharmProjects/untitled/training_prediction_interictal/'
  training_prediction_p = '/Users/PycharmProjects/untitled/training_prediction_preictal/'
  validation_prediction_i = '/Users/PycharmProjects/untitled/validation_prediction_interictal/'
  validation_prediction_p = '/Users/PycharmProjects/untitled/validation_prediction_preictal/'
  testing_prediction_i = '/Users/PycharmProjects/untitled/test_prediction_interictal/'
  testing_prediction_p = '/Users/PycharmProjects/untitled/test_prediction_preictal/'
```

```
training_data = []
validation_data = []
testing_data = []

if predict is True:
 for filename in os.listdir(training_prediction_i):
   if filename.endswith('.mat'):
     f_path = training_prediction_i + filename
     mat = scipy.io.loadmat(f_path)
     variable = get_variable(filename)
     eeg = mat[variable][0][0][0][0]
     processed_data = cnn_preprocess(eeg[0:4096], detect, predict)
     for index in range(0, len(processed_data)):
       training_data.append(processed_data[index])

 for filename in os.listdir(training_prediction_p):
   if filename.endswith('.mat'):
     f_path = training_prediction_p + filename
     mat = scipy.io.loadmat(f_path)
     variable = get_variable(filename)
     eeg = mat[variable][0][0][0][0]
     processed_data = cnn_preprocess(eeg[0:4096], detect, predict)
     for index in range(0, len(processed_data)):
       training_data.append(processed_data[index])

 for filename in os.listdir(validation_prediction_i):
   if filename.endswith('.mat'):
     f_path = validation_prediction_i + filename
     mat = scipy.io.loadmat(f_path)
     variable = get_variable(filename)
     eeg = mat[variable][0][0][0][0]
     processed_data = cnn_preprocess(eeg[0:4096], detect, predict)
     for index in range(0, len(processed_data)):
       validation_data.append(processed_data[index])

 for filename in os.listdir(validation_prediction_p):
   if filename.endswith('.mat'):
     f_path = validation_prediction_p + filename
     mat = scipy.io.loadmat(f_path)
     variable = get_variable(filename)
     eeg = mat[variable][0][0][0][0]
     processed_data = cnn_preprocess(eeg[0:4096], detect, predict)
     for index in range(0, len(processed_data)):
       validation_data.append(processed_data[index])

 for filename in os.listdir(testing_prediction_i):
   if filename.endswith('.mat'):
     f_path = testing_prediction_i + filename
     mat = scipy.io.loadmat(f_path)
     variable = get_variable(filename)
     eeg = mat[variable][0][0][0][0]
     processed_data = cnn_preprocess(eeg[0:4096], detect, predict)
```

```
    for index in range(0, len(processed_data)):
      testing_data.append(processed_data[index])

  for filename in os.listdir(testing_prediction_p):
    if filename.endswith('.mat'):
      print (filename)
      f_path = testing_prediction_p + filename
      mat = scipy.io.loadmat(f_path)
      variable = get_variable(filename)
      eeg = mat[variable][0][0][0][0]
      processed_data = cnn_preprocess(eeg[0:4096], detect, predict)
      for index in range(0, len(processed_data)):
        testing_data.append(processed_data[index])

if detect is True:
  for filename in os.listdir(training):
    if filename.endswith('.txt'):
      f_path = training + filename
      text_file = open(f_path, "r")
      lines = text_file.readlines()
      results = map(int, lines)
      text_file.close()
      processed_data = cnn_preprocess(results, detect, predict)
      for index in range(0, len(processed_data)):
        training_data.append(processed_data[index])

  for filename in os.listdir(validation):
    if filename.endswith('.txt'):
      f_path = validation + filename
      text_file = open(f_path, "r")
      lines = text_file.readlines()
      results = map(int, lines)
      text_file.close()
      processed_data = cnn_preprocess(results, detect, predict)
      for index in range(0, len(processed_data)):
        validation_data.append(processed_data[index])

  for filename in os.listdir(testing):
    if filename.endswith('.txt'):
      f_path = testing + filename
      text_file = open(f_path, "r")
      lines = text_file.readlines()
      results = map(int, lines)
      text_file.close()
      processed_data = cnn_preprocess(results, detect, predict)
      for index in range(0, len(processed_data)):
        testing_data.append(processed_data[index])

y_train = [1] * (23*2)
y_train += [0] * (23*2)
y_val = [1] * (23*2)
y_val += [0] * (23*2)
```

```
y_test = [1] * (23*2)
y_test += [0] * (23*2)

X_train = np.array(training_data)
X_val = np.array(validation_data)
X_test = np.array(testing_data)

y_val = np.array(y_val)
y_train = np.array(y_train)
y_test = np.array(y_test)

y_train = y_train.astype(np.uint8)
y_test = y_test.astype(np.uint8)
y_val = y_val.astype(np.uint8)

X_train = X_train.reshape(-1, 1, 224, 224)
X_val = X_val.reshape(-1, 1, 224, 224)
X_test = X_test.reshape(-1, 1, 224, 224)

X_train = X_train / np.float(224)
X_val = X_val / np.float(224)
X_test = X_test / np.float(224)

return X_train, y_train, X_val, y_val, X_test, y_test

def convolutional_neural_network(num_epochs, detect, predict):

X_train, y_train, X_val, y_val, X_test, y_test = load_cnn_dataset(detect, predict)
input_var = T.tensor4('inputs')
target_var = T.ivector('targets')
network = build_cnn(input_var)

prediction = lasagne.layers.get_output(network)
loss = lasagne.objectives.categorical_crossentropy(prediction, target_var)
loss = loss.mean()

params = lasagne.layers.get_all_params(network, trainable=True)
updates = lasagne.updates.nesterov_momentum(loss, params, learning_rate=0.01,
momentum=0.9)

test_prediction = lasagne.layers.get_output(network, deterministic=True)
test_loss = lasagne.objectives.categorical_crossentropy(test_prediction, target_var)
test_loss = test_loss.mean()
test_acc = T.mean(T.eq(T.argmax(test_prediction, axis=1), target_var),
dtype=theano.config.floatX)
train_fn = theano.function([input_var, target_var], loss, updates=updates)
val_fn = theano.function([input_var, target_var], [test_loss, test_acc])

batches = 4

print("Starting training...")
# We iterate over epochs:
```

```
for epoch in range(num_epochs):
  # In each epoch, we do a full pass over the training data:
  train_err = 0
  train_batches = 0
  start_time = time.time()
  for batch in iterate_minibatches(X_train, y_train, batches, shuffle=True):
    inputs, targets = batch
    train_err += train_fn(inputs, targets)
    train_batches += 1l
  print("Training took {:.3f}s".format(time.time() - start_time))

print("Testing...")
batch_num = 0
test_err = 0
test_acc = 0
test_batches = 0
test_time = time.time()
for batch in iterate_minibatches(X_test, y_test, batches, shuffle=False):
  batch_num += 1
  print(batch_num)
  inputs, targets = batch
  err, acc = val_fn(inputs, targets)
  test_err += err
  test_acc += acc
  test_batches += 1
print("Final results:")
print(" test loss:\t\t\t{:.6f}".format(test_err / test_batches))
print(" test accuracy:\t\t{:.2f} %".format(test_acc / test_batches * 100))
print("Testing took {:.3f}s".format(time.time() - test_time))


def main(model='mlp', num_epochs=10):
  if model == 'cnn':
    convolutional_neural_network(num_epochs, True, False)
  elif model == 'lamstar':
    lamstar(False, True, False)

def iterate_minibatches(inputs, targets, batchsize, shuffle=False):
  assert len(inputs) == len(targets)
  if shuffle:
    indices = np.arange(len(inputs))
    np.random.shuffle(indices)
  for start_idx in range(0, len(inputs) - batchsize + 1, batchsize):
    if shuffle:
      excerpt = indices[start_idx:start_idx + batchsize]
    else:
      excerpt = slice(start_idx, start_idx + batchsize)
    yield inputs[excerpt], targets[excerpt]

def build_cnn(input_var=None):
  network = lasagne.layers.InputLayer(shape=(None, 1, 224, 224), input_var=input_var)
  network = lasagne.layers.Conv2DLayer(network, num_filters=96, filter_size=(7, 7), stride=2)
```

```
  network = lasagne.layers.MaxPool2DLayer(network, pool_size=(3, 3), stride=3,
ignore_border=False)
  network = lasagne.layers.DenseLayer(network, num_units=2,
nonlinearity=lasagne.nonlinearities.softmax)
  return network

if __name__ == '__main__':
  # USAGE:
  #  To run Convolutional neural network:
  #    run: 'python NeuralNetwork.py 'cnn' <number_of_epochs>
  #    e.g. python NeuralNetwork.py cnn 10
  #
  #  To run LAMSTAR network:
  #    run: 'python NeuralNetwork.py 'lamstar'
  #
  kwargs = {}
  if len(sys.argv) > 1:
    kwargs['model'] = sys.argv[1]
  if len(sys.argv) > 2:
    kwargs['num_epochs'] = int(sys.argv[2])
  main(**kwargs)
```

A.8.3. Cancer Detection (D Bose)

Part 1: CNN: The code below uses https://github.com/sdemyanov/ConvNet. Copyright (c) 2014 Sergey Demyanov.

1) *Using CNN :-*

```
close all; clear;
% cd(fileparts(mfilename('fullpath')));
% funtype = 'gpu';
% funtype = 'cpu';
funtype = 'matlab';

disp(funtype);

if (strcmp(funtype, 'gpu') || strcmp(funtype, 'cpu'))
 kMexFolder = './c++/build';
 kBuildFolder = fullfile(kMexFolder, funtype);
 if (ispc)
  mexfiles = fullfile(kBuildFolder, '*.mexw64');
 elseif (isunix)
  mexfiles = fullfile(kBuildFolder, '*.mexa64');
 end;
 copyfile(mexfiles, kMexFolder, 'f');
 addpath(kMexFolder);
end;
addpath('./matlab');
addpath('./data');
% load d;
```

```
load data;

kWorkspaceFolder = './workspace';
if (~exist(kWorkspaceFolder, 'dir'))
 mkdir(kWorkspaceFolder);
end;

kTrainNum = 166;
%kTrainNum = 12800;
%kTrainNum = 2000;
kOutputs = 2;%size(TrainY, 2);
for i = 1:kTrainNum
  train_x(:,:,i) = single(reshape(X_in(:, i),10,10));
  train_y(i,:)  = single(t(:,i))';
end

kSampleDim = ndims(train_x);
kXSize = size(train_x);
kXSize(kSampleDim) = [];
if (kSampleDim == 3)
 kXSize(3) = 1;
end;

kTestNum = 50;
% test_x = single(reshape(X_in(:, 1:kTestNum),10,10));
% test_y = single(t(:,1:kTestNum));

kOutputs = 2;%size(TrainY, 2);
for i = 1:kTestNum
  test_x(:,:,i) = single(reshape(X_in(:, 166+i),10,10));
  test_y(i,:)  = single(t(:,166+i))';
end

clear params;
params.epochs = 1;
params.alpha = 0.1;
% this is the parameter for invariant backpropagation
% keep it 0 for standard backpropagation
params.beta = 0;
params.momentum = 0.9;
params.lossfun = 'logreg';
params.shuffle = 1;
params.seed = 0;
dropout = 0;

% norm_x = squeeze(mean(sqrt(sum(sum(train_x.^2))), kSampleDim));

% !!! IMPORTANT NOTICES FOR GPU VERSION !!!
% Outputmaps number should be divisible on 16
% For speed use only the default value of batchsize = 128

% This structure gives pretty good results on MNIST after just several epochs
```

```
layers = {
 struct('type', 'i', 'mapsize', kXSize(1:2), 'outputmaps', kXSize(3))
 % remove the following layer in the Matlab version - it is not implemented there
 %struct('type', 'j', 'mapsize', [28 28], 'shift', [1 1], ...
 %    'scale', [1.40 1.40], 'angle', 0.10, 'defval', 0)
 struct('type', 'c', 'filtersize', [3 3], 'outputmaps', 16)
 struct('type', 's', 'scale', [2 2], 'function', 'max', 'stride', [2 2])
% struct('type', 'c', 'filtersize', [5 5], 'outputmaps', 64, 'padding', [2 2])
% struct('type', 's', 'scale', [3 3], 'function', 'max', 'stride', [2 2])
 struct('type', 'f', 'length', 256, 'dropout', dropout)
 struct('type', 'f', 'length', kOutputs, 'function', 'soft')
};

weights = single(genweights(layers, params, funtype));
EpochNum = 50;
errors = zeros(EpochNum, 1);
time1 = 0;
time2 = 0;
for i = 1 : EpochNum
 disp(['Epoch: ' num2str((i-1) * params.epochs + 1)])
 [weights, trainerr,t1] = cnntrain(layers, weights, params, train_x, train_y, funtype);
 time1 = time1 + t1;
 disp([num2str(mean(trainerr(:, 1))) ' loss']);
 [err, bad, pred,t2] = cnntest(layers, weights, params, test_x, test_y, funtype);
 time2 = time2 + t2;
 disp([num2str(err*100) '% error']);
 errors(i) = err;
 params.alpha = params.alpha * 0.95;
 params.beta = params.beta * 0.95;
end;
plot(errors);
disp('Done!');
```

Part 2: LAMSTAR — 1 (MATLAB)

```
%% LAMSTAR_main.m
% File for setting up the LAMSTAR Network
tic;
% clear all; clc
% tic;
load 'OvarianCancerQAQCdataset.mat';

ind = rankfeatures(Y,grp,'CRITERION','ttest','NUMBER',100);
x = Y(ind,:);
t = double(strcmp('Cancer',grp));
t = [t; 1-t];
[x,t] = ovarian_dataset;

X_in = x;
[row, col] = size(X_in);
numSubWords = 100;
```

```
numTraining = 156;
 val = randperm(216);
train = val(1:166);
test = val(167:216);
% load data.mat
X_norm = normalizeData(X_in);
% X_norm = X_train;
% for j=1:216
%  count = 1;
%  for i=1:10:100
%    data(count,count) = sum(X_norm(i:i+9,j).^2);
%    count = count + 1;
%  end
% end
% Forming Sub Words
% X_train is the list of sub-words for all the 216 datasets
for i = 1:size(train,2)
  for j = 1:numSubWords
    X_train(i,j) = X_norm(j,train(i));
  end
end
% Forming Sub Words
% X_test is the list of sub-words for all the 216 datasets
for i = 1:size(test,2)
  for j = 1:numSubWords
    X_test(i,j) = X_norm(j,test(i));
  end
end
index = 1;
% for iter = 10:10:200
%   tic;
  % Creating SOM Modules for respective subwords
  for i=1:numSubWords
    [~,edges] = histcounts(X_train(:,i),100);
    range = [-Inf edges Inf];
    [N,edges] = histcounts(X_train(:,i),range);
    SOM{i}.Neuron = size(N,2);
    SOM{i}.Range = edges;
    SOM{i}.Number = N;
    SOM{i}.Weight = [];
  end
```

A.8.4. Depth Information from 2D Images (J C Somaundaram)

Part 1: Seting up of the CNN Code

The toolbox used for Convolutinal Neural Network (CNN) is ConvNet, provided by Sergey Demyanov. The codes can be found on the following link: https://github.com/sdemyanov/ConvNet.

```
%%Depth Prediction
%JOHN CALEB SOMASUNDARAM
%UIN:652266896
%MS - ECE
clc
clear
tic
d=dir('C:\Users\Sulochana\Documents\MATLAB\KinectColor');
d=d(3:end);
for i=1:size(d,1)
  temp=imread(d(i).name);
  im(i).name=temp;
end
im=im';
de=dir('C:\Users\Sulochana\Documents\MATLAB\RegisteredDepthData');
de=de(3:end);
k=1;
for i=1:2:size(de,1)
  tempe=imread(de(i).name);
  label = 1:16;
  tempD = (imquantize(tempe./1000,label));
  dep(k).name=tempD;
  k=k+1;
end
dep=dep
% Patching the image around the superpixel centroid
 for i=1:size(d,1)
  [slicimg(i).name, Am, Sp, d] = slic((im(i).name), 400, 25, 1);
  stats=regionprops(slicimg(i).name,'Centroid');
  centroids(i).name = cat(1,stats.Centroid);
  padimg(i).name = padarray(slicimg(i).name, [122 122], 'both');
  centroids1(i).name = centroids(i).name + 122;
  for j=1:size(centroids1.name,1)
    startP = int32(centroids1(i).name(1,:) - 122),
    endP = startP + 223;
    patch(i).name(j).index = padimg(1).name(startP(1):endP(1), startP(2):endP(2));
  end
end

  %Get the depth mean at the centroid patch
for i = 1:size(d,1);
 paddepimg(i).name = padarray(dep(i).name, [122 122], 'both');
```

```
 for j=1:size(centroids1.name,1)
   startP = int32(centroids1(i).name(j,:) - 122);
   endPP = startP + 223;
   endP = min(724,endPP);
   patchdep(i).name(j).index = mean(mean(paddepimg(i).name(startP(1):endP(1),
startP(2):endP(2))));
 end
end

% Training and Testing Dataset
 while i<=849
  tempp=[];
  for j=1:399
   tempest=patch(i).name(j).index;
   tempp=[tempp;tempest];
  end
% Training and Testing Dataset
 while i<=849
  tempp=[];
  for j=1:399
   tempest=patch(i).name(j).index;
   tempp=[tempp;tempest];
  end
  new=reshape(tempp,224,224,(i*399));
  new=permute(new,[2 1 3]);
  i=i+1;
 end
 traindata=new(:,:,(1:319200));
 testdata=new(:,:,(319200:338751));
 quantte=[];
 for i=1:1
  for j=1:399
  quantt = patchdep(i).name(j).index;
  quantte = [quantte;quantt];
  end
 end
 trainlabel=quantte(1:319,200);
 testlabel=quantte(319,200:338,751);
Feature Extraction
for i=1:size(d,1)
  [map(i).name]=laws(im(i).name,3);
end
hormask=[1,2,1;0,0,0;-1,-2,-1];
vertmask=[1,0,-1;2,0,-2;1,0,-1];
for i=1:size(d,1)
 for k=1:6
   theta=30*(k);
   norm=(theta/180)*pi;
   convoima(i).name=hormask*cos(norm)+vertmask*sin(norm);
   output(i).name{k}=rgb2gray(convn(im(i).name,convoima(i).name,'same'));
 end
end
```

```
for i=1:size(d,1)
feat(i).name=[map(i).name,output(i).name];
end

%% CNN Unary branch:
close all; clear mex;
cd(fileparts(mfilename('fullpath')));
%funtype = 'gpu';
% funtype = 'cpu';
funtype = 'matlab';

% disp(funtype);
```

Part 2: Setting up the LAMSTAR Code

```
%%LAMSTAR UNARY BRANCH
%% LAMSTAR_main.m
% File for setting up the LAMSTAR Network
 clear all; clc
tic;
load Depth_data.mat
numSubWords = 22; %22
X_train = traindata;
flag = zeros(1,numSubWords);
% Forming Sub Words
for i = 1:size(X_train,3)
  tempX = reshape(X_train(:,:,i),11,11);
  for j = 1:numSubWords
    if j<=11
      X_in{i}(j,:) = tempX(j,:);
    else
      X_in{i}(j,:) = tempX(:,j-11)';
    end
  end
end
 % Normalizing the inputs
check(1,:) = zeros(1,11);
for i = 1:size(X_train,3)
  for j = 1:numSubWords
    if (sum(X_in{i}(j,:)) ~= sum(check(1,:)))
      X_norm{i}(j,:) = X_in{i}(j,:) ./ sqrt(sum(X_in{i}(j,:).^2));
    else
      X_norm{i}(j,:) = zeros(1,11);
    end
  end
end
%%%%%%%%%%%%%%%%%%%%%%%%%%%%%%
% Dynamic Building of neurons
%%%%%%%%%%%%%%%%%%%%%%%%%%%%%%
% Building of the first neuron is done as Kohonen Layer neuron
%(this is for all the subwords in the first input pattern for all SOM modules
```

```
i = 1;
ct = 1;
while (i<=numSubWords),
  cl = 0;
  for t = 1:11,
    if (X_norm{ct}(i,t)==0),
      cl = cl+1;
    end
  end
  if (cl == 11),
    Z{ct}(i) = 0;
  elseif (flag(i) == 0),
    W{i}(:,ct) = rand(11,1);
    flag(i) = ct;
    W_norm{i}(:,ct) = W{i}(:,ct)/sqrt(sum(W{i}(:,ct).^2));
    Z{ct}(i)= X_norm{ct}(i,:)*W_norm{i};
    alpha = 0.8;
    tol = 1e-5;
    while(Z{ct}(i) <= (1-tol)),
      W_norm{i}(:,ct) = W_norm{i}(:,ct) + alpha*(X_norm{ct}(i,:)' - W_norm{i}(:,ct));
      Z{ct}(i) = X_norm{ct}(i,:)*W_norm{i}(:,ct);
    end
  end
  r(ct,i) = 1;
  i = i+1;
end

% For param = 0.9:0.05:0.9
  ct = 1;
  r(ct,:) = 1;
  ct = ct+1;
  while (ct <= size(X_train,3)),  %Size of input training data
    for i = 1:numSubWords,
      cl = 0;
      for t = 1:11,
        if (X_norm{ct}(i,t)==0),
          cl = cl+1;
        end
      end
      if (cl == 11),
        Z{ct}(i) = 0;
      else
        r(ct,i) = flag(i);
        r_new=0;
        for k = 1:max(r(ct,i)),
          Z{ct}(i) = X_norm{ct}(i,:)*W_norm{i}(:,k);
          ct
          if Z{ct}(i)>=0.9999,
            r_new = k;
            flag(i) = r_new;
```

```
        r(ct,i) = flag(i);
        break;
      end
    end
    if (r_new==0),
      flag(i) = flag(i)+1;
      r(ct,i) = flag(i);
      W{i}(:,r(ct,i)) = rand(11,1);
      %flag(i) = r
      W_norm{i}(:,r(ct,i)) = W{i}(:,r(ct,i))/sqrt(sum(W{i}(:,r(ct,i)).^2));
      Z{ct}(i) = X_norm{ct}(i,:)*W_norm{i}(:,r(ct,i));
      alpha = 0.8;
      tol = 1e-5;
      while(Z{ct}(i) <= (1-tol)),
        W_norm{i}(:,r(ct,i)) = W_norm{i}(:,r(ct,i)) + alpha*(X_norm{ct}(i,:)' –
       %W_norm{i}(:,r(ct,i)));
        Z{ct}(i) = X_norm{ct}(i,:)*W_norm{i}(:,r(ct,i));
      end%%%End of while
    end%%%End of if
    %r_new
    %disp('Flag')
    %flag(i)
  end%%%%End of if
 end
 ct = ct+1;
end
save W_norm W_norm
%-------------------------------------------------------------
% Form the 18 element vector 'd' for each input dataset
for i = 1:72000,
  tempVec = zeros(1,18);
  temp_depth = ceil(trainlabel(i));
  tempVec(temp_depth) = 1;
  d(i,:) = tempVec;
end

%%%%%%%%%%%%%%%%
% Link Weights
%%%%%%%%%%%%%%%%
ct = 1;
m_r = max(r);
% Initializing the Link Weight Matrix by
% the maximum number of neurons in SOM layer x 2(Output Neurons)
for i = 1:numSubWords,
  L_w{i} = zeros(m_r(i),18);
end
```

A.8.5. Scene Classification (N Koudinya)

The CNN code is a Python Thaeno Keras code

Preprocessing

```
import cv2
    import glob from os import path
    import os
    import errno
# No Hierarchical Storing # Resize the Input Images and save them to a user defined path # Use this when the src folder has just .jpg files with no other file hierarch y # All the resized images will be dumped to one destination folder
    def imgResizeWithOutHier(srcPath, destPath, reSampleSize):
      # Loop Variable
      loopVar = 0

 # Find and select all the Images, resize and write them to the destPath
      for imgs in glob.glob(srcPath + '/*jpg'):
        filePath, ext = path.split(imgs)
        image = cv2.imread(imgs)
        image = cv2.resize(image, reSampleSize)
        cv2.imwrite(destPath + ext, image)
        print(' Writing Image: %i' % loopVar)
        loopVar += 1

    # For now hardcoding for this problem! (coding for this train hierarchy) # With Hierarchical Storing (with out recursive copying) # Resize the Input Images and save them to a user defined pat # Use this when the src folder has a custom hierarchy in which .jpg files are stored# All the resized images will be dumped with source file hierarchy
    def imgResizeWithHier(srcRootPath, destRootPath, reSampleSize):

      # Loop Count
      loopVar = 0
      loopWrite = 0

    # Traverse through the directory tree and write the resized images with hierarchy in destination directory
      for dirName, subdirList, fileList in os.walk(srcRootPath):
        for fname in fileList:

          # Source path
          imgDir = dirName
          imgExt = fname
          imgPath = imgDir + '/' + imgExt

          # To separate srcrootPath folder from full path
          destHier = imgDir.split(srcRootPath)
          destDir = destRootPath + str(destHier[1]) + '/'

          destPath = destDir + imgExt
          print(destPath)
```

```
    # Create directory if it doesnt exists and eliminate the race condition if neccessary
    checkDir = os.path.dirname(destDir)
    if not os.path.exists(checkDir):
      try:
        os.makedirs(checkDir)
      except OSError as exception:
        if exception.errno != errno.EEXIST:
          raise

    # Read images and resize them
    img = cv2.imread(imgPath)
    reSize = (64, 64)
    img = cv2.resize(img, reSize)
    cv2.imwrite(destPath, img)
```

Main ( )

```
from dataParser import getData
from datetime import datetime
from dataParser import kerasDataFormat
from utilityModule import writeToPickle
from utilityModule import writeToFile
from utilityModule import recordTime
from cnnNetwork import cnnClassifier

def main():
    # Start time for loading the data, creating a container and writing the output to a file
    dataLoadStartTime = datetime.now()

    # Load Training Data (with appropriate data structure) and write to a txt file and a pickle file
    trainData = getData('train')
    trnPklFile = '/home/koundinya/Koundi/UIC/Projects/DeepLearning/MiniPlaces-
Theano/Output Folder/trainDataPickleFile.plk'
    trnTxtFile = '/home/koundinya/Koundi/UIC/Projects/DeepLearning/MiniPlaces-
Theano/Output Folder/trainDataTextFile.txt'
    writeToFile(trainData, trnTxtFile)
    writeToPickle(trainData, trnPklFile)
    print('Writing Finished!')

    # Load Validation Data (with appropriate data structure) and write to a file
    valData = getData('val')
    valPklFile = '/home/koundinya/Koundi/UIC/Projects/DeepLearning/MiniPlaces-
Theano/Output Folder/valDataPickleFile.plk'
    valTxtFile = '/home/koundinya/Koundi/UIC/Projects/DeepLearning/MiniPlaces-
Theano/Output Folder/valDataTextFile.txt'
    writeToFile(valData, valTxtFile)
    writeToPickle(valData, valPklFile)
    print('Writing Finished!'



    )
```

```
    # Load Validation Data (with appropriate data structure) and write to a file
    testData = getData('test')
    testPklFile = '/home/koundinya/Koundi/UIC/Projects/DeepLearning/MiniPlaces-
Theano/Output Folder/testDataPickleFile.plk'
    testTxtFile = '/home/koundinya/Koundi/UIC/Projects/DeepLearning/MiniPlaces-
Theano/Output Folder/testDataTextFile.txt'
    writeToFile(testData, testTxtFile)
    writeToPickle(testData, testPklFile)
    print('Writing Finished!')

    # Format/structure the data for Keras library
    trnKerasFormat = kerasDataFormat(trainData, 'train')
    valKerasFormat = kerasDataFormat(valData, 'val')
    X_train = trnKerasFormat[0]
    Y_train = trnKerasFormat[1]
    X_val = valKerasFormat[0]
    Y_val = valKerasFormat[1]

    # End time for loading the data, creating a container and writing the output to a file
  if __name__ == '__main__':
    main()
```

Data Parser

```
  from utilityModule import writeToFile
  import glob
  import cv2
  import numpy
  from utilityModule import fileLength
  from SceneRecognition.utilityModule import encode

  # Training File Path and length
  trnIpFile = '/home/koundinya/Koundi/UIC/Projects/DeepLearning/MiniPlaces-
Theano/Data/development_kit/data/train.txt'
  trnImgFolder = '/home/koundinya/Koundi/UIC/Projects/DeepLearning/MiniPlaces-
Theano/Data/Data/images/train'
  trainLen = fileLength(trnIpFile)

  # Validation File Path and length
  valIpFile = '/home/koundinya/Koundi/UIC/Projects/DeepLearning/MiniPlaces-
Theano/Data/development_kit/data/val.txt'
  valImgFolder = '/home/koundinya/Koundi/UIC/Projects/DeepLearning/MiniPlaces-
Theano/Data/Data/images/val'
  valLength = fileLength(valIpFile)

  # Testing File Path
  testImgFolder = '/home/koundinya/Koundi/UIC/Projects/DeepLearning/MiniPlaces-
Theano/Data/Data/images/test'

# Get Data for training and validation (both Images and associated Class labels) from input text
file
  def getDataFromFile(fname, length, label):
```

```
# Input File
datafileName = fname
dataFile = open(datafileName)

# Find the length of the file
length = length

# Empty Dictionary
data = {}

# Read by line and store Images, Class labels in a dictionary for i in range(length):
  ipDataByLine = dataFile.readline()
  ipDescrp = ipDataByLine.split()
  imagePath = '/home/koundinya/Koundi/UIC/Projects/DeepLearning/MiniPlaces-
Theano/Data/Data/images' + '/' + ipDescrp[0]
  imageClassLabl = int(ipDescrp[1])

  # Read the image (OpenCV)
  image = cv2.imread(imagePath)
  # Store the data
  data[i] = (image, imageClassLabl)

  # Show progress
  if label == 'train':
    print('Percentage Completion of Training Data Modelling is: %f' %
  elif label == 'val':
    print('Percentage Completion of Validation Data Modelling is: %f' % i)
  else:
    print('Percentage of Completion is : %f' %i)
return data

# Get data for testing from test folder
def getTestData(fname):

  # Empty List
  testData = []
  loopVar = 0

  for images in glob.glob(fname+'/*.jpg'):
    img = cv2.imread(images)
    testData.append(img)

    # Show progress
    print('Percentage Completion of Testing Data Modelling is: %f' % loopVar)
    loopVar = loopVar + 1

  return testData

def kerasDataFormat(data, label):
```

```
    X = []
    Y = []
    totalSamples = len(data)

    for i in range(totalSamples):
      imgData = data[i][0]
      X.append(imgData)
      labels = encode(data[i][1])
      Y.append(labels)
      print("The current Iteration for Keras Data Model is: ", i)
    X = numpy.asarray(X)
    X = X.reshape(totalSamples, 3, 128, 128)
    Y = numpy.asarray(Y)
    if label == 'train':
      imgPath = '/home/koundinya/Desktop/Link to MiniPlaces-Theano/Output
Folder/kerasFormatForTrnImg.txt'
      labelPath = '/home/koundinya/Desktop/Link to MiniPlaces-Theano/Output
Folder/kerasFormatForTrnLab.txt'
      writeToFile(X,imgPath)
      writeToFile(Y, labelPath)
    if label == 'val':
      imgPath = '/home/koundinya/Desktop/Link to MiniPlaces-Theano/Output
Folder/kerasFormatForValImg.txt'
      labelPath = '/home/koundinya/Desktop/Link to MiniPlaces-Theano/Output
Folder/kerasFormatForValLab.txt'
      writeToFile(X,imgPath)
      writeToFile(Y, labelPath)

    return X, Y
  # Pass train, validation and test data to main function
  def getData(label):

    if label == 'train':
      trainData = getDataFromFile(trnIpFile, trainLen, label)
      print("Loading Training data - Completed!")
      return trainData
    elif label == 'val':
      valData = getDataFromFile(valIpFile, valLength, label)
      print("Loading Validation data - Completed!")
      return valData
    elif label=='test':
      testData = getTestData(testImgFolder)
      print("Loading Testing data - Completed!")
      return testData
    else:
      print("Unknown Label: %s Please check your entry" % label)

  Convolutional Network
  from keras.models import Sequential
  from keras.layers.core import Dense, Dropout, Activation, Flatten
  from keras.layers.convolutional import Convolution2D, MaxPooling2D
```

```
from keras.optimizers import SGD
from keras.regularizers import l2, activity_l1l2
```

A.8.6. Fingerprint Recognition 1 (A Daggubati)

Part 1: Preprocessing Code for LAMSTAR

```
% Image Preprocessing  %Extracting the ridges and bifurcation from a fingerprint image  %Read
Input Image
binary_image=im2bw(imread('C:\Users\anuhsa\fp.jpg'));
%Small region is taken to show output clear
binary_image = binary_image(120:400,20:250);
figure;imshow(binary_image);title('Input image');

%Thinning
thin_image=~bwmorph(binary_image,'thin',Inf);
figure;imshow(thin_image);title('Thinned Image');

%Minutiae extraction
s=size(thin_image);
N=3;%window size
n=(N-1)/2;
r=s(1)+2*n;
c=s(2)+2*n;
double temp(r,c);
temp=zeros(r,c);bifurcation=zeros(r,c);ridge=zeros(r,c);
temp((n+1):(end-n),(n+1):(end-n))=thin_image(:,:);
outImg=zeros(r,c,3);%For Display
outImg(:,:,1) = temp .* 255;
outImg(:,:,2) = temp .* 255;
outImg(:,:,3) = temp .* 255;
for x=(n+1+10):(s(1)+n-10)
 for y=(n+1+10):(s(2)+n-10)
   e=1;
   for k=x-n:x+n
     f=1;
     for l=y-n:y+n
       mat(e,f)=temp(k,l);
       f=f+1;
     end
     e=e+1;
   end;
   if(mat(2,2)==0)
     ridge(x,y)=sum(sum(~mat));
     bifurcation(x,y)=sum(sum(~mat));
   end
 end;
end;
```

```
% RIDGE END FINDING
[ridge_x ridge_y]=find(ridge==2);
len=length(ridge_x);
%For Display
for i=1:len
  outImg((ridge_x(i)-3):(ridge_x(i)+3),(ridge_y(i)-3),2:3)=0;
  outImg((ridge_x(i)-3):(ridge_x(i)+3),(ridge_y(i)+3),2:3)=0;
  outImg((ridge_x(i)-3),(ridge_y(i)-3):(ridge_y(i)+3),2:3)=0;
  outImg((ridge_x(i)+3),(ridge_y(i)-3):(ridge_y(i)+3),2:3)=0;

  outImg((ridge_x(i)-3):(ridge_x(i)+3),(ridge_y(i)-3),1)=255;
  outImg((ridge_x(i)-3):(ridge_x(i)+3),(ridge_y(i)+3),1)=255;
  outImg((ridge_x(i)-3),(ridge_y(i)-3):(ridge_y(i)+3),1)=255;
  outImg((ridge_x(i)+3),(ridge_y(i)-3):(ridge_y(i)+3),1)=255;
end

%BIFURCATION FINDING
[bifurcation_x bifurcation_y]=find(bifurcation==4);
len=length(bifurcation_x);
%For Display
for i=1:len
  outImg((bifurcation_x(i)-3):(bifurcation_x(i)+3),(bifurcation_y(i)-3),1:2)=0;
  outImg((bifurcation_x(i)-3):(bifurcation_x(i)+3),(bifurcation_y(i)+3),1:2)=0;
  outImg((bifurcation_x(i)-3),(bifurcation_y(i)-3):(bifurcation_y(i)+3),1:2)=0;
  outImg((bifurcation_x(i)+3),(bifurcation_y(i)-3):(bifurcation_y(i)+3),1:2)=0;
  outImg((bifurcation_x(i)-3):(bifurcation_x(i)+3),(bifurcation_y(i)-3),3)=255;
  outImg((bifurcation_x(i)-3):(bifurcation_x(i)+3),(bifurcation_y(i)+3),3)=255;
  outImg((bifurcation_x(i)-3),(bifurcation_y(i)-3):(bifurcation_y(i)+3),3)=255;
  outImg((bifurcation_x(i)+3),(bifurcation_y(i)-3):(bifurcation_y(i)+3),3)=255;
end
figure;imshow(outImg);title('Minutiae');
```

A.8.7. Fingerprint Recognition 2 (A Ponguru)

Convolution Neural Network:

```
from __future__ import print_function
import sys
import os
import time
import numpy as np
import theano
import theano.tensor as T
import lasagne
# Download and prepare the dataset
def load_dataset():
  # We first define a download function, supporting both Python 2 and 3.
  if sys.version_info[0] == 2:
    from urllib import urlretrieve
  else:
```

```
  from urllib.request import urlretrieve
  def download(filename, source= http://biometrics.idealtest.org/):
INTERRUPTED

# This script supports three types of models. For each one, we define a
# function that takes a Theano variable representing the input and returns
# the output layer of a neural network model built in Lasagne.
def build_mlp(input_var=None):
  # This creates an MLP of two hidden layers of 800 units each, followed by
  # a softmax output layer of 10 units. It applies 20% dropout to the input
  # data and 50% dropout to the hidden layers.
  # Input layer, specifying the expected input shape of the network
  # (unspecified batchsize, 1 channel, 28 rows and 28 columns) and
  # linking it to the given Theano variable `input_var`, if any:
  l_in = lasagne.layers.InputLayer(shape=(None, 1, 28, 28),
              input_var=input_var)
  # Apply 20% dropout to the input data:
  l_in_drop = lasagne.layers.DropoutLayer(l_in, p=0.2)
  # Add a fully-connected layer of 800 units, using the linear rectifier, and
  # initializing weights with Glorot's scheme (which is the default anyway):
  l_hid1 = lasagne.layers.DenseLayer(
    l_in_drop, num_units=800,
    nonlinearity=lasagne.nonlinearities.rectify,
    W=lasagne.init.GlorotUniform())
  # We'll now add dropout of 50%:
  l_hid1_drop = lasagne.layers.DropoutLayer(l_hid1, p=0.5)
  l_hid2 = lasagne.layers.DenseLayer(
    l_hid1_drop, num_units=800,
    nonlinearity=lasagne.nonlinearities.rectify)
  # 50% dropout again:
  l_hid2_drop = lasagne.layers.DropoutLayer(l_hid2, p=0.5)
  # Finally, we'll add the fully-connected output layer, of 10 softmax units:
  l_out = lasagne.layers.DenseLayer(
    l_hid2_drop, num_units=10,
    nonlinearity=lasagne.nonlinearities.softmax)
```

A.8.8. Face Recognotion (S Gangineni)

LNN1/LNN2 setup Setup

```
% Face Detection and recognition using LAMSTAR and Modified LAMSTAR
% Reading of a RGB image
close all;
i=imread('Individual1_01.jpg');
I=rgb2gray(i);
BW=im2bw(I);
figure,imshow(BW)

%minimisation of background portion
[n1 n2]=size(BW);
```

```
  r=floor(n1/10);
  c=floor(n2/10);
  x1=1;x2=r;
  s=r*c;
  for i=1:10
          y1=1;
          y2=c;
          for j=1:10
                  if (y2<=c | y2>=9*c) | (x1==1 | x2==r*10)
                          loc=find(BW(x1:x2, y1:y2)==0);
                          [o p]=size(loc);
                          pr=o*100/s;
                          if pr<=100
                                  BW(x1:x2, y1:y2)=0;
                                  r1=x1;r2=x2;s1=y1;s2=y2;
                                  pr1=0;
end imshow(BW);
end
y1=y1+c;
y2=y2+c;
end
    x1=x1+r;
    x2=x2+r;
  end
   figure,imshow(BW)
  %detection of face
  L = bwlabel(BW,8);
  BB  = regionprops(L, 'BoundingBox');
  BB1=struct2cell(BB); BB2=cell2mat(BB1);
  [s1 s2]=size(BB2);
  mx=0;
  for k=3:4:s2-1
          p=BB2(1,k)*BB2(1,k+1);
          if p>mx & (BB2(1,k)/BB2(1,k+1))<1.8
                  mx=p;
                  j=k;
  end
  end

  figure,imshow(I);
  hold on;

  rectangle('Position',[BB2(1,j-2),BB2(1,j-
  1),BB2(1,j),BB2(1,j+1)],'EdgeColor','r')

  %getting eigen faces
function [wi, AvgImage, efaces] = get_eigenfaces(X, top_k)
N=64;
M = 135;
if size(X,2) ~=N*N
   display('error');
```

```
    return;
   end
st.size = M;
for i = 1:M
   st.data{i} = reshape(X(i,:), [N,N]);
   end
AvgImage=zeros(N);
for k=1:20
      AvgImage   =AvgImage  + (1/M)*st.data{k};
   end
%% normalize (remove mean)
for k=1:20
   st.dataAvg{k}  = st.data{k}-AvgImage;
   end
A = zeros(N*N,M);% (N*N)*M   1000*10
for k=1:20
      A(:,k) = st.dataAvg{k}(:);
   end
% covariance matrix small dimension (transposed)
C = A'*A;
% figure(4);
% imagesc(C);
% title('covariance');
%% eigen vectros  in small dimension
[Veigvec, Deigval]  = eig(C);% v M*M e M*M only 20 eigen values
% eigan face in large dimension  A*veigvec is eigen vector of Clarge
Vlarge = A*Veigvec;% 2500*M*M*M  =2500 *M
% reshape to eigen face
efaces_tmp=[];
for k=1:20
    c  = Vlarge(:,k);
    efaces_tmp{k} = reshape(c,N,N);
   end
x=diag(Deigval);
[~,xci]=sort(x,'descend');% largest eigenval
nsel=top_k; % select  eigen faces
for mi=1:M % image number
   for k=1:nsel   % eigen face for coeff number
      wi(mi,k) =   sum(A(:,mi).* efaces_tmp{xci(k)}(:)) ;
      end
   end
efaces = [];
for k = 1:nsel
   efaces{k} = efaces_tmp{xci(k)};
fprintf('eigenfaces.txt', efaces{k});
   end
facerecognition.m
   close all;
   clear all;
   clc;
   eigen_faces='eigen
```

```
  faces.txt';
  delimiterIn=' ';
  headerlinesIn=1;
  A=importdata(eigen_faces,delimiterIn,headerlinesIn);
  for class=1:1:15
        face=[];

        if class==1
              face = ImageWord1;
        elseif class==2
              face = ImageWord2;
              ;
        elseif class==13
              face = ImageWord13;
        elseif class==14
              face = ImageWord14;
        else face = ImageWord15;
        end
end
finalvector = [ 1 0 0 0 0 0 0 0 0 0 0 0 0 0 0 %Individual-1
                0 1 0 0 0 0 0 0 0 0 0 0 0 0 0 %Individual-2
                0 0 1 0 0 0 0 0 0 0 0 0 0 0 0 %Individual-3
                0 0 0 1 0 0 0 0 0 0 0 0 0 0 0 %Individual-4
                0 0 0 0 1 0 0 0 0 0 0 0 0 0 0 %Individual-5
                0 0 0 0 0 1 0 0 0 0 0 0 0 0 0 %Individual-6
                0 0 0 0 0 0 1 0 0 0 0 0 0 0 0 %Individual-7
                0 0 0 0 0 0 0 1 0 0 0 0 0 0 0 %Individual-8
                0 0 0 0 0 0 0 0 1 0 0 0 0 0 0 %Individual-9
                0 0 0 0 0 0 0 0 0 1 0 0 0 0 0 %Individual-10
                0 0 0 0 0 0 0 0 0 0 1 0 0 0 0 %Individual-11
                0 0 0 0 0 0 0 0 0 0 0 1 0 0 0 %Individual-12
                0 0 0 0 0 0 0 0 0 0 0 0 1 0 0 %Individual-13
                0 0 0 0 0 0 0 0 0 0 0 0 0 1 0 %Individual-14
                0 0 0 0 0 0 0 0 0 0 0 0 0 0 1]; %Individual-15
   N_Sub = 20;
   N_Numneuron = 10;
  N_OPNeuron = 15;
```

Part 2: CNN Setup (per using CaffeeNetConv code)

```
#face_full_conv.prototxt

# Fully convolutional network version of CaffeNet.
name: "CaffeNetConv"
input: "data"
input_dim: 1
input_dim: 3
input_dim: 64
input_dim: 64
layer {
```

```
 name: "conv1"
 type: "Convolution"
 bottom: "data"
 top: "conv1"
 convolution_param {
  num_filters: 4
  kernel_size: 5
  stride: 1
 }
}

layer {
 name: "pool1"
 type: "Pooling"
 bottom: "conv1"
 top: "pool1"
 pooling_param {
  pool: MAX
  stride: 2
 }
}

layer {
 name: "conv2"
 type: "Convolution"
 bottom: "pool1"
 top: "conv2"
 convolution_param {
  num_filters: 4
  kernel_size: 5
  stride: 1
 }
}

layer {
 name: "pool2"
 type: "Pooling"
 bottom: "conv2"
 top: "pool2"
 pooling_param {
  pool: MAX
  stride: 2
 }
}
layer {
 name: "relu1"
 type: "ReLU"
 bottom: "pool2"
 top: "conv2"
}
```

```
layer {
 name: "prob"
 type: "Softmax"
 bottom: "relu1"
 top: "prob"
}
#image preprocessing
from PIL import Image
import numpy as np
import random

d .... ....(INTERRUPTED).
```

A.8.9. Butterfly Species Recognition (V R S S Kadi)

Part 1: LAMSTAR and Modified LAMSTAR — Source Code

```
%Code written in Matlab

function [ images ] = preprocessing()
 imagefiles = dir('*.jpg');
 nfiles = length(imagefiles);
 for ii=1:nfiles
   currentfilename = imagefiles(ii).name;
   RGB = imread(currentfilename);
   I = rgb2gray(RGB);
   Iblur1 = imgaussfilt(I);
   Iblur2 = medfilt2(Iblur1);
   BW = im2bw(Iblur2, 0.6);
   mask = ones(size(BW));
   contour = activecontour(BW,mask,'edge');
   images{ii} = contour;
 end
end

function [featureVec]=features(contenttype, images)
cd(strcat('/Users/Susmitha/neural_netwroks/project/LAMSTAR/',contenttype));
flst=dir('*.jpg');

ImageWord=[];
contentfilename=[];
for j=1:length(flst)
  fn=flst(j).name;
  disp(sprintf('workin on <%s>',fn));

OriginalImage = imread(fn);
GrayOrgImage = RGB2gray(OriginalImage);

% Each Color Component Image
R = OriginalImage(:,:,1);
```

```
G = OriginalImage(:,:,2);
B = OriginalImage(:,:,3);

% Color Histogram
R = reshape(R,size(R,1)*size(R,2),1);
G = reshape(G,size(G,1)*size(G,2),1);
B = reshape(B,size(B,1)*size(B,2),1);

[Rn1,Rx1] = imhist(R);
[Gn1,Gx1] = imhist(G);
[Bn1,Bx1] = imhist(B);

NormRn1 = Rn1;
NormGn1 = Gn1;
NormBn1 = Bn1;

Mean=[];Variance=[];Skew=[];

% First,Second and Third order statistics for each color component
% scaling the values of mean, variance and skew for some values between 0
% and 1

Mean(1)= mean(NormRn1);
Mean(2)= mean(NormGn1);
Mean(3)= mean(NormBn1);

Variance(1) = var(NormRn1);
Variance(2) = var(NormGn1);
Variance(3) = var(NormBn1);

Skew(1)=skewness(NormRn1);
Skew(2)=skewness(NormGn1);
Skew(3)=skewness(NormBn1);

if (Mean(1)>=0)&(Mean(1)<1000)
  Mean(1)=1;
else
  if (Mean(1)>1000)&(Mean(1)<=2000)
    Mean(1)=2;
  else Mean(1)=3;
  end
end


if (Mean(2)>=0)&(Mean(2)<1000)
  Mean(2)=1;
else
  if (Mean(2)>1000)&(Mean(2)<=2000)
    Mean(2)=2;
  else Mean(2)=3;
  end
end
```

```
if (Mean(3)>=0)&(Mean(3)<1000)
 Mean(3)=1;
else
 if (Mean(3)>1000)&(Mean(3)<=2000)
  Mean(3)=2;
 else Mean(3)=3;
 end
end

if (Variance(1)>=0)&(Variance(1)<50e+5)
 Variance(1)=0;
else
 if (Variance(1)>50e+5)&(Variance(1)<=100e+5)
  Variance(1)=1;
 else
  if (Variance(1)>100e+5)&(Variance(1)<=150e+5)
   Variance(1)=2;
  else Variance(1)=3;
  end
 end
end

if (Variance(2)>=0)&(Variance(2)<50e+5)
 Variance(2)=0;
else
 if (Variance(2)>50e+5)&(Variance(2)<=100e+5)
  Variance(2)=1;
 else
  if (Variance(2)>100e+5)&(Variance(2)<=150e+5)
   Variance(2)=2;
  else Variance(2)=3;
  end
 end
end

if (Variance(3)>=0)&(Variance(3)<50e+5)
 Variance(3)=0;
else
 if (Variance(3)>50e+5)&(Variance(3)<=100e+5)
  Variance(3)=1;
 else
  if (Variance(3)>100e+5)&(Variance(3)<=150e+5)
   Variance(3)=2;
  else Variance(3)=3;
  end
 end
end

%Color vector

ColorVec =[Mean Variance];
```

```
% taking discrete wavelet transform of the gray image... for one level.

[CA CH CV CD] = dwt2(GrayOrgImage,'haar');

CA = (CA + abs(min(min(CA))))/(max(max(CA))+abs((min(min(CA)))));
CH = (CH + abs(min(min(CH))))/(max(max(CH))+abs((min(min(CH)))));
CV = (CV + abs(min(min(CV))))/(max(max(CV))+abs((min(min(CV)))));
CD = (CD + abs(min(min(CD))))/(max(max(CD))+abs((min(min(CD)))));

CA = reshape(CA,size(CA,1)*size(CA,2),1);
CH = reshape(CH,size(CH,1)*size(CH,2),1);
CV = reshape(CV,size(CV,1)*size(CV,2),1);
CD = reshape(CD,size(CD,1)*size(CD,2),1);

texturevec(1) = mean(CA);
texturevec(2) = mean(CH);
texturevec(3) = mean(CV);
texturevec(4) = mean(CD);

%Geometric features
geometricvec(1) = bwarea(images{j});
geometricvec(2) = bwperim(images{j});
geometricvec(3) = sqrt(4 * geometricvec(1)/ pi);

texturevec = round(texturevec*15);
ColorVec = round(ColorVec*15);
geometricvec = round(geometricvec*15);


ImageWord(j,:) = [ColorVec texturevec geometricvec];

a = ImageWord(j,:);

end

featureVec = ImageWord;


% function [returnword]= runlamstar()

% number of subwords in each lamstar network
clear all
clc

load 'preprocessedfile'

% Arranging the input words in the format we need
% Preparing the Input Vector

for class=1:1:10
  ClassWords=[];
  if class==1
```

```
   ClassWords = ImageWord1;
  elseif class==2
   ClassWords = ImageWord2;
  elseif class==3
   ClassWords = ImageWord3;
  elseif class==4
   ClassWords = ImageWord4;
  elseif class==5
   ClassWords = ImageWord5;
  elseif class==6
   ClassWords = ImageWord6;
  elseif class==7
   ClassWords = ImageWord7;
  elseif class==8
   ClassWords = ImageWord8;
  elseif class==9
   ClassWords = ImageWord9;
  else ClassWords = ImageWord10;
  end
  for i=1:1:size(ClassWords,1)
   Wordstring=[];
   for j=1:1:6
    subword = ClassWords(i,j);
    tempstring = dec2bin(subword,2);
    Wordstring = strcat(Wordstring,tempstring);
   end
   Actualword(class,i,:)=int8(Wordstring-'0');
  end
end

% Deciding the Target Vector
% we have 10 class here

targetvector = [ 1 0 0 0 0 0 0 0 0 0
       0 1 0 0 0 0 0 0 0 0
       0 0 1 0 0 0 0 0 0 0
       0 0 0 1 0 0 0 0 0 0
       0 0 0 0 1 0 0 0 0 0
       0 0 0 0 0 1 0 0 0 0
       0 0 0 0 0 0 1 0 0 0
       0 0 0 0 0 0 0 1 0 0
       0 0 0 0 0 0 0 0 1 0
       0 0 0 0 0 0 0 0 0 1];

N1_Subword = 16;
N1_NumElmtSub =10;

N1_LinkWeight=[];
for i=1:1:N1_Subword
  for j=1:1:N1_Numofneuron
   for k=1:1:N1_OutputNeurons
     N1_LinkWeight(i,j,k)= .0001*(2*rand-1);
```

```
    end
   end
  end

 % Normalize the Weights

 for k=1:1:N1_OutputNeurons
   Normvalue = sqrt(sum(sum(N1_LinkWeight(:,:,k).^2)));
   if Normvalue~=0
    for i=1:1:N1_Subword
     for j=1:1:N1_Numofneuron
       N1_LinkWeight(i,j,k)= N1_LinkWeight(i,j,k)/Normvalue;
     end
    end
   end
 end

 % Intializing the SOM layer Weights

 N1_SomWeight=[];
 for i=1:1:N1_Subword
  for j=1:1:N1_NumElmtSub
   for k=1:1:N1_Numofneuron
     N1_SomWeight(i,j,k) = .0001*(2*rand-1);
   end
  end
 end

 % Normalizing the Weights

 for i=1:1:N1_Subword
  for k=1:1:N1_Numofneuron
   Normvalue = sqrt(sum(N1_SomWeight(i,:,k).^2));
   if Normvalue~=0
    for j=1:1:N1_NumElmtSub
     N1_SomWeight(i,j,k) = N1_SomWeight(i,j,k)/Normvalue;
    end
   end
  end
 end
 firstrand = round(rand*(size(ImageWord2,1)-20));
 secondrand = round(rand*(size(ImageWord3,1)-20));
 p=[1:20 size(ImageWord1,1)+firstrand+1:size(ImageWord1,1)+firstrand+
 20 size(ImageWord1,1)+size(ImageWord2,1)+secondrand+1:size(ImageWord1,1)+
 secondrand+size(ImageWord2,1)+20];

 OInputWordpatterns=[];
 ODesiredOutputPatterns=[];

 for i=1:1:60
   for i=1:1:150
  if p(i)<=size(ImageWord1,1)
```

```
    OInputWordpatterns(i,:) = Actualword(1,p(i),:);
    ODesiredOutputPattern(i,:)= [1 0 0];
  else
    if p(i)<=(size(ImageWord2,1)+size(ImageWord1,1))
      OInputWordpatterns(i,:) = Actualword(2,(p(i)-size(ImageWord1,1)),:);
      ODesiredOutputPattern(i,:)= [0 1 0];
    else OInputWordpatterns(i,:) = Actualword(3,(p(i)-size(ImageWord1,1)-
size(ImageWord2,1)),:);
       ODesiredOutputPattern(i,:)= [0 0 1];
    end
   end
  end
end

flag=0; numCycle=0; alfa=.7; beta0=1; Error=[]; Err=[];
punishdelta=0.5;rewarddelta=3;
Er1=[];
Winner=[];
while flag==0
  numCycle=numCycle+1;
  alfa = alfa0/numCycle;


  if mod(numCycle,15)==0
   alfa = alfa0/(numCycle/15);
   betta = betta0/(numCycle/15);
  end

 permute the order of the input words and the training class

  p = randperm(60);

  InputWordpatterns=[];
  DesiredOutputPatterns=[];

  for i=1:1:60
   for i=1:1:832
    InputWordpatterns(i,:)= OInputWordpatterns(p(i),:);
    DesiredOutputPattern(i,:)=ODesiredOutputPattern(p(i),:);

    if p(i)<=size(ImageWord1,1)
      InputWordpatterns(i,:) = Actualword(1,p(i),:);
      DesiredOutputPattern(i,:)= [1 0 0];
    else
      if p(i)<=(size(ImageWord2,1)+size(ImageWord1,1))
       InputWordpatterns(i,:) = Actualword(2,(p(i)-size(ImageWord1,1)),:);
       DesiredOutputPattern(i,:)= [0 1 0];
     else InputWordpatterns(i,:) = Actualword(3,(p(i)-size(ImageWord1,1)-size(ImageWord2,1)),:);
       DesiredOutputPattern(i,:)= [0 0 1];
     end
    end
end
```

```
% SOM layers Weight Adjustments done here.

% temp = InputWordpatterns(:,37:64);
% InputWordpatterns=[];
% InputWordpatterns=temp;
%
for i=1:1:size(InputWordpatterns,1)

 identified=0;
 alfa=0.7;

 while identified==0

  alfa=0.9*alfa;

  KohOutputs = zeros(N2_Subword,N2_Numofneuron);

  InputPattern=[];
  DesiredPattern=[];
  InputPattern = InputWordpatterns(i,:);
  DesiredPattern = DesiredOutputPattern(i,:);

  Winner=[];
  for j=1:1:N1_Subword
   SubWord =InputWordpatterns((j-1)*2+1:(j-1)*2+2);
   Normvalue =sqrt(sum(SubWord.^2));
   if Normvalue~=0
   SubWord = SubWord/Normvalue;
   end

   for k=1:1:N1_Numofneuron
    sumx=0;
    for z=1:1:N1_NumElmtSub
     sumx = sumx + SubWord(z)*N1_SomWeight(j,z,k);
    end
    % KohOut(j,k)= SubWord.*N1_SomWeight(j,:,k);
    KohOut(j,k)=sumx;
   end

   % Finding the winner
   [WinnerVal WinnerIndex] = max(KohOut(j,:));

   % Winner take all
   KohOutputs(j,WinnerIndex)=1;

   Winner(j)=WinnerIndex;

   % Change the weights
   for k=1:N1_Numofneuron
    for z=1:1:N1_NumElmtSub
     diff = SubWord(z)-N1_SomWeight(j,z,k);
     N1_SomWeight(j,z,k) = N1_SomWeight(j,z,k)+ alfa*(diff);
```

```
      end;
    end;

    % Normalize the changed weights
    for k=1:1:N1_Numofneuron
      Normvalue = sqrt(sum(N1_SomWeight(j,:,k).^2));
      if Normvalue~=0
       for z=1:1:N1_NumElmtSub
        N1_SomWeight(j,z,k) = N1_SomWeight(j,z,k)/Normvalue;
       end
      end
    end
  end

  % adjusting weights in the decision layer
  % Punishing/rewarding the link weights based on the result

  % If the result is favourable then reward all the link-weights of
  % the winning neurons to the output winning neuron and all other
  % link weights connecting to this particular output neuron is
  % punished

  % If the result is not favourable then punish all the link-weights
  % of the winning neuron to the ouput winning neuron


  % Here winning neuron index is Dindex


  % find the sum of link weights of all the winners that corresponds
  % to the neurons in the output layer.
ef IoUofTwoSameImages(region1, region2) ………….
```

Part 2: CNN — Code written in Python's Keras (Theano based Python Library)

```
#cnn.py

from __future__ import absolute_import
from __future__ import print_function
import numpy as np
np.random.seed(1337) # for reproducibility

from six.moves import cPickle
from keras.datasets import mnist
from keras.models import Sequential
from keras.layers.core import Dense, Dropout, Activation, Flatten
from keras.layers.convolutional import Convolution2D, MaxPooling2D

from keras.utils import np_utils
from loadData import load_data
```

```
batch_size = 50
nb_classes = 10
nb_epoch = 200

# input image dimensions
img_rows, img_cols = 150, 150
# number of convolutional filters to use
nb_filters = 10
# size of pooling area for max pooling
nb_pool = 5
# convolution kernel size
nb_conv = 10

path = "/Users/Susmitha/neural_networks/project/data.pkl"
# the data, shuffled and split between tran and test sets
(X_train, y_train), (X_test, y_test) = load_data(path)
X_train = X_train.reshape(X_train.shape[0], 1, img_rows, img_cols)
X_test = X_test.reshape(X_test.shape[0], 1, img_rows, img_cols)
X_train = X_train.astype("float32")
X_test = X_test.astype("float32")
X_train /= 255
X_test /= 255
print('X_train shape:', X_train.shape)
print(X_train.shape[0], 'train samples')
print(X_test.shape[0], 'test samples')

# convert class vectors to binary class matrices
Y_train = np_utils.to_categorical(y_train, nb_classes)
Y_test = np_utils.to_categorical(y_test, nb_classes)

model = Sequential()

model.add(Convolution2D(nb_filters, nb_conv, nb_conv,
        border_mode='full',
        input_shape=(1, img_rows, img_cols)))
model.add(Activation('relu'))
model.add(Convolution2D(nb_filters, nb_conv, nb_conv))
model.add(MaxPooling2D(pool_size=(nb_pool, nb_pool)))
model.add(Activation('relu'))
model.add(Convolution2D(nb_filters, nb_conv, nb_conv))
model.add(MaxPooling2D(pool_size=(nb_pool, nb_pool)))
model.add(Activation('relu'))
model.add(Activation('relu'))
model.add(Dropout(0.25))
model.add(Dense(nb_classes))
model.add(Activation('softmax'))

model.compile(loss='categorical_crossentropy', optimizer='adadelta')
model.fit(X_train, Y_train, batch_size=batch_size, nb_epoch=nb_epoch, show_accuracy=True,
verbose=1, validation_data=(X_test, Y_test))
score = model.evaluate(X_test, Y_test, show_accuracy=True, verbose=0)
print('Test score:', score[0])
```

```
print('Test accuracy:', score[1])

#loadData.py

from __future__ import absolute_import
from __future__ import print_function

import tarfile
import os
import numpy as np

import gzip
from six.moves import cPickle
import sys

def get_file(fname, origin, untar=False):
  if not os.path.exists(datadir):
    os.makedirs(datadir)
  if untar:
    untar_fpath = os.path.join(datadir, fname)
    fpath = untar_fpath + '.tar.gz'
  else:
    fpath = os.path.join(datadir, fname)
  return fpath

def load_data(path):
  path = get_file(path)

  if path.endswith(".gz"):
    f = gzip.open(path, 'rb')
  else:
    f = open(path, 'rb')

  if sys.version_info < (3,):
    data = cPickle.load(f)
  else:
    data = cPickle.load(f, encoding="bytes")

  f.close()

  return data # (X_train, y_train), (X_test, y_test)
```

A.8.10. Leaf Classification (P Bondili)

Convolutional Neural Networks (Python, Library Used: Lasagne)

```
#cnn_leaves.py
from __future__ import print_function
import sys
import os
```

```
import time
import numpy as np
import theano
import theano.tensor as T
import lasagne
import gzip
import pylab
from PIL import Image
import glob
def load2d(x_train, img_rows, img_cols, image_dim):
# return reshaped array
  return x_train.reshape(x_train.shape[0], image_dim, img_rows, img_cols).astype("float32")
def get_images(image_path, image_extension=const.EXTENSION, size=200):
  all_paths = glob.glob(image_path + image_extension)
  images = []
  basenames = []
  # load images
  for path in all_paths:
    stacked = stack_features(path)
    basenames.append(os.path.basename(path))
    images.append(stacked)  INTERRUPTED

def build_cnn(input_var=None):
  # As a third model, we'll create a CNN of two convolution + pooling stages
  # and a fully-connected hidden layer in front of the output layer.
  network = lasagne.layers.InputLayer(shape=(None,1, 200, 200),
              input_var=input_var)
  network = lasagne.layers.Conv2DLayer(
     network, num_filters=5, filter_size=(10, 10),
     nonlinearity=lasagne.nonlinearities.rectify,
     W=lasagne.init.GlorotUniform())
  network = lasagne.layers.MaxPool2DLayer(network, pool_size=(2, 2))
  network = lasagne.layers.Conv2DLayer(
     network, num_filters=5, filter_size=(10, 10),
     nonlinearity=lasagne.nonlinearities.rectify)
  network = lasagne.layers.MaxPool2DLayer(network, pool_size=(2, 2))
                INTERRUPTSD

  # Prepare Theano variables for inputs and targets
  input_var = T.tensor4('inputs')
  target_var = T.ivector('targets')
  network = build_cnn(input_var)
  prediction = lasagne.layers.get_output(network)
  loss = lasagne.objectives.categorical_crossentropy(prediction, target_var)
  loss = loss.mean()
  params = lasagne.layers.get_all_params(network, trainable=True)
  updates = lasagne.updates.nesterov_momentum(
     loss, params, learning_rate=0.01, momentum=0.9)
  test_prediction = lasagne.layers.get_output(network, deterministic=True)
  test_loss = lasagne.objectives.categorical_crossentropy(test_prediction,
                    target_var)
  test_loss = test_loss.mean()
```

```
 test_acc = T.mean(T.eq(T.argmax(test_prediction, axis=1), target_var),
        dtype=theano.config.floatX)
 train_fn = theano.function([input_var, target_var], loss, updates=updates)
 val_fn = theano.function([input_var, target_var], [test_loss, test_acc])
INTERRUPTED
```

A.8.11. Traffic Sign Recognition (D Somasundaram)

LAMSTAR Network (setup)

```
function img = edu_imgpreprocess(I, selected_col,selected_ln)
Igray = rgb2gray(I);
Ibw = im2bw(Igray,graythresh(Igray));
Iedge = edge(uint8(Ibw));
se = strel('square',3);
Iedge2 = imdilate(Iedge, se);
Ifill= imfill(Iedge2,'holes');
[Ilabel num] = bwlabel(Ifill);
Iprops = regionprops(Ilabel);
Ibox = [Iprops.BoundingBox];
[y,x]=size(Ibox);
x=x/4;
Ibox = reshape(Ibox,[4 x]);
Ic = [Iprops.Centroid];
[z,w]=size(Ic);%
w=w/2;%
Ic = reshape(Ic,[2 w]);
Ic = Ic';
Ic(:,3) = (mean(Ic.^2,2)).^(1/2);
Ic(:,4) = 1:w;
Ic2 = sortrows(Ic,2);
for cnt = 1:selected_ln
Ic2((cnt-1)*selected_col+1:cnt*selected_col,:) = sortrows(Ic2((cnt-
1)*selected_col+1:cnt*selected_col,:),4);
end
Ic3 = Ic2(:,1:2);
ind = Ic2(:,4);
for cnt = 1:selected_ln*selected_col
img{cnt} = imcrop(Ibw,Ibox(:,ind(cnt)));
end
function bw2 = edu_imgcrop(bw)
% Find the boundary of the image
[y2temp x2temp] = size(bw);
x1=1;
y1=1;
x2=x2temp;
y2=y2temp;
% Finding left side blank spaces
cntB=1;
while (sum(bw(:,cntB))==y2temp)
```

```
x1=x1+1;
cntB=cntB+1;
end
% Finding right side blank spaces
cntB=1;
while (sum(bw(cntB,:))==x2temp)
y1=y1+1;
cntB=cntB+1;
end
% Finding upper side blank spaces
cntB=x2temp;
while (sum(bw(:,cntB))==y2temp)
x2=x2-1;
cntB=cntB-1;
end
% Finding lower side blank spaces
cntB=y2temp;
while (sum(bw(cntB,:))==x2temp)
y2=y2-1;
cntB=cntB-1;
end
% Crop the image to the edge
bw2=imcrop(bw,[x1,y1,(x2-x1),(y2-y1)]);
function lett = edu_imgresize(bw2)
% This function will take the cropped binary image and change it to 10 x 10
% character representation in single vector.
bw_1010=imresize(bw2,[10,10]);
for cnt=1:10
for cnt2=1:10
Atemp=sum(bw_7050((cnt*10-9:cnt*10),(cnt2*10-9:cnt2*10)));
lett((cnt-1)*5+cnt2)=sum(Atemp);
end
end
let=((100-lett)/100)
fid = fopen('imageresize.txt','w');
lett=lett';
fprintf(fid,'%6.2f \n',lett);
fclose(fid);
```

INTERRUPTED…….

A.8.12. Programming-Language Classification (E Wolfson)

Lamstar Setup Code (Including Generator Code)

```
// BY ERIC WOLFSON FALL 2015 FOR FINAL PROJECT OF CS 559
#include <iostream>
#include <utility>
#include <algorithm>
#include <string>
```

```
#include <vector>
#include <sstream>
#include <cstdlib>
#include <math.h>
#include <time.h>
#define NUM_POSSIBLE_VARIABLES 26

#define NUM_INPUT_NEURONS 600
#define NUM_HIDDEN_NEURONS 4
#define NUM_OUTPUT_NEURONS 2

#define NUM_IDEAL_COMBINATIONS 4
#define NUM_TRAINING_PATTERNS 300

#define MULT_FACTOR 1.5873

#define MAX_ITERATIONS 40000

// LAMSTAR
#define NUM_LAMSTAR_TEST_COMBINATIONS 400
#define NUM_LAMSTAR_TRAINING_PATTERNS 1000
#define som_init_tolerance 0.0001
#define som_subsequent_tolerance 0.05
#define SUBWORD_SIZE 150
#define NUM_SUBWORDS_PER_INPUT_VECTOR 4
#define INC_LINK_WEIGHT 1.0
#define DEC_LINK_WEIGHT 1.0

// FLIP BETWEEN UNMODIFIED/MODIFIED LAMSTAR HERE:
static const bool modified_lamstar_usage = false;
static const double euler_const = 2.71828182845904523536;
static const double learn_rate = 0.7;
static const double momentum = 0.3;
static const double end_error = 0.1;
static const double test_success_error = 0.49;
static const std::string language_indicator[NUM_IDEAL_COMBINATIONS] = {"C: ","PYTHON:
","RUBY: ","OTHER: "};

enum language_type
{
  C_LANGUAGE,
  PYTHON_LANGUAGE,
  RUBY_LANGUAGE
};

// IGNORE the second ruby, it is just a placeholder for other in that slot
static const language_type lang_order[NUM_IDEAL_COMBINATIONS] =
{
 C_LANGUAGE,
 PYTHON_LANGUAGE,
 RUBY_LANGUAGE,
 RUBY_LANGUAGE,
```

```
};
static const double
ideal_output_vector[NUM_IDEAL_COMBINATIONS][NUM_OUTPUT_NEURONS] =
{
  // C
  {0.0,1.0},
  // PYTHON
  {1.0,0.0},
  // RUBY
  {1.0,1.0},
  // other
  {0.0,0.0}
};

// BP
double compute_activation(double x)
{
  return (1.0/(1.0+pow(euler_const,-x)));
}

double compute_activation_derivative(double x)
{
  double exp_temp = pow(euler_const,x);
  return exp_temp/((1.0+exp_temp)*(1.0+exp_temp));
}

// LAMSTAR
struct s_word
{
  double vals[SUBWORD_SIZE];
};

//LAMSTAR NEURON for SOM MODULE
struct SOM_neuron
{
  double inps[SUBWORD_SIZE];
  double outp;
  bool is_winner;
};
// Snippet complexity:
// -) if statements
// -) for loops
// -) while loops
// -) assignment with operations and literals
// -) conditions in if statements and loops
// -) declarations/parameters
// -) return values

// GENERATOR CODE BEGINS HERE

enum line_type
{
```

```
  LINE_PARAM,
  LINE_DECLR,
  LINE_ASSGN,
  LINE_OPERN,
  LINE_IFSTT,
  LINE_WLOOP,
  LINE_FLOOP
};
enum data_type
{
  TYPE_INT,
  TYPE_FLOAT
};
enum cond_type
{
  COND_EQ,
  COND_NEQ,
  COND_LT,
  COND_LTE,
  COND_GT,
  COND_GTE
};
enum oper_type
{
  OPER_ADD,
  OPER_MULT,
  OPER_SUB
};

struct struct_tuple
{
  int a,b;
};

struct variable
{
  char symbol;
  data_type dt;
};

struct literal
{
  int whole_part;
  int decimal_part;
};

struct varlit_pair
{
  variable v;
  literal l;
};
```

```
struct condition
{
  cond_type ct;
  varlit_pair vlp;
  int id;
  int parent;
};

struct oper_statement
{
  oper_type op;
  variable vd;
  varlit_pair vlps;
  int id;
  int parent;
};

struct for_statement
{
  condition c;
  varlit_pair i;
  oper_statement o;
  int id;
  int parent;
};

int roll(int low, int high)
{
  // check boundary
  if (low < 0 || high < 0)
    return 0;

  if (low == 0 && high == 0)
    return 0;

  return (rand() % (high - low + 1)) + low;
}
literal genLiteral(data_type dt, int mwp, int mdp)
{
  literal l = {roll(0,mwp),roll(0,mdp)};
  if (dt == TYPE_INT)
    l.decimal_part = 0;
  return l;
}

std::string int2String(int s)
{
  std::stringstream ss;
  ss << s;
  return ss.str();
}
```

```
std::string getCTypeString(data_type d)
{
 switch(d)
 {
  case(TYPE_INT):
    return "int ";
  case(TYPE_FLOAT):
    return "float ";
  default:
    break;
 }
 // never happens...
 return "void ";
}

std::string getLiteralString(data_type dt, literal l)
{
 if (dt == TYPE_INT)
  return int2String(l.whole_part);
 return int2String(l.whole_part) + "." + int2String(l.decimal_part);
}

std::string getCOperString(oper_type o)
{
 switch(o)
 {
  case(OPER_ADD):
   return "+";
  case(OPER_SUB):
   return "-";
  default:
   break;
 }

 return "*";
}

std::string getCondString(cond_type c)
{
 switch (c)
 {
  case(COND_EQ):
    return "==";
  case(COND_GT):
    return ">";
  case(COND_GTE):
    return ">=";
  case(COND_LT):
    return "<";
  case(COND_LTE):
    return "<=";
  default:
```

```
        break;
    }

    return "!=";
}
```

A.8.13. Data Classification from Transcribed Spoken Text (A Kumar)

Part 1: Lamstar Code

LamstarNeuralNetwork.java

```
package uic.edu.neuralnetwork.lamstar;

import java.math.BigDecimal;
import java.util.ArrayList;
import java.util.Calendar;
import java.util.LinkedHashMap;
import java.util.List;

import uic.edu.neuralnetwork.shared.container.Edge;
import uic.edu.neuralnetwork.shared.container.Layer;
import uic.edu.neuralnetwork.shared.container.Neuron;
import uic.edu.neuralnetwork.shared.container.Neuron.ActivationMode;
import uic.edu.neuralnetwork.shared.utils.CommonUtils;

public class LamstarNeuralNetwork extends ForwardFeedNeuralNetwork{

        private boolean normalizedLinkWeights;

        public LamstarNeuralNetwork(int totalInputSubwords, int
totalInputNeuronsPerSubword, int totalOutputNeurons,
                        BigDecimal learningRate, int learningRateMode, int maxIterations,
BigDecimal threshold, boolean normalizeLinkWeights) {
                super(totalInputSubwords, totalInputNeuronsPerSubword,
totalOutputNeurons, learningRate, learningRateMode, maxIterations, threshold);

                //Lamstar can be implemented using normalized link weights
                this.normalizedLinkWeights = normalizeLinkWeights;

                //We care about summation of the input to see what is the winner in kohonen
layer hence need summation mode
                Neuron.setOutputActivation(ActivationMode.SUMMATION_FUNCTION);

                //Although initial weights are randomized, we must normalize the storage
weights (not the link weights)
                normalizeStorageWeights();
        }

        //Normalize the random weights assigned to each neuron in each kohonen layer (just one
neuron per kohonen layer initially
```

```
	private void normalizeStorageWeights(){
		for(Layer kohonenLayer : kohonenLayers){
			for(Neuron neuron : kohonenLayer){
				List<BigDecimal> weights = new
				ArrayList<BigDecimal>();
				for(Edge neighbor : neuron.backwardNeighbors()){
					weights.add(neighbor.weight());
				}

				weights = CommonUtils.normalize(weights);
				List<Edge> backwardNeighbors =
				neuron.backwardNeighbors();
				for(int cnt = 0; cnt < weights.size(); cnt++){
					Edge neighbor = backwardNeighbors.get(cnt);
					BigDecimal weight = weights.get(cnt);
					neighbor.setWeight(weight);

	neighbor.target().forwardNeighbor(neighbor.source().id()).setWeight(weight);
				}
			}
		}
	}

	private void updateWeightsForWinningNeuron(Neuron maximumNeuron, BigDecimal
learningRate, List<BigDecimal> subword){
		BigDecimal output = maximumNeuron.output();
		LinkedHashMap<Integer, BigDecimal> normalizedWeightsMap = new
LinkedHashMap<Integer, BigDecimal>();

		//while the only neuron is not close enough to output of 1, keep updating weights
		while(output.compareTo(new BigDecimal(0.99999)) < 0){
			//this.totalIterations++;
			//the lone neuron that we deem as the winner, need to iterate its
subword neighbors and update the weight for each, as (w + alpha*(x-w))
			for(int cnt1 = 0; cnt1 <
			maximumNeuron.backwardNeighbors().size(); cnt1++){
				Edge neighbor =
				maximumNeuron.backwardNeighbors().get(cnt1);
				BigDecimal value = subword.get(cnt1);

				//extract normalized weight for current neighbor
				BigDecimal weight = neighbor.weight();

				//delta = (x - w)
				BigDecimal deltaWeight = value.subtract(weight);

				//delta = alpha * delta = alpha * (x - w)
				deltaWeight = learningRate.multiply(deltaWeight);
				neighbor.setDeltaWeight(deltaWeight);
```

```
                //w = w + delta = w + alpha(x - w)
                BigDecimal newWeight =
                neighbor.weight().add(deltaWeight);

                //update the new weight into map. Dont update actual
weight until we normalize so that we maintain the previous weight states correctly
                //otherwise the previous weight state would be recorded as
the unnormalized weight rather than the true previous normalized weight value
                normalizedWeightsMap.put(neighbor.target().id(),
newWeight);
            }
            //compute the normalized weight values for the backward neighbors
(subword neighbors) and store back into map
            normalizedWeightsMap =
CommonUtils.normalize(maximumNeuron.backwardNeighbors(), normalizedWeightsMap);

            //finally update the backward neighbors with the normalized weight
values
            for(int neuronId : normalizedWeightsMap.keySet()){
                Edge backwardNeighbor =
                maximumNeuron.backwardNeighbor(neuronId);
                BigDecimal normalizedWeight =
                normalizedWeightsMap.get(neuronId);
                backwardNeighbor.setWeight(normalizedWeight);

                Edge forwardNeighbor =
backwardNeighbor.target().forwardNeighbor(maximumNeuron.id());
                forwardNeighbor.setWeight(normalizedWeight);
            }

            //update output of the only neuron to check again if it's close enough to
1.0 yet
            maximumNeuron.applySummation();
            maximumNeuron.applyActivationFunction();
            output = maximumNeuron.output();
        }
    }

    //only update the winning neuron. It's link weight is rewarded if it should have fired and
punished if it should not have fired.
    private void updateLinkWeightsForWinningNeuron(Neuron maximumNeuron,
List<BigDecimal> expectedOutput){
        BigDecimal deltaWeight = new BigDecimal(0.05).multiply(new
BigDecimal(20));
        //this.totalIterations += 20;

        for(int cnt1 = 0; cnt1 < maximumNeuron.forwardNeighbors().size(); cnt1++){
            Edge neighbor = maximumNeuron.forwardNeighbors().get(cnt1);
            neighbor.setDeltaWeight(deltaWeight);

            Edge backwardNeighbor =
            neighbor.target().backwardNeighbor(maximumNeuron.id());
```

```
					backwardNeighbor.setDeltaWeight(deltaWeight);

					BigDecimal expectedValue = expectedOutput.get(cnt1);

					//punish if winning neuron should not have fired for this output neuron
					if(expectedValue.compareTo(BigDecimal.ZERO) == 0){
						//BigDecimal newWeight =
						neighbor.weight().subtract(deltaWeight);
						BigDecimal newWeight = neighbor.weight();

						//if normalized version of lamstar, then divide by number of
times that neuron has won
						if(normalizedLinkWeights)
							newWeight = CommonUtils.ratio(newWeight,
new BigDecimal(maximumNeuron.noOfWins()));

						newWeight = newWeight.subtract(deltaWeight);

						neighbor.setWeight(newWeight);

						backwardNeighbor.setWeight(newWeight);
					} else { //output is one so reward since winning neuron should have
fired for this output neuron
						BigDecimal newWeight =
						neighbor.weight().add(deltaWeight);
						neighbor.setWeight(newWeight);

						backwardNeighbor.setWeight(newWeight);
					}
				}
	}

	private boolean isOutputComplete(List<BigDecimal> expectedOutput){

			List<BigDecimal> actualOutput = new ArrayList<BigDecimal>();
			for(int cnt1 = 0; cnt1 < expectedOutput.size(); cnt1++){
					BigDecimal summation = BigDecimal.ZERO;
					for(Layer kohonenLayer : kohonenLayers){
						Neuron maximumNeuron =
						kohonenLayer.maximumActivatedNeuron();
						BigDecimal weight =
						maximumNeuron.forwardNeighbors().get(cnt1).weight();
						summation = summation.add(weight);
					}
					actualOutput.add(summation);
			}

			for(int cnt = 0; cnt < expectedOutput.size(); cnt++){
					BigDecimal expected = expectedOutput.get(cnt);
					BigDecimal actual = actualOutput.get(cnt);
```

```
					if(expected.compareTo(BigDecimal.ZERO) == 0){
						if(actual.compareTo(new BigDecimal(-1)) >= 0) return false;
						continue;
					}

					if(actual.compareTo(BigDecimal.ONE) < 0) return false;

				}
				return true;
		}

		@Override
		public LinkedHashMap<String, BigDecimal> train(List<List<List<BigDecimal>>>
inputs, List<List<BigDecimal>> expectedOutputs) {
				Calendar calStart = Calendar.getInstance();

				List<List<List<BigDecimal>>> normalizedInputs = new
ArrayList<List<List<BigDecimal>>>();
				for(List<List<BigDecimal>> input : inputs){
					List<List<BigDecimal>> normalizedInput = new
ArrayList<List<BigDecimal>>();
					for(List<BigDecimal> subword : input){
						normalizedInput.add(CommonUtils.normalize(subword));
					}
					normalizedInputs.add(normalizedInput);
				}

				//maintains which outputs are incomplete. When all outputs are complete, then
this is empty and we stop training since that means we have converged.
				List<List<BigDecimal>> incompleteOutputs = new
ArrayList<List<BigDecimal>>();
				for(List<BigDecimal> output : expectedOutputs)
incompleteOutputs.add(output);

				for(int iteration = 0; iteration < maxIterations; iteration++){
					this.totalIterations++;

					int currentIndex = iteration % inputs.size();
					List<List<BigDecimal>> normalized =
normalizedInputs.get(currentIndex);
					List<BigDecimal> expectedOutput =
expectedOutputs.get(currentIndex);

					//The input is normalized and so are the storage weights (input to
kohonen layer weights), so lets feedforward so that we have outputs at the kohonen layer
					feedForward(normalized);

					//if the expected and actual outputs are close enough, then mark as
completed training for that expected output
					if(incompleteOutputs.contains(expectedOutput) &&
isOutputComplete(expectedOutput)) incompleteOutputs.remove(expectedOutput);
```

```
                    //if no more outputs are incomplete then we have converged so end
the training
                    if(incompleteOutputs.isEmpty()) break;

                    //choose the output neuron with maximum activation w*x. Why?
Because this is the neuron for which the weight and input vectors are closest to each other.
                    for(int cnt = 0; cnt < kohonenLayers.size(); cnt++){
                         //extract the subword and current kohonen layer to examine
                         Layer kohonenLayer = kohonenLayers.get(cnt);
                         List<BigDecimal> subword = normalized.get(cnt);
                         Layer inputLayer = inputLayers.get(cnt);

                         BigDecimal alpha = learningRate(learningRate, iteration);

                         //pick the neuron in each kohonen layer that has the max
                         output
                         Neuron maximumNeuron =
                         kohonenLayer.maximumActivatedNeuron();

                         //if just one neuron exists in the kohonen layer and it's the
first input, then lets adjust weights to make the lone neuron in each kohonen layer the winner
                         if(kohonenLayer.size() == 1 && iteration == 0){
                              //declare the winning neuron
                              maximumNeuron.declaredWinner();

                              //while the only neuron is not close enough to
output of 1, keep updating weights.

                              updateWeightsForWinningNeuron
(maximumNeuron, alpha, subword);

                              //Now that we have the winning neuron lets
update its output to 1.0 and the other neurons to 0.0
                              //updateNeuronOutputsForKohonenLayer
(maximumNeuron, kohonenLayer);

                              //now let's update the link weights
                              updateLinkWeightsForWinningNeuron
(maximumNeuron, expectedOutput);

                              continue;
                         }
                         //otherwise, this is a subsequent pattern input, not the first
input

                         //the winning neuron of all the neurons in the current
kohonen layer has its link weights updated if its value is at least 0.95
                         if(maximumNeuron.output().compareTo(new
BigDecimal(0.95)) >= 0){
                              //declare the winning neuron
                              maximumNeuron.declaredWinner();
```

```
                                                //successful winning neuron so no need to update
weights, just the link weights (that is, the weights going to the output layer)
                                                updateLinkWeightsForWinningNeuron
(maximumNeuron, expectedOutput);
                                                continue;

                                        }

                                        //otherwise the winning neuron is not within 0.05 of 1.0 and
hence need to update the weight vector for it. This means we need to create a new neuron and
declare that as the winner.
                                        Neuron newNeuron = new Neuron();
                                        kohonenLayer.addNeuron(newNeuron);

                                        //declare the winning neuron
                                        newNeuron.declaredWinner();

                                        //connect it to all the corresponding input layer neurons,
including normalized weights
                                        List<BigDecimal> normalizedWeights = new
ArrayList<BigDecimal>();
                                        for(@SuppressWarnings("unused") Neuron inputNeuron :
inputLayer){
                                                BigDecimal newWeight = random();
                                                normalizedWeights.add(newWeight);
                                        }
                                        normalizedWeights =
CommonUtils.normalize(normalizedWeights);

                                        for(int cnt1 = 0; cnt1 < inputLayer.size(); cnt1++){
                                                Neuron inputNeuron = inputLayer.neuron(cnt1);
                                                BigDecimal normalizedWeight =
                                                normalizedWeights.get(cnt1);
                                                newNeuron.addBackwardNeighbor(newNeuron,
                                                inputNeuron, normalizedWeight);
                                                inputNeuron.addForwardNeighbor(inputNeuron,
                                                newNeuron, normalizedWeight);
                                        }

                                        //next add link weights to the output layer
                                        for(Neuron outputNeuron : outputLayer){
                                                BigDecimal newWeight = random();
                                                newNeuron.addForwardNeighbor(newNeuron,
outputNeuron, newWeight);
                                                outputNeuron.addBackwardNeighbor
(outputNeuron, newNeuron, newWeight);
                                        }

                                        //finally, update the output value of the new winning neuron
                                        newNeuron.applySummation();
                                        newNeuron.applyActivationFunction();
```

```
                                    //while the winning neuron is not close enough to output of
1, keep updating weights
                                    updateWeightsForWinningNeuron(newNeuron,
newNeuron.output(), subword);

                                    //Now that we have the winning neuron lets update its
output to 1.0 and the other neurons to 0.0
                                    //updateNeuronOutputsForKohonenLayer(newNeuron,
kohonenLayer);

                                    //now let's update the link weights
                                    updateLinkWeightsForWinningNeuron(newNeuron,
expectedOutput);
                        }
                }

                buildTrainedWeightsMap();
                printTrainedWeights();

                Calendar calEnd = Calendar.getInstance();

                this.duration = calEnd.getTimeInMillis() - calStart.getTimeInMillis();
                this.error = BigDecimal.ZERO;
                printStatistics();
                return trainedWeights;
        }

        @Override
        public void test(List<List<List<BigDecimal>>> inputs, List<List<BigDecimal>>
expectedOutputs) {
                int correct = 0;
                for(int cnt = 0; cnt < inputs.size(); cnt++){
                        List<List<BigDecimal>> input = inputs.get(cnt);
                        List<List<BigDecimal>> normalized = new
ArrayList<List<BigDecimal>>();

                        for(List<BigDecimal> subword : input){
                                normalized.add(CommonUtils.normalize(subword));
                        }

                        List<BigDecimal> expectedOutput = null;
                        if(expectedOutputs != null)
                                expectedOutput = expectedOutputs.get(cnt);

                        feedForward(normalized);

                        for(Layer kohonenLayer : kohonenLayers){
                                Neuron maximumNeuron =
                                kohonenLayer.maximumActivatedNeuron();
                                for(Neuron neuron : kohonenLayer){
                                        if(neuron == maximumNeuron)
                                                neuron.setOutput(BigDecimal.ONE);
```

```
                    else
                                neuron.setOutput(BigDecimal.ZERO);
            }
        }

        outputLayer.feedForward();

        System.out.println();
        System.out.println();

        printWinnerStatistics();

        System.out.println();
        System.out.println();

        printOutputs(normalized, expectedOutput, outputLayer.outputs());

        if(isCorrect(expectedOutput, outputLayer.outputs())) correct++;
    }

    System.out.println();
    System.out.println();

    BigDecimal accuracy = CommonUtils.ratio(new BigDecimal(correct), new
BigDecimal(inputs.size()));
    System.out.println("Accuracy: " + accuracy);

}

private boolean isCorrect(List<BigDecimal> expectedOutput, List<BigDecimal>
actualOutput){
    for(int cnt = 0; cnt < expectedOutput.size(); cnt++){
        BigDecimal expected = expectedOutput.get(cnt);
        BigDecimal actual = actualOutput.get(cnt);

        if(expected.compareTo(BigDecimal.ZERO) == 0){
            if(actual.compareTo(new BigDecimal(0)) > 0) return false;
            continue;
        }

        if(actual.compareTo(BigDecimal.ONE) < 0) return false;
    }
    return true;
}

private void printWinnerStatistics(){
    for(int cnt = 0; cnt < kohonenLayers.size(); cnt++){
        Layer kohonenLayer = kohonenLayers.get(cnt);
        System.out.print("[SOM][" + (cnt + 1) + "]");
        for(Neuron neuron : kohonenLayer){
            int neuronId = neuron.id();
            int noOfWins = neuron.noOfWins();
```

```
                                    System.out.print("[Neuron][" + neuronId + "][" +
                                    noOfWins + "]");
                              }
                              System.out.println();
                  }
        } ...............
INTERRUPTED
```

Lastar Code Incorporates the Following Text Classicication Code

TextClassification.java

```
package uic.edu.textclassification.lamstar;

import java.io.File;
import java.math.BigDecimal;
import java.util.ArrayList;
import java.util.LinkedHashMap;
import java.util.List;

import nlp.cs.uic.edu.CorpusUtilities.parser.ParserUtil;
import nlp.cs.uic.edu.CorpusUtilities.util.PunctuationUtil;
import nlp.cs.uic.edu.shared_utilities.shared_containers.Pair;
import nlp.cs.uic.edu.shared_utilities.shared_helpers.FileUtil;
import nlp.cs.uic.edu.shared_utilities.shared_parsers.DynamicTextReader;
import nlp.cs.uic.edu.shared_utilities.shared_parsers.DynamicTextWriter;
import uic.edu.characterrecognition.parser.Parser;
import uic.edu.neuralnetwork.lamstar.LamstarNeuralNetwork;
import uic.edu.neuralnetwork.shared.utils.CommonUtils;
import uic.edu.neuralnetwork.lamstar.ForwardFeedNeuralNetwork.LearningRateMode;

public class TextClassification {
          public static void main(String [] args){
                    boolean isModifiedLamstar = false;

                    int sentenceLengthLimit = 3;

                    File unprocessedDataFile = null;

                    File preprocessedDataFile = null;

                    File indexedDataFile = null;

                    List<File> unprocessedDataFiles = null;

                    List<List<List<BigDecimal>>> subwords = null;
                    List<List<BigDecimal>> expectedOutputs = null;

                    LinkedHashMap<String,String> labelMap = null;
                    Pair<List<List<List<BigDecimal>>>, List<List<BigDecimal>> >
modelData = null;
```

```
LinkedHashMap<String,String> vocabulary = null;

labelMap = new LinkedHashMap<String, String>();
labelMap.put("Based on data", "0 0");
labelMap.put("Based on template", "0 1");
labelMap.put("Windows Management", "1 0");

unprocessedDataFiles = new ArrayList<File>();
unprocessedDataFiles.add(new
File("../TextClassification/src/main/java/uic/edu/textclassification/lamstar/data/unprocessedtrainin
gdata.data"));
unprocessedDataFiles.add(new
File("../TextClassification/src/main/java/uic/edu/textclassification/lamstar/data/unprocessedtesting
data.data"));

vocabulary = buildVocabulary(unprocessedDataFiles, labelMap, 3);

unprocessedDataFile = unprocessedDataFiles.get(0);

preprocessedDataFile = new
File("../TextClassification/src/main/java/uic/edu/textclassification/lamstar/data/preprocessedtraini
ngdata.data");

indexedDataFile = new
File("../TextClassification/src/main/java/uic/edu/textclassification/lamstar/data/trainingdata.data")
;

modelData = preprocessAndExtractModelData(unprocessedDataFile,
preprocessedDataFile, indexedDataFile, sentenceLengthLimit, vocabulary, labelMap);

subwords = modelData.getFirst();
expectedOutputs = modelData.getSecond();

uic.edu.neuralnetwork.lamstar.NeuralNetwork lamstar = new
LamstarNeuralNetwork(sentenceLengthLimit, 16, 2, new BigDecimal(0.80),
LearningRateMode.CONSTANT, 10000, new BigDecimal(0.00001), isModifiedLamstar);
lamstar.train(subwords, expectedOutputs);

unprocessedDataFile = unprocessedDataFiles.get(1);

preprocessedDataFile = new
File("../TextClassification/src/main/java/uic/edu/textclassification/lamstar/data/preprocessedtestin
gdata.data");

indexedDataFile = new
File("../TextClassification/src/main/java/uic/edu/textclassification/lamstar/data/testingdata.data");

modelData = preprocessAndExtractModelData(unprocessedDataFile,
preprocessedDataFile, indexedDataFile, sentenceLengthLimit, vocabulary, labelMap);
subwords = modelData.getFirst();
expectedOutputs = modelData.getSecond();
```

```
                    lamstar.test(subwords, expectedOutputs);

//                  unprocessedDataFiles = new ArrayList<File>();
//                  unprocessedDataFiles.add(new
File("../TextClassification/src/main/java/uic/edu/textclassification/lamstar/data/unprocessedaggreg
atetrainingdata.data"));
//                  unprocessedDataFiles.add(new
File("../TextClassification/src/main/java/uic/edu/textclassification/lamstar/data/unprocessedaggreg
atetestingdata.data"));
//
//                  vocabulary = buildVocabulary(unprocessedDataFiles, labelMap, 3);
//
//                  labelMap = new LinkedHashMap<String, String>();
//                  labelMap.put("Aggregate neighborhood", "0 0");
//                  labelMap.put("Aggregate time", "0 1");
//                  labelMap.put("Aggregate crime-type", "1 0");
//                  labelMap.put("Aggregate location-type", "1 1");
//
//                  unprocessedDataFile = unprocessedDataFiles.get(0);
//                  preprocessedDataFile = new
File("../TextClassification/src/main/java/uic/edu/textclassification/lamstar/data/preprocessedaggre
gatetrainingdata.data");
//                  indexedDataFile = new
File("../TextClassification/src/main/java/uic/edu/textclassification/lamstar/data/aggregatetrainingd
ata.data");
//
//                  modelData = preprocessAndExtractModelData(unprocessedDataFile,
preprocessedDataFile, indexedDataFile, sentenceLengthLimit, vocabulary, labelMap);
//
//                  subwords = modelData.getFirst();
//                  expectedOutputs = modelData.getSecond();
//
//                  uic.edu.neuralnetwork.lamstar.NeuralNetwork aggregateLamstar = new
LamstarNeuralNetwork(sentenceLengthLimit, 16, 2, new BigDecimal(0.80),
LearningRateMode.CONSTANT, 10000, new BigDecimal(0.00001), true);
//                  aggregateLamstar.train(subwords, expectedOutputs);
//
//                  unprocessedDataFile = unprocessedDataFiles.get(1);
//                  preprocessedDataFile = new
File("../TextClassification/src/main/java/uic/edu/textclassification/lamstar/data/preprocessedaggre
gatetestingdata.data");
//                  indexedDataFile = new
File("../TextClassification/src/main/java/uic/edu/textclassification/lamstar/data/aggregatetestingda
ta.data");
//
//                  modelData = preprocessAndExtractModelData(unprocessedDataFile,
preprocessedDataFile, indexedDataFile, sentenceLengthLimit, vocabulary, labelMap);
//
//                  subwords = modelData.getFirst();
//                  expectedOutputs = modelData.getSecond();
//
//                  aggregateLamstar.test(subwords, expectedOutputs);
```

```
//
//                    unprocessedDataFiles = new ArrayList<File>();
//                    unprocessedDataFiles.add(new
File("../TextClassification/src/main/java/uic/edu/textclassification/lamstar/data/unprocessedfiltertr
ainingdata.data"));
//                    unprocessedDataFiles.add(new
File("../TextClassification/src/main/java/uic/edu/textclassification/lamstar/data/unprocessedfilterte
stingdata.data"));
//
//                    vocabulary = buildVocabulary(unprocessedDataFiles, labelMap, 3);
//
//                    labelMap = new LinkedHashMap<String, String>();
//                    labelMap.put("Filter neighborhood", "0 0");
//                    labelMap.put("Filter time", "0 1");
//                    labelMap.put("Filter crime-type", "1 0");
//                    labelMap.put("Filter location-type", "1 1");
//
//                    unprocessedDataFile = unprocessedDataFiles.get(0);
//                    preprocessedDataFile = new
File("../TextClassification/src/main/java/uic/edu/textclassification/lamstar/data/preprocessedfiltert
rainingdata.data");
//                    indexedDataFile = new
File("../TextClassification/src/main/java/uic/edu/textclassification/lamstar/data/filtertrainingdata.d
ata");
//
//                    modelData = preprocessAndExtractModelData(unprocessedDataFile,
preprocessedDataFile, indexedDataFile, sentenceLengthLimit, vocabulary, labelMap);
//
//                    subwords = modelData.getFirst();
//                    expectedOutputs = modelData.getSecond();
//
//                    uic.edu.neuralnetwork.lamstar.NeuralNetwork filterLamstar = new
LamstarNeuralNetwork(sentenceLengthLimit, 16, 2, new BigDecimal(0.80),
LearningRateMode.CONSTANT, 10000, new BigDecimal(0.00001), true);
//                    filterLamstar.train(subwords, expectedOutputs);
//
//                    unprocessedDataFile = unprocessedDataFiles.get(1);
//                    preprocessedDataFile = new
File("../TextClassification/src/main/java/uic/edu/textclassification/lamstar/data/preprocessedfiltert
estingdata.data");
//                    indexedDataFile = new
File("../TextClassification/src/main/java/uic/edu/textclassification/lamstar/data/filtertestingdata.da
ta");
//
//                    modelData = preprocessAndExtractModelData(unprocessedDataFile,
preprocessedDataFile, indexedDataFile, sentenceLengthLimit, vocabulary, labelMap);
//
//                    subwords = modelData.getFirst();
//                    expectedOutputs = modelData.getSecond();
//
//                    filterLamstar.test(subwords, expectedOutputs);
        }
```

```
	public static Pair<List<List<List<BigDecimal>>>, List<List<BigDecimal>> > preprocessAndExtractModelData(File unprocessedDataFile, File preprocessedDataFile, File indexedDataFile, int sentenceLengthLimit, LinkedHashMap<String,String> vocabulary, LinkedHashMap<String,String> labelMap){
		LinkedHashMap<String,String> unprocessedData = new DynamicTextReader(unprocessedDataFile).readMapping();

		List<String> preprocessed = preprocess(unprocessedData, labelMap, sentenceLengthLimit);

		write(preprocessed, preprocessedDataFile);

		List<String> indexed = extractIndex(preprocessed, vocabulary);

		write(indexed, indexedDataFile);

		LinkedHashMap<List<BigDecimal>,List<BigDecimal>> inputOutputMap = Parser.Parse(indexedDataFile);
		List<List<BigDecimal>> inputs = new ArrayList<List<BigDecimal>>(inputOutputMap.keySet());
		List<List<List<BigDecimal>>> subwords = Parser.toSubwords(inputs, 16);
		List<List<BigDecimal>> expectedOutputs = new ArrayList<List<BigDecimal>>(inputOutputMap.values());

		return new Pair<List<List<List<BigDecimal>>>, List<List<BigDecimal>> >(subwords,expectedOutputs);
	}

	public static LinkedHashMap<String,String> buildVocabulary(List<File> unprocessedDataFiles, LinkedHashMap<String,String> labelMap, int sentenceLengthLimit){
		List<String> preprocessed = new ArrayList<String>();
		for(File unprocessedDataFile : unprocessedDataFiles){
			LinkedHashMap<String,String> unprocessedData = new DynamicTextReader(unprocessedDataFile).readMapping();
			List<String> preprocessedData = preprocess(unprocessedData, labelMap, sentenceLengthLimit);
			preprocessed.addAll(preprocessedData);
		}
		return dataToIndex(preprocessed);
	}

	public static void write(List<String> data, File outputFile){
		FileUtil.deleteFile(outputFile);
		DynamicTextWriter writer = new DynamicTextWriter(outputFile, DynamicTextWriter.APPEND_ON);
		writer.write(data.toArray(new String[data.size()]), "\n");
	}

	public static List<String> preprocess(LinkedHashMap<String,String> unprocessedData, LinkedHashMap<String,String> labelMap, int sentenceLengthFilter){
		File stopWordsFile = new File("../TextClassification/src/main/java/uic/edu/textclassification/lamstar/data/stopwords.txt");
```

```
                List<String> stopWords = new DynamicTextReader(stopWordsFile).readList();

                File contractionWordsFile = new
File("../TextClassification/src/main/java/uic/edu/textclassification/lamstar/data/contractions.txt");
                LinkedHashMap<String,String> contractions = new
DynamicTextReader(contractionWordsFile).readMapping();

                List<String> preprocessed = new ArrayList<String>();
                for(String line : unprocessedData.keySet()){
                        String processed = line.toLowerCase();
                        processed = ParserUtil.replaceLineTokens(processed, contractions);
                        processed = ParserUtil.removeLineTokens(processed, stopWords);
                        processed = ParserUtil.lemmatize(processed);
                        processed = ParserUtil.removeSpecialCharacters(processed);
                        processed = PunctuationUtil.removeAllPunctuation(processed);
                        int sentenceLength = processed.split(" ").length;
                        if(sentenceLength != sentenceLengthFilter) continue;
                        preprocessed.add(processed);
                        preprocessed.add(labelMap.get(unprocessedData.get(line)));
                }
                return preprocessed;
        }

        public static LinkedHashMap<String,String> dataToIndex(List<String> data){
                int j = 1;
                LinkedHashMap<String,String> vocabulary = new LinkedHashMap<String,
String>();
                for(int cnt = 0; cnt < data.size(); cnt++){
                        String line = data.get(cnt);
                        if(cnt%2 == 1) continue;
                        String[] tokens = line.split(" ");
                        for(String token : tokens){
                                String index = vocabulary.get(token);
                                if(index == null){
                                        String binary = CommonUtils.toBinary(j++,16);
                                        vocabulary.put(token, binary);
                                }
                        }
                }
                return vocabulary;
        }

        public static List<String> extractIndex(List<String> data,
LinkedHashMap<String,String> vocabulary){
                for(int cnt = 0; cnt < data.size(); cnt++){
                        String line = data.get(cnt);
                        if(cnt%2 == 1) continue;
                        String[] tokens = line.split(" ");
                        String indexed = "";
                        for(String token : tokens) indexed = indexed +
                        vocabulary.get(token) + " ";
                        indexed = indexed.substring(0, indexed.length() - 1);
```

```
                        data.set(cnt, indexed);
                    }
                    return data;
            }
}
```

PART 2: Code for Support Vector Machine (SVM) Classifier — Also See Attached Actual Transcribed Script (Unprocessed) at End of Code

ClassifierHelper.java

```
package nlp.cs.uic.edu.Classifier.classifier;

import java.io.File;
import java.util.ArrayList;

import nlp.cs.uic.edu.Classifier.shared.TextReader;
import weka.classifiers.Classifier;
import weka.classifiers.Evaluation;
import weka.classifiers.evaluation.NominalPrediction;
import weka.classifiers.evaluation.Prediction;
import weka.classifiers.functions.SMO;
import weka.core.Instances;
import weka.core.tokenizers.NGramTokenizer;
import weka.filters.Filter;
import weka.filters.unsupervised.attribute.StringToWordVector;

public class ClassifierHelper {
            public static void classify(File file){
                    // Set the tokenizer
                    NGramTokenizer tokenizer = new NGramTokenizer();
                    tokenizer.setNGramMinSize(1);
                    tokenizer.setNGramMaxSize(1);
                    tokenizer.setDelimiters("\\W");

                    Instances dataset = dataSet(file);
                    StringToWordVector filter = new StringToWordVector();
                    try {
                            filter.setInputFormat(dataset);
                    } catch (Exception e1) {
                            e1.printStackTrace();
                    }
                    filter.setTokenizer(tokenizer);
                    filter.setWordsToKeep(1000000);
                    filter.setDoNotOperateOnPerClassBasis(true);
                    filter.setLowerCaseTokens(true);

                    Instances outputset = null;

                    // Filter the input instances into the output ones
                    try {
                            outputset = Filter.useFilter(dataset,filter);
```

```
		} catch (Exception e1) {
			// TODO Auto-generated catch block
			e1.printStackTrace();
		}

		// Do 10-split cross validation
		Instances[][] split = crossValidationSplit(outputset, 10);

		Instances[] trainingSplits = split[0];
		Instances[] testingSplits = split[1];

		Classifier supportVectorMachineClassifier = new SMO();
		ArrayList<Prediction> predictions = new ArrayList<Prediction>();
		for(int row = 0; row < trainingSplits.length; row++){
			try {
				Evaluation validation =
ClassifierHelper.classify(supportVectorMachineClassifier, trainingSplits[row],
testingSplits[row]);
				predictions.addAll(validation.predictions());
				System.out.println(supportVectorMachineClassifier.toString());

			} catch (Exception e) {
				// TODO Auto-generated catch block
				e.printStackTrace();
			}
		}

		double accuracy = accuracy(predictions);

		System.out.println("Accuracy of " +
supportVectorMachineClassifier.getClass().getSimpleName() + ": "
				+ String.format("%.2f%%", accuracy)
				+ "\n---------------------------------");

	}

	public static Instances dataSet(File file){
		return TextReader.read(file);
	}

	public static Evaluation classify(Classifier model, Instances trainingSet, Instances
testingSet) throws Exception {
		Evaluation evaluation = new Evaluation(trainingSet);

		model.buildClassifier(trainingSet);
		evaluation.evaluateModel(model, testingSet);

		return evaluation;
	}

	public static double accuracy(ArrayList<Prediction> predictions) {
		double correct = 0;
```

```
            for (int i = 0; i < predictions.size(); i++) {
                    NominalPrediction np = (NominalPrediction) predictions.get(i);
                    if (np.predicted() == np.actual()) {
                            correct++;
                    }
            }

            return 100 * correct / predictions.size();
    }

    public static Instances[][] crossValidationSplit(Instances data, int numberOfFolds) {
            Instances[][] split = new Instances[2][numberOfFolds];

            for (int i = 0; i < numberOfFolds; i++) {
                    split[0][i] = data.trainCV(numberOfFolds, i);
                    split[1][i] = data.testCV(numberOfFolds, i);
            }

            return split;
    }
}
```

Unprocessed Transcript of Conversation used for Classification:

unprocessedtrainingdata.data

Can you show me in separate windows?	Windows Management
I don't need this chart, can you move it?	Windows Management
I want to keep this one.	Windows Management
This one is not useful in my purpose.	Windows Management
Can you widen the *x*-axis?	Windows Management
Can we remove this graph?	Windows Management
Can we remove the 02-P_N_G graph?	Windows Management
Can we see the 01-P_N_G one?	Windows Management
Sorry, can you minimize U_I_C?	Windows Management
So can we remove this graph from the screen?	Windows Management
Can we align the 2013 graph so it's easier?	Windows Management
Can you place the plot where it was on the screen?	Windows Management
Ok so can you close all these graphs?	Windows Management
Can I look at 10-3-P_N_G plot?	Windows Management
Sorry, could you make it a little smaller?	Windows Management
Could you stack them on the side?	Windows Management
Could you move it over just a little bit?	Windows Management
Can you show me separate graphs by year?	Windows Management
Can I like save it or put it over there?	Windows Management
You can close these graphs as I won't be needing them anymore.	Windows Management
Yeah I don't need this one here.	Windows Management
Did we have a graph around here for that?	Windows Management
Could you maximize the Loop map?	Windows Management
Can you bring up the 02-5-P_N_G and 02-4-P_N_G?	Windows Management

Can you show me the distribution of crime-type?	Based on data
Can you do number-of-crime for month-of-year?	Based on data
Can you show me the number-of-crime in each year?	Based on data
Can you show me the number-of-crime based on location-type?	Based on data
What about number-of-crime according to day-of-the-week?	Based on data
With this graph I want to know which time-of-day is the number-of-crime very high?	Based on data
Can you have crime-type for month-of-year?	Based on data
Can you give analysis through the day-of-week?	Based on data
Can you give me that graph of the crime-type each year?	Based on data
Can we see all number-of-crime by each neighborhood?	Based on data
During what time-of-day is the number-of-crime maximum?	Based on data
Ok so what crime-type is the number-of-crime?	Based on data
Ok is there a map of where the crimes occurred in those neighborhoods?	Based on data
Could I see number-of-crime by month-of-year?	Based on data
Could you get this number-of-crime information by crime-type?	Based on data
Is there a graph for just all four neighborhoods?	Based on data
Can you show me burglary and assault?	Based on template
Can we see the map with deceptive-practice?	Based on template
Can we have the map of thefts?	Based on template
Could I get these same charts but just for battery?	Based on template
Can we just focus on Loop for this data?	Based on template
So let's look at 12-P_M to 6-P_M block in terms of number-of-crime.	Based on template
Can we just focus on Loop for this data?	Based on template
So let's look at 12-P_M to 6-P_M block in terms of number-of-crime.	Based on template

A.8.14. Speech Recognition (M Racha)

PART 1: CNN (LeNet) Code Used in is a theano.tensor Program

COMPUTATIONAL LANGUAGE USED: MATLAB

Main.m

```
clc;
clear all;
Fs=16000;
[TrainData,TestData]= ReadData;
CharData=[( 'Violet', 'Blue', 'Green', 'Yellow', 'Orange', 'Red', 'White', 'Black', 'Pink', 'Brown')];

for k= 1:150
t=0.04;
j=1;
for i=1:16000
if(abs(TrainData(i))>t)
   y1(j)=TrainData(i);
   j=j+1;
end
```

```
end
y2=y1/(max(abs(y1)));
y3=[y2,zeros(1,1500-length(y2))];
y=filter([1 -0.95],1,y3');        %pre-emphasis filter

%%frame blocking
blocklen=400;    %25ms block
overlap=160;
block(1,:)=y(1:400);
for i=1:18
  block(i+1,:)=y(i*240:(i*240+blocklen-1));
end
w=hamming(blocklen);
y1=w*y
 p=12;% no of coefficnets
Mscoeff(i,:) = mfscf(p,x(i),16000);  % spectral coefficients
end
rand('state',0)
cnn.layers = {
  struct('type', 'i') %input layer
  struct('type', 'c', 'outputmaps', 4, 'kernelsize', 1) %convolution layer
  struct('type', 's', 'scale', 2) %Max pooling layer
  struct('type', 'c', 'outputmaps', 8, 'kernelsize', 1) %convolution layer
  struct('type', 's', 'scale', 2) %Max pooling layer
  struct('type', 'c', 'outputmaps', 12, 'kernelsize', 1) %convolution layer
  struct('type', 'f', 'outputs', 10) %fully connected
};
opts.alpha = 0.1;
opts.batchsize = 50;
opts.numepochs = 10;
train_label = zeros(150,1);
test_label = zeros(50,1);
for i = 1:150
temp = i%15;
train_label = temp;
end
cnn = cnn_setup(cnn, Mscoeff, train_label);
cnn = cnn_train(cnn, Mscoeff, train_label, opts);
[er, bad] = cnn_test(cnn, testData, test_label);
end
```

mfscf.m

```
function [mfccMatrix]=mfcf(num,s,Fs)
%Computes and returns the mfsc coefficients for a speech signal s
n=512;      %Number of FFT points
Tf=0.025;     %Frame duration in seconds
N=Fs*Tf;     %Number of samples per frame
fn=25;      %Number of mel filters
```

```
l=length(s);  %total number of samples in speech
Ts=0.01;      %Frame step in seconds
FrameStep=Fs*Ts;  %Frame step in samples
a=1;
b=[1, -0.97];   %a and b are high pass filter coefficients
noFrames=floor(l/FrameStep);  %Maximum no of frames in speech sample
FMatrix=zeros(noFrames-2, num); %Matrix to hold cepstral coefficients
lifter=1:num;        %Lifter vector index
lifter=1+floor((num)/2)*(sin(lifter*pi/num));%raised sine lifter version

if mean(abs(s)) > 0.01
  s=s/max(s);          %Normalises to compensate for mic vol differences
end
%Segment the signal into overlapping frames and compute MFCC coefficients
for i=1:noFrames-2
  frame=s((i-1)*FrameStep+1:(i-1)*FrameStep+N);
 %Holds individual frames
  Ce1=sum(frame.^2);   %Frame energy
  Ce2=max(Ce1,2e-22);    %floors to 2 X 10 raised to power -22
  Ce=log(Ce2);
  framef=filter(b,a,frame);  %High pass pre-emphasis filter
  F=framef.*hamming(N);
 %multiplies each frame with hamming window
  FFTo=fft(F,N);      %computes the fft
  melf=melbankm(fn,n,Fs);  %creates 24 filter, mel filter bank
  halfn=1+floor(n/2);
  spectr1=log10(melf*abs(FFTo(1:halfn)).^2);
%result is mel-scale filtered
  spectr=max(spectr1(:),1e-22);
  mfscMatrix(i, :)=spectr';  %assigns mfsc coeffs to succesive rows
end
```

ReadData.m

```
function [TrainData,TestData]=ReadData;
neuralData= load('speech_dataset.mat'); % this file has the 200 input signals i.e. 20 different
speakers
for i=1:15
for j= 1:10
TrainData (i,:) = neuralData(i,j);
end
end
for i=15:20
for j=1:10
TestData(i,: ) = neuralData(i,j);
end
end
end
```

cnn_setup.m

```
function net = cnn_setup( net,x,y )
% cnn
 inputmaps=1;
 [d1,d2,~]=size(x);
 mapsize=[d1,d2];
 for l=1:numel(net.layers)
   if strcmp(net.layers{l}.type,'s')
     mapsize=mapsize/net.layers{l}.scale;
     for i=1:inputmaps
       net.layers{l}.bias{i}=0;
     end
   end
   if strcmp(net.layers{l}.type,'c')
     mapsize=mapsize-net.layers{l}.kernelsize+1;
     in=inputmaps*net.layers{l}.kernelsize^2;
     out=net.layers{l}.outputmaps*net.layers{l}.kernelsize^2;
     for j=1:net.layers{l}.outputmaps
       for i=1:inputmaps
         net.layers{l}.kernel{i}{j}=(rand(net.layers{l}.kernelsize)-0.5)*2*sqrt(6/(in+out));
end
       net.layers{l}.bias{j}=0;
     end
     inputmaps=net.layers{l}.outputmaps;
       end
 end
 fvnum=prod(mapsize)*inputmaps;
 onum=size(y,1);

 net.ff_bias=zeros(onum,1);
 net.ff_weight=(rand(onum,fvnum)-0.5)*2*sqrt(6/fvnum+onum);
end
```

cnn_train.m

```
function net = cnn_train( net,x,y,opts )
%cnn
 m=size(x,3);
```

INTERRUPTED

……………

CONTINUED HERE

cnn_ff.m

```
function net = cnn_ff( net,x)
%cnn  n=numel(net.layers);
 net.layers{1}.out{1}=x;
 inputmaps=1;
 for l=2:n
```

```
    if strcmp(net.layers{l}.type, 'c')      %net.layers{l}.outputmaps
     for j=1:net.layers{l}.outputmaps
      z=zeros(size(net.layers{l-1}.out{1})-[(net.layers{l}.kernelsize)-1 (net.layers{l}.kernelsize)-1 0]);
       for i=1:inputmaps
         z=z+convn(net.layers{l-
1}.out{i},net.layers{l}.kernel{i}{j},'valid'
end
       net.layers{l}.out{j}=sigm(z+net.layers{l}.bias{j});%sigmoid
     end
     inputmaps=net.layers{l}.outputmaps;
    elseif strcmp(net.layers{l}.type, 's')
     for j=1:inputmaps%
       z=convn(net.layers{l-1}.out{j},ones(net.layers{l}.scale)/net.layers{l}.scale^2,'valid');
       net.layers{l}.out{j}=z(1:net.layers{l}.scale:end,1:net.layers{l}.scale:end,:);
     end
    end
  end
  net.fv=[];
%reshape
  for j=1:numel(net.layers{n}.out)
    s=size(net.layers{n}.out{j});
    net.fv=[net.fv;reshape(net.layers{n}.out{j},s(1)*s(2),s(3))];
  end
  net.out=sigm(net.ff_weight*net.fv+repmat(net.ff_bias,1,size(net.fv,2)));
end
```

cnn_bp.m

function net = cnn_bp(net,y) .....

INTERRUPTED

PART 2: LAMSTAR Computaional Language Used: MATLAB

Main.m

```
clc;
clear all;
Fs=16000;
[TrainData,TestData]= ReadData;
CharData=[( 'Violet', 'Blue', 'Green', 'Yellow', 'Orange', 'Red', 'White', 'Black', 'Pink',
'Brown')];
for k= 1:150
t=0.04;
j=1;
for i=1:16000
if(abs(TrainData(i))>t)
   y1(j)=TrainData(i);
   j=j+1;
end
end
y2=y1/(max(abs(y1)));
```

```
y3=[y2,zeros(1,1500-length(y2))];
y=filter([1 -0.95],1,y3');       %pre-emphasis filter
%%frame blocking
blocklen=400;   %25ms block
overlap=160;
block(1,:)=y(1:400);
for i=1:18
  block(i+1,:)=y(i*240:(i*240+blocklen-1));
end
p=12;      % no of coefficnets
Mcoeff(i,:) = mfccf(p,y(i),16000);
end;
Nsom=20;
NneuronSub=12;
NneuronSOM=10;
SOMS= SelfOrganizedMap;
end
```

mfccf.m

```
function [mfccMatrix]=mfcf(num,s,Fs)
%Computes and returns the mfcc coefficients for a speech signal s
n=512;      %Number of FFT points
Tf=0.025;     %Frame duration in seconds
N=Fs*Tf;     %Number of samples per frame
fn=25;      %Number of mel filters
l=length(s);   %total number of samples in speech
Ts=0.01;     %Frame step in seconds
FrameStep=Fs*Ts;  %Frame step in samples
a=1;
b=[1, -0.97];   %a and b are high pass filter coefficients

noFrames=floor(l/FrameStep);  %Maximum no of frames in speech sample
FMatrix=zeros(noFrames-2, num); %Matrix to hold cepstral coefficients
lifter=1:num;      %Lifter vector index
lifter=1+floor((num)/2)*(sin(lifter*pi/num));%raised sine lifter version

if mean(abs(s)) > 0.01
  s=s/max(s);         %Normalises to compensate for mic vol differences
end

%Segment the signal into overlapping frames and compute MFCC coefficients
for i=1:noFrames-2
  frame=s((i-1)*FrameStep+1:(i-1)*FrameStep+N);
 %Holds individual frames
  Ce1=sum(frame.^2);    %Frame energy
  Ce2=max(Ce1,2e-22);    %floors to 2 X 10 raised to power -22
  Ce=log(Ce2);
  framef=filter(b,a,frame);  %High pass pre-emphasis filter
  F=framef.*hamming(N);
 %multiplies each frame with hamming window
  FFTo=fft(F,N);      %computes the fft
  melf=melbankm(fn,n,Fs);  %creates 24 filter, mel filter bank
```

```
  halfn=1+floor(n/2);
  spectr1=log10(melf*abs(FFTo(1:halfn)).^2);
%result is mel-scale filtered
  spectr=max(spectr1(:),1e-22);
  c=dct(spectr);      %obtains DCT, changes to cepstral domain
  c(1)=Ce;        %replaces first coefficient
  coeffs=c(1:num);      %retains first num coefficients
  ncoeffs=coeffs.*lifter';  %Multiplies coefficients by lifter value
  mfccMatrix(i, :)=ncoeffs';  %assigns mfcc coeffs to succesive rows
end
```

SelfOrganizedMap.m

```
%Lamstar neural network
function SOM= SelfOrganizedMap

  SelfOrganizingMap[]_SOMCollection;
  SelfOrganizingMap_OutputNeuron;
   LinkWeight[][]=0;
      currentSOM=0;
  Train(input)
    datasets=input.length;
     size=input[1].length;
    SOMCollection=new SelfOrganizingMap[20];
for i=0:SOMCollection.length
        SOMCollection[i]=new SelfOrganizingMap(12,datasets);
    OutputNeuron=new SelfOrganizingMap(20,datasets);
    LinkWeight=new double[20][datasets];
    WinCount=new int[20][datasets];

    Subwords=new double[20][datasets][12];
for subwordIndex=1:20
for SetIndex=1:datasets
      Subwords[subwordIndex][SetIndex]=splitInput(input[SetIndex],subwordIndex);
end
for subwordIndex=1:20
      out=Subword+subwordIndex;
for SetIndex=0:datasets

for i=0:12
        out= Subwords([subwordIndex][SetIndex][i]);
end
end
end
end
```

INTERRUPTED

….

CONTINUED

```
%Linked weights
for i=1:LinkWeight.length
for j=1:LinkWeight[i].length
```

```
    Test(double(input));
    FinalSet=new(double[20]);
for subwordIndex=1:20
    firingNeuron=0
firingNeuron = SOMCollection[subwordIndex].winner(splitInput(input,subwordIndex));
FinalSet[subwordIndex]=LinkWeight[subwordIndex][firingNeuron];
end
% Test results
  result=OutputNeuron.winner(FinalSet);
end
end
   splitInput(double( input, x))
   subword()=new_double(12);
    index=0;
for i=x*12:(x+1)*12
     subword[index++]=input[i];
end
   punish(neuronNumber){
   LinkWeight[currentSOM][neuronNumber]-=0.5;

  reward(neuronNumber){
   LinkWeight[currentSOM][neuronNumber]+=1;
       WinCount[currentSOM][neuronNumber]+=1;
       fori=1:LinkWeight[currentSOM].length
if(i!=neuronNumber)
       punish(i);
end
end
end
```

A.8.15. Music Genre Classification (C Deshpande)

CNN/Python Code

```
File 1
import sys, os.path, json
import gaia2.fastyaml as yaml
from optparse import OptionParser
def convertJsonToSig(filelist_file, result_filelist_file):
  fl = yaml.load(open(filelist_file, 'r'))
  result_fl = fl
  errors = []
  for trackid, json_file in fl.iteritems():
    try:
      data = json.load(open(json_file))
      if 'tags' in data['metadata']:
        del data['metadata']['tags']
      if 'smpl_rt' in data['metadata']['audio_prop']:
        del data['metadata']['audio_prop']['smpl_rt']
      sig_file = os.path.splitext(json_file)[0] + '.sig'
```

```
    yaml.dump(data, open(sig_file, 'w'))
    result_fl[trackid] = sig_file
   except:
    errors += [json_file]
  yaml.dump(result_fl, open(result_filelist_file, 'w'))
  print "Failed to convert", len(errors), "files:"
  for e in errors:
   print e
  return len(errors) == 0
if __name__ == '__main__':
  parser = OptionParser(usage = '%prog [options] filelist_file result_filelist_file\n' +
"""
Converts json files found in filelist_file into *.sig yaml files compatible with
Gaia. The result files are written to the same directory where original files were
located.
"""
   )
  options, args = parser.parse_args()
  try:
   filelist_file = args[0]
   result_filelist_file = args[1]
  except:
   parser.print_help()
   sys.exit(1)
  convertJsonToSig(filelist_file, result_filelist_file)
```

File 2

```
def dumpFeaturesIntoJson(recordingID, jsonOutputFolder, genre):
  url = 'http://marsyasweb.appspot.com/download/data_sets/' + recordingID + '/low-level'
  response = urllib.urlopen(url).read()
  try:
   lowlevel = json.loads(response)
   outputFilename = jsonOutputFolder + '/' + genre +'/' + recordingID +'.json'

   with open(outputFilename, 'w+') as outfile:
    json.dump(lowlevel, outfile)

   return True
  except:
   return False

  #print lowlevel
```

File 3

```
def b_l(featureDict):
  return
featureDict['rhythm']['b_l']['median']


def dis(featureDict):
  return
featureDict['lowlevel']['dis']['median']
```

```
def t_d(featureDict):
  return
featureDict['tonal']['t_d_strength']

def t_e_t(featureDict):
  return
featureDict['tonal']['t_e_t_deviation']

def readThem2List(jsonPath):
  with open(jsonPath) as data_file:
    data = json.load(data_file)

    bl = b_l(data)
    ds = dis(data)
    td = t_d(data)
    te = t_e_t(data)

  return bl, ds, td, te
```

File 4

```
def groundtruthMaker(className, groundtruthDict):
  rDict = {}
  rDict['className'] = className
  rDict['groundTruth'] = groundtruthDict
  rDict['type'] = 'singleClass'
  rDict['version'] = 1.0
  #rStr = 'className: ' + className + '\n' + groundtruthStr + '\n' + 'type: singleClass' + '\n' +
'version: 1.0'
  return rDict
```

File 5

```
import compmusic as cm
import os
from os import listdir
from os.path import isfile, join

def jingjuRecordingIDreader(folder):
  mp3Files = []
  recordingIDs = []
  for name in listdir(folder):
    if not name.startswith('.'):
      name = "/Users/Chinmayi/Documents/Neural/Classical/No.5/" + name + '/'
      files = [ join(name, f) for f in listdir(name) if isfile(join(name,f)) and f.endswith('.mp3')]
      mp3Files = mp3Files + files

  ii = 1
  length = len(mp3Files)
  for f in mp3Files:
    recordingIDs.append(cm.file_metadata(f)['meta']['recordingid'])
    print 'reading recording ID ', ii, 'of total', length
    ii += 1
```

```
  return recordingIDs

File 6
import compmusic as cm
from compmusic import dunya as dy

dy.conn.set_token('0186a989507de593d7e83e530a7a5c1280507217')
def rockRecordingIDfetcher():
  '''this function get all recordingIDs for all rock artistis
  no need to query concerts for the recording IDs, because the rock
  api is well developped.'''
  # get artists
  rockArtists = dy.rock.get_artists()

  # get artist mbids
  rockMBIDs = []
  for rockArtist in rockArtists:
    rockMBIDs.append(rockArtist['mbid'])

  # get recordingID
  rockRecordingIDs = []
  ii = 1
  length = len(rockMBIDs)

  print 'fetching rock recording Ids... ...'
  for mbid in rockMBIDs:
    rdic = dy.rock.get_artist(mbid)
    rdic = rdic['recordings']

    if len(rdic) != 0:
      for recording in rdic:
        rockRecordingIDs.append(recording['mbid'])

    print 'fetching rock artist number ', ii, 'of total ', length
    ii += 1

return rockRecordingIDs
def jazzRecordingIDfetcher():
  '''this function get all recordingIDs for all jazz artistis
  no need to query releases for the recording IDs, because the jazz
  api is well developped.'''
  # get artists
  jazzArtists = dy.jazz.get_artists()

  # get artist mbids
  jazzMBIDs = []
  for jazzArtist in jazzArtists:
    jazzMBIDs.append(jazzArtist['mbid'])

  # get recordingID
  jazzRecordingIDs = []
  ii = 1
```

```
  length = len(jazzMBIDs)

  print 'fetching jazz recording Ids... ...'
  for mbid in jazzMBIDs:
    rdic = dy.jazz.get_artist(mbid)
    rdic = rdic['recordings']

    if len(rdic) != 0:
     for recording in rdic:
       jazzRecordingIDs.append(recording['mbid'])

    print 'fetching jazz artist number ', ii, 'of total ', length
    # if ii/float(length) > jj/20:
#      print 'fetched ', jj, '/', 20
#      jj += 1
    ii += 1
  return jazzRecordingIDs

def classicalRecordingIDfetcher():
  '''this function get all recordingIDs for all markam artistis
  we need to query releases firstly'''
  # get artists
  classicalArtists = dy.classical.get_artists()

  # get artist mbids
  classicalMBIDs = []
  for classicalArtist in classicalArtists:
    classicalMBIDs.append(classicalArtist['mbid'])

  # get recordingID
  classicalRecordingIDs = []
  ii = 1
  length = len(classicalMBIDs)
print 'fetching classical recording Ids... ...'
  for mbid in classicalMBIDs:
    rdic = dy.classical.get_artist(mbid)
    # print rdic

    if 'releases' in rdic:
      rdic = rdic['releases'] # release of the artist

      if len(rdic) != 0:
       for release in rdic:
         releaseDict = dy.classical.get_release(release['mbid'])
         recordingArray = releaseDict['recordings'] # recordings of the release
         if len(recordingArray) != 0:
          for recording in recordingArray:
            classicalRecordingIDs.append(recording['mbid'])

    print 'fetching markam artist number ', ii, 'of total ', length
    ii += 1
  return classicalRecordingIDs
```

A.8.16. Credit Card Fraud Detection (F Wang)

LNN-2 Code

```
ModifiedLamstarNetwork.m
% function lamstar = ModifiedLamstarNetwork(inputData, extraData, train_extra)
lamstar=[];
lamstar.SOMs=[];
numSubwords=16;

% lamstar.OutputNeurons=zeros(20,numSubwords);
LinkWeight1=zeros(20,numSubwords);
LinkWeight2=zeros(20,numSubwords);
% defaultWeight=[];
% defaultWeight=[defaultWeight -10];
% defaultWeight=[defaultWeight 10];
% offset = (defaultWeight(1) + defaultWeight(2))/2.0;
% range = abs(defaultWeight(2) - defaultWeight(1));
% linkweight1 = (rand(numSubwords,1) -0.5 )* range + offset;
% linkweight2 = (rand(numSubwords,1) -0.5 )* range + offset;
% lamstar.OutputNeurons=[linkweight1 linkweight2];

tolerance=0.05;
trainingData = generateLamstarData( inputData, 1, 4, 1);
trainingData(4).data=train_extra;

numGroup=size(trainingData,2);
SOMs=[];
defaultWeight=[];
defaultWeight=[defaultWeight 0];
defaultWeight=[defaultWeight 1];
alpha=0.8;

%training network
for i=1:numGroup
  numCases=size(trainingData(i).data,2);
  groupData=trainingData(i).data;
  for j=1:numCases
    data=groupData(j).input;
    output=groupData(j).output;
    %neuron weights
    if i==1&&j==1
     for k=1:numSubwords
       neurons=[];
       SOM=[];
       subword=data(k,:);
       offset = (defaultWeight(1) + defaultWeight(2))/2.0;
       range = abs(defaultWeight(2) - defaultWeight(1));
       weight = (rand(1,8) -0.5 )* range + offset;
       weight=weight./norm(weight);
       weight=weight+alpha.*(subword-weight);
```

```
      weight=weight./norm(weight);
      neuron.weight=weight;
      neuron.win=1;
      neurons=[neurons neuron];
      SOM.neurons=neurons;
      SOM.number=k;
      SOM.winNeuron=1;
      SOM.value=weight*(subword');
      SOMs=[SOMs SOM];
      if(output(1,1)>0.95)
        LinkWeight1(1,k)=0.05*20;
      else
        LinkWeight1(1,k)=-0.05*20;
      end
      if(output(1,2)>0.95)
        LinkWeight2(1,k)=0.05*20;
      else
        LinkWeight2(1,k)=-0.05*20;
      end
      LinkWeight1(1,k)=LinkWeight1(1,k)/1;
      LinkWeight2(1,k)=LinkWeight2(1,k)/1;
    end
    lamstar.SOMs=SOMs;

  else
   for k=1:numSubwords
     neuronIndex=1;
     subword=data(k,:);
     SOM_old=SOMs(k);
     numNeurons=size(SOM_old.neurons,2);
     flag=0;
     for s=1:numNeurons
       z=SOM_old.neurons(s).weight*(subword');
       if abs(1-z)<tolerance
         SOM=SOM_old;
         SOM.winNeuron=s;
         SOM.value=z;
         SOM.neurons(s).win=SOM.neurons(s).win+1;
         SOMs(k)=SOM;
         flag=1;
         neuronIndex=s;
         break;
       end
     end
     if flag==0
       offset = (defaultWeight(1) + defaultWeight(2))/2.0;
       range = abs(defaultWeight(2) - defaultWeight(1));
       weight = (rand(1,8) -0.5 )* range + offset;
       weight=weight./norm(weight);
       weight=weight+alpha.*(subword-weight);
       weight=weight./norm(weight);
       neuron.weight=weight;
```

```
          neuron.win=1;
          neurons=SOM_old.neurons;
          neurons=[neurons neuron];
          SOM=[];
          SOMs(k).neurons=neurons;
          SOMs(k).winNeuron=(numNeurons+1);
          SOMs(k).value=weight*(subword');
%            SOMs(k)=SOM;
          neuronIndex=(numNeurons+1);
        end
        if(output(1,1)>0.95)
          LinkWeight1(neuronIndex,k)=LinkWeight1(neuronIndex,k)+0.05*20;
        else
          LinkWeight1(neuronIndex,k)=LinkWeight1(neuronIndex,k)-0.05*20;
        end
        if(output(1,2)>0.95)
          LinkWeight2(neuronIndex,k)=LinkWeight2(neuronIndex,k)+0.05*20;
        else
          LinkWeight2(neuronIndex,k)=LinkWeight2(neuronIndex,k)-0.05*20;
        end
        LinkWeight1(neuronIndex,k)=
       LinkWeight1(neuronIndex,k)/(SOMs(k).neurons(neuronIndex).win);
        LinkWeight2(neuronIndex,k)=
       LinkWeight2(neuronIndex,k)/(SOMs(k).neurons(neuronIndex).win);
      end
      lamstar.SOMs=SOMs;
    end
    lamstar.linkweight1=LinkWeight1;
    lamstar.linkweight2=LinkWeight2;
  end
end

%testing
testingData = generateLamstarData( inputData, 30, 40, 2);
% testingData = generateLamstarExtraData( extraData, 2, 40, 2);
numGroup=size(testingData,2);
correct_number=0;
for i=1:numGroup
  numCases=size(testingData(i).data,2);
  groupData=testingData(i).data;
  for j=1:numCases
    data=groupData(j).input;
    output=groupData(j).output;
    sum1=0;
    sum2=0;
    for k=1:numSubwords
      neurons=lamstar.SOMs(k).neurons;
      numNeurons=size(neurons,2);
      subword=data(k,:);
      zmax=0;
      z_index=1;
      for s=1:numNeurons
```

```
      weight=neurons(s).weight;
      z=weight*(subword');
      if(zmax<z)
        zmax=z;
        z_index=s;
      end
    end
    sum1=sum1+lamstar.linkweight1(z_index,k);
    sum2=sum2+lamstar.linkweight2(z_index,k);
  end
  if sum1>0
    ans(1,1)=1;
  else
    ans(1,1)=0;
  end
  if sum2>0
    ans(1,2)=1;
  else
    ans(1,2)=0;
  end
  diff=abs(ans-output);
  if diff<0.01
    correct_number=correct_number+1;
  else
  end
 end
end
numCases=size(testingData(1).data,2);
correct_number=correct_number*1.0/numGroup/numCases*100;
result=[num2str(correct_number),'%'];
display(result)

end
```

A.8.17. Predicting Site for Oil Drilling from Permeability Data (S A Hussain)

LAMSTAR LNN-1 Code

```
% load the data
[input,inp_headers]=xlsread('well_619_IP_TRG','Input');
[output,out_header]=xlsread('well_619_IP_TRG','Target'
trnind=ceil(size(input,1)*3/4);


trninp=input(1:trnind,:);
tstinp=input(trnind+1:end,:);
```

```
trnout=output(1:trnind,:);
tstout=output(trnind+1:end,:);

% [srtinp,srtind]=sort(trninp);
% neu_ind=round(linspace(trnind*.1,trnind*.9,9))
% for i = 1:size(srtinp,2)
%     % neuron classification
%     neu_ran{i}=[srtinp(1,i);srtinp(neu_ind,i);srtinp(end,i)];
% end

% for i=1:9,
%     figure(i)
%     semilogy(srtinp(:,i),10.^output(srtind(:,i)))
%     title(inp_headers{i})
%     corrcoef(trninp(:,i),trnout);
% end

neu_range{1}=[1 1.5 2.0];
neu_range{2}=[0.1 0.15 0.2 0.25];
neu_range{3}=[0.1 0.15 0.2 0.25];
neu_range{4}=[2.2 2.3 2.4 2.5 2.6];
neu_range{5}=[0.05 0.1 0.15 0.2];
neu_range{6}=[8.41 8.42 8.43 8.44 8.45 8.46 8.47 8.48];
neu_range{7}=[0.02 0.04 0.06 0.08 0.1];
neu_range{8}=[0.02 0.04 0.06 0.08 0.1];
neu_range{9}=[10 15 20];
out_neu_range=[0 1 2];
for j=1:length(neu_range)
    L{j}=zeros(length(neu_range{j})+1,4);
    win_no{j}=zeros(1,length(neu_range{j})+1)
end

for ii=1:10
    % for each training pattern or iteration for individual depth
    for i=1:length(trninp)
        if i==18
            i
        end
        % determining the winning output neuron by comparing
        % and selecting the range in which the output value
% 'permeability' falls
        outwinneu=(trnout(i)<=out_neu_range
        );
        % find the index of the winning output neuron for output layer
        outwinneu_ind=find(outwinneu);
        If isempty~(outwinneu_ind),
            z_out{i}=outwinneu_ind(1);
        else
```

```
                z_out{i}=length(outwinneu)
                end

            for j=1:length(neu_range)
                % for each SOM layer, find the winning neuron by comparing
                % and deciding as to which range the input Subword
                % would fall inpwinneu=(trninp(i,j)<=neu_range{j})
                ;
                % find the index of that neuron inpwinneu_ind=find(inpwinneu);
                % store the index for that input subword for that
                layer if ~isempty(inpwinneu_ind),
                    zwinno{i}(j)=inpwinneu_ind(1);
                else
                    zwinno{i}(j)=length(inpwinneu)+1;
                end
                % winning neuron from layer j for input pattern i
                k=zwinno{i}(j);
                % Calculating the no of times a neuron is winning
                win_no{j}(k)=win_no{j}(k)+1;

                % LINK WEIGHTS CALCULATIONS
                % for each winning neuron 'k' in layer j to each
                % winning neuron m in only one output layer
                % reward the Link weight by a value 0.2 for each
                iteration
                % and penalized the Link Weight by a value 0.1 for each
                % iteration for a total of 10
                iterations for m=1:length(outwinneu)+1
                    if m==z_out{i}
                        L{j}(k,m)=L{j}(k,m)+0.2;
                        Ls{j}(k,m)=L{j}(k,m)/win_no{j}(k)
                    else
                        L{j}(k,m)=L{j}(k,m)+0.1;
                        Ls{j}(k,m)=L{j}(k,m)/win_no{j}(k)
                    end
                end
        end
    end
end

    su=0;
    for i=1:length(tstinp);


            if ~isempty(outwinneu_ind),
                z_out{i}=outwinneu_ind(1);
            else
                z_out{i}=length(outwinneu)
```

```
            end
            for   j=1:length(neu_range)
                  % for each  SOM layer, find the winning neuron by comparing
                  % and deciding as  to which  range the input Subword
                  % would fall
                  inpwinneu=(trninp(i,j)<=neu_range{j})
                  ;
                  % find the index of that neuron
                  inpwinneu_ind=find(inpwinneu);
                  % store the index for that input subword for that
                  layer  if   ~isempty(inpwinneu_ind),
                        zwinno{i}(j)=inpwinneu_ind(1);
                  else
                        zwinno{i}(j)=length(inpwinneu)+1;
                  end
                  % winning neuron from layer j for input pattern i
                  k=zwinno{i}(j);
                  % Calculating the no of times a neuron is winning
                  win_no{j}(k)=win_no{j}(k)+1;

                  % LINK WEIGHTS CALCULATIONS
                  % for each  winning neuron 'k'  in  layer   j to  each
                  % winning  neuron  m  in  only one  output layer
                  % reward the  Link  weight by  a  value 0.2 for  each iteration
                  % and penalized the Link  Weight by a value 0.1 for each
                  % iteration for a total of 10
                  iterations for m=1:length(outwinneu)+1
                        if m==z_out{i}
                              L{j}(k,m)=L{j}(k,m)+0.2;
                              Ls{j}(k,m)=L{j}(k,m)/win_no{j}(k)
                        else
                              L{j}(k,m)=L{j}(k,m)+0.1;
                              Ls{j}(k,m)=L{j}(k,m)/win_no{j}(k)
                        end
                  end
         end
      end
end

      su=0;
      for  i=1:length(tstinp);
            for j=1:length(neu_range)
                  inpwinneu=(tstinp(i,j)<=neu_range{j})
                  ; inpwinneu_ind=find(inpwinneu);
                  if ~isempty(inpwinneu_ind),
                        z_win{i}(j)=inpwinneu_ind(1),
                  else
                        z_win{i}(j)=length(inpwinneu)+1,
```

```
            end
            kw=z_win{i}(j);
            Li(j,:)=Ls{j}(kw,:);
        end
        Li_sum=sum(Li)
        outwinneu=(tstout(i)<=out_neu_range)
        ; outwinneu_ind=find(outwinneu);
        if ~isempty(outwinneu_ind),
            z_out{i}=outwinneu_ind(1);
        else
            z_out{i}=length(outwinneu)+1;
        end
        win_ind(i)=find(Li_sum==max(Li_sum));
        succ(i)=(win_ind(i)==z_out{i});
        su=succ(i)+su
    end

        end i
        win_ind(i)=find(Li_sum==max(Li_sum));
        succ(i)=(win_ind(i)==z_out{i});
        su=succ(i)+su

                su_pe=su/length(t stinp)*100 bar(1:length(suc c),succ)
                title('Success    for each depth') xlabel('Depth')
                ylabel('0<---failure ---- Success --->1') axis([0  90  -0.2 1.2])
```

A.8.18. Predicting Forest Fires (S R K Muralidharan)

Part 1: LAMSTAR Network (Matlab)

Source Code: MATLAB R2015a
Reference: Principles of Artificial neural Networks, 3rd edition by Dr. Daniel Graupe, Chapter 9
Lamstar.m

```
clear all;
close all;
clc;
load ('forest2.mat');
disp('Training');
X_train = X';
[row, col] = size(X_train);
numSubWords = 16;
nBit = 8;
alpha = 0.9;
tol = 1e-5;
thresh = 0.9999;
flag = zeros(1,numSubWords);
```

```
disp('Forming Sub Words');
tic; % to determine the training time
for i = 1:size(X_train,2)
tempX = reshape(X_train(:,i), nBit, nBit);
for j = 1:numSubWords
if (j <= nBit)
X_in{i}(j,:) = tempX(j,:);
else
X_in{i}(j,:) = tempX(:,j - nBit)';
end
end
check(1,:) = zeros(1, nBit);
for k = 1:numSubWords
for t = 1 : nBit
if (X_in{i}(k,t) ~= check(1,t))
X_norm{i}(k,:) = X_in{i}(k,:) / sqrt(sum(X_in{i}(k,:).^2));
 else
X_norm{i}(k,:) = zeros(1,nBit);
end
end
end
end
%
% for i = 1:size(X_train,2)
% tempX = reshape(X_train(:,i), nBit, nBit);
% for j = 1:numSubWords
% if j <= nBit
% X_in{i}(j,:) = tempX(j,:);
% else
% X_in{i}(j,:) = tempX(:,j - nBit)';
% end
% end
disp('Dynamic Allocation of neurons');
i = 1;
ct = 1;
% while (i <= numSubWords)
% i = 1;
% ct = 1;
% while (i <= numSubWords)
cl = 0;
for t = 1 : nBit
if (X_norm{ct}(i,t)==0)
cl = cl+1;
end
end
disp('Weights}
if (cl == nBit)
Z{ct}(i) = 0;
```

```
elseif (flag(i) == 0)
W{i}(:,ct) = rand(nBit, 1);
flag(i) = ct;
W_norm{i}(:,ct) = W{i}(:,ct)/sqrt(sum(W{i}(:,ct).^2));
Z{ct}(i)= X_norm{ct}(i,:)*W_norm{i};
while(Z{ct}(i) <= (1-tol)),
W_norm{i}(:,ct) = W_norm{i}(:,ct) + alpha*(X_norm{ct}(i,:)' - W_norm{i}(:,ct));
Z{ct}(i) = X_norm{ct}(i,:)*W_norm{i}(:,ct);
end
end
r(ct,i) = 1;
i = i+1;
end
r(ct,:) = 1;
ct = ct+1;
while (ct <= size(X_train,2))
for i = 1 : numSubWords
cl = 0;
for t = 1 : nBit
if (X_norm{ct}(i,t) == 0)
cl = cl+1;
end
end
if (cl == nBit)
Z{ct}(i) = 0;
else
r(ct,i) = flag(i);
r_new=0;
for k = 1:max(r(ct,i)),
Z{ct}(i) = X_norm{ct}(i,:)*W_norm{i}(:,k);
if Z{ct}(i) >= thresh
r_new = k;
flag(i) = r_new;
r(ct,i) = flag(i);
break;
end
end
if (r_new == 0)
flag(i) = flag(i) + 1;
r(ct,i) = flag(i);
W{i}(:,r(ct,i)) = rand(nBit,1);
%flag(i) = r
W_norm{i}(:,r(ct,i)) = W{i}(:,r(ct,i))/sqrt(sum(W{i}(:,r(ct,i)).^2));
Z{ct}(i) = X_norm{ct}(i,:)*W_norm{i}(:,r(ct,i));
while(Z{ct}(i) <= (1-tol)),
W_norm{i}(:,r(ct,i)) = W_norm{i}(:,r(ct,i)) + alpha*(X_norm{ct}(i,:)' - W_norm{i}(:,r(ct,i)));
Z{ct}(i) = X_norm{ct}(i,:)*W_norm{i}(:,r(ct,i));
end
```

```
end
end
end
ct = ct+1;
end
save W_norm W_norm
% Link Weights
outNum = size(y,2);
ct = 1;
m_r = max(r);
%W_norm{i}(:,r(ct,i)) = W{i}(:,r(ct,i))/sqrt(sum(W{i}(:,r(ct,i)).^2));
%Z{ct}(i) = X_norm{ct}(i,:)*W_norm{i}(:,r(ct,i));
%while(Z{ct}(i) <= (1-tol)),
%W_norm{i}(:,r(ct,i)) = W_norm{i}(:,r(ct,i)) + alpha*(X_norm{ct}(i,:)' - W_norm{i}(:,r(ct,i)));
%Z{ct}(i) = X_norm{ct}(i,:)*W_norm{i}(:,r(ct,i));
if exist('C:\Users\SriRamKumar\Downloads\lamstar\L_w.mat', 'file')
load L_w;
else
for i = 1:numSubWords
L_w{i} = zeros(m_r(i),outNum);
end
end
ct = 1;
disp('Output');
Z_out = zeros(size(X_train,2), outNum);
while (ct <= size(X_train,2))
L = zeros(size(X_train,2), outNum);
for i = 1 : numSubWords
% count = size(find(r(:,i) == r(ct,i)) , 1);
if (r(ct,i)~=0)
for j = 1 : outNum
if (y(ct,j)==0)
L_w{i}(r(ct,i),j) = L_w{i}(r(ct,i),j) - 20;
%L_w{i}(r(ct,i),j) = (L_w{i}(r(ct,i),j) / count) - 20;
else
L_w{i}(r(ct,i),j) = L_w{i}(r(ct,i),j) + 20;
% L_w{i}(r(ct,i),j) = (L_w{i}(r(ct,i),j) / count) + 20;
 end
end
L(i,:) = L_w{i}(r(ct,i),:);
% L(i,:) = L_w{i}(r(ct,i),:)/count;
end
end
Z_out(ct,:) = sum(L);
ct = ct+1;
end
t=toc;
save L_w L_w
```

disp(['Training done in ' num2str(t) ' sec']);

Testing_LM

```
Testing_LM.m
function Testing_LM
clear all;
load W_norm
load L_w
load ('forest2.mat');
```

INTERRUPTED…….

PART 2: CNN (using https://github.com/rasmusbergpalm/DeepLearnToolbox)

```
clear all;
close all;
clc;
load ('forest2.mat');
[testsrow, testcol] = size(tsdata);
[trainrow, traincol] = size(trdata);
tsdata = double(reshape(tsdata',8,8,testcol));
% test col size is 64 and its reshaped as 8 x 8
trdata = double(reshape(trdata',8,8,traincol));
% train col size is 64 and its reshaped as 8 x 8
tslabel = double(tslabel'); %testing label
trlabel = double(trlabel'); %training label
rand('state',0)
for i = 1:25 % max number of iterations or epochs is not greater than 25
cnn = [];
cnn.layers = { % CNN structure
sruct('type', 'i') %input layer is 8 x 8
struct('type', 'c', 'outputmaps', 8, 'kernelsize', 5) %design of the convolution layer done by toolbox
struct('type', 's', 'scale', 2) %sub sampling layer
% with subsample window size as 2 x 2
% with pooling layer size as 2 x 2
%struct('type', 'c', 'outputmaps', 15, 'kernelsize', 2) %convolution layer
};
opts.numberepochs = i;
opts.a = 0.85; % alpha is 0.85 or the learning rate is 0.85
opts.bs = 8;
cnn = cnnsetup(cnn, trdata, trlabel);
cnn = cnntrain(cnn, trdata, trlabel, opts);
er(i) = cnntest(cnn, tsdata, tslabel); % error
disp('Convolutional Neural Network');
end
save er er;
%plot mean squared error
plot(er, 'LineWidth', 2);
```

```
ylabel('Mean squared error (%)');
xlabel('Number of epoch');
cnnapplygrads.m
function net = cnnapplygrads(net, opts)
for l = 2 : numel(net.layers)
if strcmp(net.layers{l}.type, 'c')
for j = 1 : numel(net.layers{l}.a)
for ii = 1 : numel(net.layers{l - 1}.a)
net.layers{l}.k{ii}{j} = net.layers{l}.k{ii}{j} - opts.alpha * net.layers{l}.dk{ii}{j};
end
net.layers{l}.b{j} = net.layers{l}.b{j} - opts.alpha * net.layers{l}.db{j};
end
end
end
net.ffW = net.ffW - opts.alpha * net.dffW;
net.ffb = net.ffb - opts.alpha * net.dffb;
end
cnnbp.m
function net = cnnbp(net, y)
n = numel(net.layers);
% error
net.e = net.o - y;
% loss function
net.L = 1/2* sum(net.e(:) .^ 2) / size(net.e, 2);
%% backprop deltas
net.od = net.e .* (net.o .* (1 - net.o)); % output delta
net.fvd = (net.ffW' * net.od); % feature vector delta
if strcmp(net.layers{n}.type, 'c') % only conv layers has sigm function
net.fvd = net.fvd .* (net.fv .* (1 - net.fv));
end
% reshape feature vector deltas into output map style
sa = size(net.layers{n}.a{1});
fvnum = sa(1) * sa(2);
for j = 1 : numel(net.layers{n}.a)
net.layers{n}.d{j} = reshape(net.fvd(((j - 1) * fvnum + 1) : j * fvnum, :), sa(1), sa(2), sa(3));
end
for l = (n - 1) : -1 : 1
if strcmp(net.layers{l}.type, 'c')
for j = 1 : numel(net.layers{l}.a)
net.layers{l}.d{j} = net.layers{l}.a{j} .* (1 - net.layers{l}.a{j}) .* (expand(net.layers{l + 1}.d{j},
[net.layers{l + 1}.scale net.layers{l + 1}.scale 1]) / net.layers{l + 1}.scale ^ 2);
end
elseif strcmp(net.layers{l}.type, 's')
for i = 1 : numel(net.layers{l}.a)
z = zeros(size(net.layers{l}.a{1}));
for j = 1 : numel(net.layers{l + 1}.a)
z = z + convn(net.layers{l + 1}.d{j}, rot180(net.layers{l + 1}.k{i}{j}), 'full');
end
```

```
net.layers{l}.d{i} = z;
end
end
end
%% calc gradients
for l = 2 : n
if strcmp(net.layers{l}.type, 'c')
for j = 1 : numel(net.layers{l}.a)
for i = 1 : numel(net.layers{l - 1}.a)
net.layers{l}.dk{i}{j} = convn(flipall(net.layers{l - 1}.a{i}), net.layers{l}.d{j}, 'valid') /
size(net.layers{l}.d{j}, 3);
end
net.layers{l}.db{j} = sum(net.layers{l}.d{j}(:)) / size(net.layers{l}.d{j}, 3);
end
end
end
net.dffW = net.od * (net.fv)' / size(net.od, 2);
net.dffb = mean(net.od, 2);
function X = rot180(X)
X = flipdim(flipdim(X, 1), 2);
end
end

cnff.m
function net = cnnff(net, x)
n = numel(net.layers);
net.layers{1}.a{1} = x;
inputmaps = 1;
```

INTERRUPTED .....

A.8.19. Predicting Price Movement in Market Microstructure (X Shi)

A partial computer code for LAMSTAR-1 (code sections for network initialization and for main output) can be found in pages 247 and 249–253 (Appendix 9.C) of D Graupe: Principles of Artificial Neural Networks, 3rd edition, World Scientific Publishing Company, 2013.

A.8.20. Fault Detection (M He)

Code for Data Preprocessing (for LNN-1, LNN-2 and BP)

```
function n = findpeaks(x)
% Find peaks.
% n = findpeaks(x)
```

```
n = find(diff(diff(x) > 0) < 0);
u = find(x(n+1) > x(n));
n(u) = n(u)+1;

function imf = emd(x)
% Empiricial Mode Decomposition (Hilbert-Huang Transform)
% imf = emd(x)
% Func : findpeaks
x = transpose(x(:));
imf = [];
while ~ismonotonic(x)
  x1 = x;
  sd = Inf;
  while (sd > 0.1) | ~isimf(x1)
    s1 = getspline(x1);
    s2 = -getspline(-x1);
    x2 = x1-(s1+s2)/2;
    sd = sum((x1-x2).^2)/sum(x1.^2); x1 = x2;
  end
  imf{end+1} = x1;
  x = x-x1;
end
imf{end+1} = x;

% FUNCTIONS

function u = ismonotonic(x)
u1 = length(findpeaks(x))*length(findpeaks(-x));
if u1 > 0, u = 0;
else,      u = 1; end
function u = isimf(x)
N = length(x);
u1 = sum(x(1:N-1).*x(2:N) < 0);
u2 = length(findpeaks(x))+length(findpeaks(-x));
if abs(u1-u2) > 1, u = 0;
else,              u = 1; end

function s = getspline(x)

N = length(x);
p = findpeaks(x);
s = spline([0 p N+1],[0 x(p) 0],1:N);
filenamein='D:\Temp Downloads\ae\steelAE_Inner_400kHz_set1_10Hz.txt';
filenameout='D:\Temp Downloads\ae\steelAE_Outer_400kHz_set2_10Hz.txt';
filenamehealth='D:\Temp Downloads\ae\steelAE_Healthy_400kHz_set1_10Hz.txt';
filenamecage='D:\Temp Downloads\ae\steelAE_Cage_400kHz_set1_10Hz.txt';
filenameball='D:\Temp Downloads\ae\steelAE_Ball_400kHz_set1_10Hz.txt';
```

```
[inner,~,~] = importdata(filenamein);
[outer,~,~] = importdata(filenameout);
[cage,~,~] = importdata(filenamecage);
[ball,~,~] = importdata(filenameball);
[health,~,~] = importdata(filenamehealth);
 innerimf=emd(inner);
outerimf=emd(outer);
cageimf=emd(cage);
ballimf=emd(ball);
helthimf=emd(health);
[row,col]=size(innerimf);
innersubword=[row,9];
for i=1:3
  rms=rms(innerimf(1,:));
  kurt=kurtosis(innerimf(1,:));
  p2p=p2p(innerimf(1,:));
  innersubword(i,:)=(rms kurt p2p);
end
innersubword=reshape((innersubword),9,1);
[row,col]=size(innerimf);
outersubword=[row,9];
for i=1:3
  rms=rms(outerimf(1,:));
  kurt=kurtsis(outerimf(1,:));
  p2p=p2p(outerimf(1,:));
  outersubword(i,:)=(rms kurt p2p);
end
outersubword=reshape((outersubword),9,1);
[row,col]=size(cageimf);
cagesubword=[row,9];
for i=1:3
  rms=rms(cageimf(1,:));
  kurt=kurtsis(cageimf(1,:));
  p2p=p2p(cageimf(1,:));
  cagesubword(i,:)=(rms kurt p2p);
end
cagesubword=reshape((cagesubword),9,1);
[row,col]=size(ballimf);
ballsubword=[row,9];
for i=1:3
  rms=rms(ballimf(1,:));
  kurt=kurtsis(ballimf(1,:));
  p2p=p2p(balllimf(1,:));
  ballsubword(i,:)=(rms kurt p2p);
end
ballsubword=reshape((ballsubword),9,1);
[row,col]=size(healthimf);
healthsubword=[row,9];
```

```
for i=1:3
  rms=rms(healthimf(1,:));
  kurt=kurtsis(healthimf(1,:));
  p2p=p2p(healthimf(1,:));
  healthsubword(i,:)=(rms kurt p2p);
end
healthsubword=reshape((healthsubword),9,1);
final=[innersubword';outersubword';cagesubword';ballsubword';healthsubword'];
traindata=final(24,:);
testdata=final(25:40,:);
```

Author Index

Subject Index

Printed in the United States
By Bookmasters